STRATEGIES FOR COMPLIANCE

Compliance is a fundamental control function within regulated industries globally. This book provides an expert introduction to corporate compliance using cases, examples and insights from the financial services sector and beyond.

The author, an experienced compliance practitioner and academic, highlights compliance challenges, using examples such as Wells Fargo, whistleblowing in the financial services and the mis-selling of payment protection insurance in the UK banking sector. The book explores strategies for creating compliant cultures and fostering regulatory trust, whilst practical guidance is provided on anticipating regulatory changes. Addressing organisational obstruction and delay, the author presents a series of valuable tools and techniques for real-world practice.

An essential professional development resource for board directors, compliance officers and other senior managers, the book also provides a unique learning and development resource for students of corporate compliance globally.

Alan Brener is a Teaching Fellow at University College London and Queen Mary University of London, UK. A qualified Chartered Accountant and member of the Institute of Chartered Accountants in England and Wales, Alan is also a Fellow of the Chartered Banker Institute, a professional body for bankers, and a member of its education and training Quality and Standards Committee. Alan has worked at a senior level in UK commercial banking for many years; most recently at Santander UK, where he was responsible, at different times, for the compliance and retail legal departments and regulatory policy. Before joining Santander in 2005, from 1996, he headed the compliance departments for the retail banking divisions of Natwest and RBS banks. From 1989 to 1996 Alan was a senior prudential and conduct of business regulator for the insurance and collective investments sectors, having previously worked on aspects of public policy at the Department of Trade and Industry. Most recently, prior to starting his PhD, Alan was on secondment from Santander helping to set up the Banking Standards Board with the objective of improving standards of conduct and professionalism within the banking industry.

STRATEGIES FOR COMPLIANCE

Tools, Techniques and Challenges
in Financial Services

Alan Brener

Routledge
Taylor & Francis Group

LONDON AND NEW YORK

First published 2021
by Routledge
2 Park Square, Milton Park, Abingdon, Oxon OX14 4RN

and by Routledge
52 Vanderbilt Avenue, New York, NY 10017

Routledge is an imprint of the Taylor & Francis Group, an informa business

© 2021 Alan Brener

British Library Cataloguing-in-Publication Data
A catalogue record for this book is available from the British Library

Library of Congress Cataloging-in-Publication Data
Names: Brener, Alan, 1955- author.
Title: Strategies for compliance : tools, techniques and challenges in financial services / Alan Brener.
Description: Abingdon, Oxon; New York, NY: Routledge, 2021. | Includes bibliographical references and index.
Identifiers: LCCN 2020035551 (print) | LCCN 2020035552 (ebook)
Subjects: LCSH: Banks and banking–State supervision. | Banking law. | Trade regulation.
Classification: LCC HG1725 .B74 2021 (print) | LCC HG1725 (ebook) | DDC 332.1068/1--dc23
LC record available at https://lccn.loc.gov/2020035551
LC ebook record available at https://lccn.loc.gov/2020035552

ISBN: 978-0-367-33774-2 (hbk)
ISBN: 978-0-367-33757-5 (pbk)
ISBN: 978-0-429-32182-5 (ebk)

Typeset in Sabon
by MPS Limited, Dehradun

For Fiona, David and my father, Leon

CONTENTS

ACKNOWLEDGEMENTS

Any work of this nature is based on the assistance and contributions of many people but I would particularly like to mention the friendship and support of Professor Iris Hse-Yu Chiu, whose guidance has been invaluable.

The process of research and writing can be trying for a family. However, the humour and help of our son David and the patience, support and love of my wife, Fiona, has made the process a pleasure.

ABBREVIATIONS

A&E	accident and emergencies
AI	Artificial Intelligence
AML	anti-money laundering
BBA	British Bankers Associate (now UK Finance)
BoE	Bank of England
CBI	Chartered Banker Institute
CBT	computer-based training
CCO	Chief Compliance Officer
CEO	Chief Executive Officer
CFO	Chief Financial Officer
CFPB	Consumer Financial Protection Bureau
CPD	continuous professional development
CSR	corporate social responsibility
DOJ	US Department of Justice
ESG	environmental, social and governance
FCA	Financial Conduct Authority
FCPA	Foreign Corrupt Practices Act of 1977
FinCEN	Financial Crimes Enforcement Network
FTC	Federal Trade Commission
FRC	Financial Reporting Council
FSA	Financial Services Authority
FTSE	Financial Times Stock Exchange Index
FX	foreign exchange
HBOS	Halifax Bank of Scotland
HILP	high impact low probability
HKMA	Hong Kong Monetary Authority
IARCP	International Association of Risk and Compliance Professionals
KYC	know your customer
LIBOR	London Inter-bank Offered Rate
MEP	mortgage endowment policy
NDA	non-disclosure agreement
NHS	National Health Service

OCC	Office of the Comptroller of the Currency
OSHA	Occupational Safety and Health Administration
PCBS	Parliamentary Commission on Banking Standards
PPI	payment protection insurance
PRA	Prudential Regulatory Authority
RCN	Royal College of Nursing
SAR	suspicious activity report
SCARP	structured capital at risk product
SEC	Securities Exchange Commission
SFO	Serious Fraud Office
SM&CR	Senior Manager and Certified Person Regime
SME	small and medium-sized enterprises
TC	training and competence
TCF	treating customers fairly

1

INTRODUCTION

Responsibility

The central issue with compliance in banking can be best summed up in an exchange before Parliamentary Commission on Banking Standards between a member of the Commission and the then Group Head of Compliance at Barclays Bank.

> Q 678 Chair (Mark Garnier MP): Whose responsibility is it to make Barclays compliant?
> Mike Walters (Group Head of Compliance, Barclays Bank): Compliance clearly is responsible and accountable for the responsibilities of compliance, and those are very clear. We carry out policy setting in the key areas that we are responsible for. We monitor whether those policies are being complied with, and we give advice on matters of the rules.
>
> Q 679 Chair: Who was responsible for the compliance at Barclays – to make Barclays compliant?
> Mike Walters: I believe that everybody at Barclays has the responsibility to do that.
>
> Q 680 Chair: So the compliance officer is not responsible for making Barclays compliant; it is everybody else. Or it is everybody including you.[1]

This exchange highlights both skepticism as to the effectiveness of the compliance function and confusion over its role: what is the extent of its responsibility? This raises the question of why have a compliance function if the scope of its role is too narrowly drawn? Does having a compliance unit add any real value? This book will explore these issues and suggest possible remedies.

The over-arching context is that the regulators need to operate via the compliance function and that of other controls since it is well-nigh impossible for regulators to operate directly upon a regulated firm. They do not know the processes, nor the products and services in any detail; and they lack both the resources and inclination to be ever present on site. They need to delegate the day-to-day job of regulation to the firm itself – it is for others, such as the compliance officer, within the firm to put the regulations into effect within the business. This is undertaken through the boards of the regulated firm, other senior executives and the various control functions. Of the latter, the compliance function is central.

What is meant by the term 'compliance' varies across jurisdictions, regulatory regimes and the types of businesses and markets involved. The next sections look at what may be encompassed by the term 'compliance' (largely in the United Kingdom and the United States), what the compliance function within a business is meant to do and the challenges faced by the function – including the need to improve the level of professionalism in compliance.

The aim of this book is to produce a conceptual framework for compliance. This concept must be capable of being set out clearly to staff within both the compliance function and the business and to other stakeholders, such as customers and regulators. Without this clear understanding of what compliance is trying to do and why, there is a strong risk of it losing direction and drifting towards ineffectiveness.

This work focuses on the United States and the United Kingdom but the issues have broader application. In addition, this work concentrates on financial services, and in particular, banking regulation. However, many of the issues have much wider application and may apply to other highly regulated industries such as pharmaceuticals, aerospace and the extractive industries.

A recent example of the how the themes in this book may apply to other industries can be seen in the action taken by Ofwat, the UK's statutory water regulator, against Southern Water in 2019. The company has had to pay a £3m fine and a further £123m in redress to its customers.[2] The firm had failed in its statutory duties to treat sewage and had dumped 'untreated effluent into beaches, rivers and streams' and misreported the relevant data. It had 'manipulated water samples for 7 years until 2017 so that the true performance of its sewage treatment works was hidden'.[3] The issues were the result of 'poor management and a failure to make the necessary investment in sewage treatment works'. 'Southern Water, which is owned by a consortium of private equity and infrastructure investors including UBS Asset Management and JPMorgan Asset Management, now faces a criminal investigation by the Environment Agency, a separate regulator, which began investigating in 2016'.[4]

The water company suffered from poor corporate governance, a weak corporate culture and the lack of an adequate compliance function.[5] The investigation found that 'senior management within the Wastewater

Operations division colluded to conceal the actual performance of [the treatment plants]. A culture of data manipulation was the norm and was accepted by staff across the division'.[6] There were also 'deficiencies in [Southern Water's] organisational culture which prevented employees from being comfortable with speaking out about inappropriate or non-compliant behaviours'.[7] These are all common themes which continue to reoccur in a variety of organisations considered in this book, including the scandal at the UK's National Health Service Mid Staffordshire Trust and the circumstances leading to the Herald of Free Enterprise ferry disaster in Zeebrugge, Belgium in 1987, as well as in the UK and US financial services industry.

By way of clarification, throughout this work the term 'compliance' is used to cover both the compliance function within a bank, no matter how it may be described in the organisation charts within individual firms, and also the task of undertaking the compliance role.

What is required of 'compliance'?

The Basel Committee requires that each 'bank should have an executive or senior staff member with overall responsibility for co-ordinating the identification and management of the bank's compliance risk and for supervising the activities of other compliance function staff'.[8] This individual is known as the 'head of compliance' or 'compliance officer'. The international standards set by the Basel Committee are then enacted by individual jurisdictions.

The UK's Financial Conduct Authority (FCA) requires that all regulated firms 'must establish, implement and maintain adequate policies and procedures sufficient to ensure compliance of the firm including its managers, employees' and so on.[9] Firms 'must, taking into account the nature, scale and complexity of its business, and the nature and range of financial services and activities undertaken in the course of that business, establish, implement and maintain adequate policies and procedures designed to detect any risk of failure by the firm to comply with its obligations under the regulatory system, as well as associated risks, and put in place adequate measures and procedures designed to minimise such risks and to enable the FCA to exercise its powers effectively under the regulatory system'.[10]

> Firms must maintain a permanent and effective compliance function which operates independently and which has the following responsibilities:
>
> (1) to monitor and, on a regular basis, to assess the adequacy and effectiveness of the measures and procedures put in place in

accordance with SYSC 6.1.2 R, and the actions taken to address any deficiencies in the firm's compliance with its obligations; and,

(2) to advise and assist the relevant persons responsible for carrying out regulated activities to comply with the firm's obligations under the regulatory system.[11]

There is also a requirement for an individual who carries out the 'compliance oversight role' (i.e. the 'compliance officer') to be a 'Senior Management Function 16' under the Senior Manager and Certified Person Regime'.[12] Besides these requirements the rules are somewhat vague about the role of the compliance officer.

The US Securities and Exchange Commission (SEC) requires investment companies and 'investment advisers to adopt written compliance procedures, review the adequacy of those procedures annually, and to designate a chief compliance officer responsible for their administration'.[13]

The US Federal Reserve explained its approach and expectations of banks and compliance officers in a letter in 2008.[14]

What is the compliance function meant to achieve?

Put simply, regulated firms are required to comply with the regulations. However, attempting to comply with the 'black-letter' law of regulations is not sufficient. There needs to be both an analysis and understanding of what the rules are trying to achieve. Sometimes this is called following the 'spirit' as well as the 'letter' of the regulations. Simply 'monitoring, assessing and advising' sets a very low standard. In reality the regulators, rightly, expect much more. Further, the regulators constitute only one of the stakeholders; albeit very a very important one. Others – such as customers, the media and politicians – with an interest in the regulated firm are likely to have their own expectations which may go beyond those of the regulators.

Compliance is much more than monitoring, assessing and advising – important though these tasks are. This book covers some of the basic requirements but also focuses on four broad, but central, expectations. These are to:

- provide a 'powerful, vocal conscience'. Compliance provides a 'voice' – an authoritative voice – within the firm, representing both stakeholders who may lack a voice and also the long term interests of the business,
- provide 'imagination of thought'. Individuals in a business, as elsewhere, should think and imagine for themselves, including looking at the wider perspective. However, for a variety of reasons – including hubris, a focus on procedure rather than substance and the simple drudgery of work – this may fail to happen. The compliance function needs to ensure that 'thought' is present and is clearly expressed and that ultimately right is done,

- act as the intelligent 'interlocutor'. Compliance explains the regulatory requirements in a form which resonates within a firm and to explain the business to the regulators. The importance of this 'communication' role cannot be overstated,
- **ensure that the business retains its 'moral compass'.** From time to time individuals in the business will be tempted, on grounds of expediency, to act wrongly. There may be strong pressures to go along with this. Compliance must resist this, often self-imposed, 'gleichschaltung' or 'accommodation' or 'alignment'. **Compliance must provide leadership and not just advice.**

All these roles may be negated by numbing ones' thoughts and instead going along with the drift, abandoning the exercise of authority and instead, keeping quiet and avoiding taking a stand.

Compliance function challenges

There have been many major compliance failures over the years in both the United Kingdom and the United States. Sharon Gilad in her empirical work found that firms, generally, have a considerable ability to self-justify and to rationalise their actions.[15] For example, The Financial Services Authority (FSA) launched a major project in the early 2000s that required regulated firms to 'treat their customers fairly' (TCF). Her work found that in many regulated firms:

> management communication of TCF messages through posters and training programs were cynical attempts at 'cosmetic compliance' – posters appeared just before a visit from the regulator, and internal communications were ... focused on providing the regulator with superficial evidence of 'cultural transformation'.[16] The research found that changes in regulation would not be 'internalised' within an organisation. The compliance function was often at the centre of this failure. The reasons for this include some or all of the factors set out in the next section some of which are developed in later chapters. Having said this, compared with, for example, in-house lawyers in regulated firms, research by UCL Centre for Ethics and Law found some evidence that compliance officers 'were more independent than in-house lawyers, who were said to have a stronger ethic of zealous loyalty to the 'client' than fidelity to the law'.[17]

Poorly and wrongly defined roles

The role of compliance varies between jurisdictions. In the United States, in financial services, compliance is closely associated with regulations relating to anti-money laundering and sanctions and preventing and reporting corporate bribery and corruption. Its work is bounded by 'black-letter law' – the more or less precise statement of the current law. In the United Kingdom, regulation is more objective-based with a set of 'Principles'.[18] There are many rules but these are also often expressed in very broad terms with the regulators relying on the regulated firm to exercise appropriate judgement and restraint. The regulators, in turn, provide guidance in the form of copious consultations and other papers as well as frequent speeches and detailed Enforcement Notices. Regulation is also 'judgement based' with the supervisory teams exercising considerable discretion.[19] The result is that almost every aspect of a bank's business appears to be regulated. This perception is a slight exaggeration but not necessarily wholly wrong.

This form of regulation poses a challenge to compliance.

> More general rules (principles) allow firms greater discretion as to what to do. With that discretion comes the need, and responsibility, for working out what they should do. Where the balance should be struck between firms thinking for themselves and the regulators providing guidance is endlessly contested, and each thinks the other should be doing more. Firms want more specific guidance; regulators think firms should work it out.[20]

The consequence is that the compliance function needs to constantly scan the regulatory 'horizon', analysing each regulatory document and speech. These need to be interpreted by compliance in the light of the firm's business and its plans and the results communicated to the senior management and board and the line managers. Compliance needs to advise on workable business solutions to address changes in regulations and regulatory emphasis. Compliance must monitor progress in implementing these changes as well as other day-to-day assessment work. The outcomes of this review work need to be communicated to senior management, the board, regulators etc. This makes compliance into both 'advisers' and 'reporters'. Many compliance staff see this as the full extent of their role.[21] However, the compliance is much more and this will be examined later.

Failure will result if compliance is excessively legalistic or the function limits itself to being some sort of internal consultancy and score-keeper. Compliance also need to serve as an 'activist'. This is the subject of much of this book.

Compliance as an 'influencer' or business lobbyist

Compliance acts as an interface between the regulators and the regulated. When it comes to policy formation, regulators seek information from a variety of sources including the regulated firms. This, of itself, provides the compliance function with an opportunity – either directly, or as a conduit for other parts of the business – to make their case. The lobbyist function is often seen as an important role since line business functions continue to see compliance as a 'business inhibitor' and may seek to withhold information and engage in a continuing battle of attrition with a function for which they have little or no regard.[22] Acting as a regulatory lobbyist has the benefit of demonstrating the 'value' of the compliance function within the firm and it also may assist the regulator. However, it may also help to distort the objectivity of compliance. It is something for both the regulators and the control function to be aware of and to watch. There is an imprecise boundary between being helpful and constructive and becoming a lobbying 'mouth-piece', with the latter undermining credibility and trust.

Lack of authority

'Authority' in this sense comes in two forms and both must be present for the compliance officer to be effective. First, using the Greek term, is 'exousian'; authority where the individual has authority bestowed upon them by the organisation. Second there is 'dynamisian' authority which derives from the individual's own innate capabilities. The former authority is obvious and can be seen in the compliance officer's position in the firm's hierarchy, their re-porting lines, the unit's budget and other resources and so on. Dynamisian authority is very different and has more to do with strength of character and the individual's 'bearing'. It may be described as 'potential power'; the 'sheathed sword'; an authority that is latent but is perceived by all. The compliance department's strength is based on these two foundations.

Lack of focus on developing and earning trust

There need to be bonds of trust between compliance and the other control functions, other senior managers and the board. It is equally important that compliance and the business is trusted by the regulators. Everything hinges on this and it is a subject considered in depth later in this work.

As will be seen from an analysis of the legal and disciplinary actions by regulators, a breakdown in trust can be catastrophic for the regulated firm and the individuals, including the compliance officer, involved.

Lack of training and need to develop professionalism

There is a growing role in banks for Artificial Intelligence (AI) and this feeds into automated trading and lending and other areas such as automated fi-nancial advice ('robo-advice'). Survey evidence indicates that compliance has had to outsource a significant part of its operations to 'buy-in' expertise in these areas.[23] Outsourcing presents a serious set of challenges for compliance since it is possible that the out-sourced and the in-house compliance function do not have congruent objectives. Additionally, the compliance officer bears personal liability and may be held, personally, to account by the regulator for the outsourced function. There is no similar accountability applied to the outsourcer.

Compliance staff must also have and display professionalism. This can be summarised as the individual displaying the 'attitudes, judgement and high standards of behaviour, integrity, knowledge and skill expected of individuals working in banking'.[24] Unfortunately, as discussed later in this work, professionalism, in compliance, is sometimes found lacking.

Professionalism is necessary when compliance is faced with two sets of problems: organisations are frequently opaque and are also afflicted by an inherent lassitude. In large and complex organisations this inertia may frustrate action with departments only wishing to be left alone to 'eat their lotus flowers'. Further, it is often very difficult in both small and large firms to know what is going on. This lack of insight may be fatal to the success of the compliance function and, ultimately, the business.

With the right attitude and the necessary skills and training compliance can often demonstrate its professionalism by identifying the issues, actively communicating them and driving action to remedy the problems. The compliance department, consequently, requires people who are have integrity and who are dynamic, naturally curious and persistent – never letting go.

All is as dust without these foundations and attributes.

Compliance as a 'ritual'

There is a strong tendency for regulation to focus on procedure. There is a range of reasons for this tendency, which fall outside the scope of this work. An inherent bias towards process is replicated within the control functions within a business. Consequently, the 'compliance function could become predominantly concerned with maintaining rituals to sustain the firm's appearance of regulatory compliance'.[25] Although processes are important, it is important that compliance considers 'outcomes' as well. Not only does it set the right objectives, but it also helps focus processes towards the right ends.

Focus on technical minutiae 'arbeitsfreude' – lack of thinking and imagination

There is always a danger that compliance staff may focus on technical minutiae, finding an 'arbeitsfreude' (or a joy in the task itself), in resolving these issues without understanding the full purpose of the requirements. This may be evident, for example, in the introduction and operation of the

UK's Senior Managers and Certified Persons Regime (SM&CR) regulations. The objective is to increase personal accountability within firms. Compliance has a major role in this new initiative. However, there is anecdotal evidence that its intent may be frustrated due to an excessive focus on the details of the regulations without ensuring that its objectives are attained. Compliance with the letter of the rules becomes the aim of compliance, with no or little assessment of whether the over-arching aims are satisfied.

There is a similar issue found with in-house lawyers. Empirical research found a significant category of these individuals who could be described as 'the Comfortably Numb'.[26] They do not perceive that they are subject to high levels of ethical pressure and have both low levels of moral attentiveness and high levels of moral disengagement.[27]

Failure to have a strategic appreciation

It is not always clear that compliance staff understand their role and purpose. Coupled with this tendency, there may be only a fragmentary knowledge of the bank's businesses and operations. This is not unusual in many organisations where the working world of individual employees may be limited to their branch or store, or their immediate unit in the office. What goes on at a desk a few feet from them is likely to be a mystery and a matter of no concern.

This limited perspective puts a control function at a severe disadvantage. If they fail to know or understand how their area fits into the whole the implications of what they see might not be appreciated and not reported. It is the role of leadership, at all levels in the organisation, to ensure that everyone understands the purpose of the organisation and how the immediate team assists in delivering this.

This is especially true of compliance. They need to understand the 'bigger picture'. There need to be regular and frequent face-to-face briefing sessions for all staff on aspects of the business, what is going on in compliance, and more generally. 'Everybody wants to feel appreciated, and to have a sense of belonging. Don't embarrass people in front of others, ... people are happiest when they have some sense of control of their circumstances, so allowing for personal initiative is great'.[28] Employees must be trusted with this information and know that they are trusted.

The risk of keeping quiet

The greatest risk is silence. All organisations rely on communication. This needs to be clear, timely and accurate. Management and boards rely on a diet of information to help guide their decisions. Customers need well presented, fair and not misleading information to make their choices. Regulators of all types can only function with insightful, relevant material. But serious problems can occur, buried within organisations, whether this be the off-shore operations of Barings bank in Singapore; the Bear Stearns High-Grade Structured Credit Fund and the High-Grade Structured Credit Enhanced Leveraged Fund, or a rogue trader in the Global Synthetic Equities trading division. They can also occur because of bad business strategic decisions, for example, by Wells Fargo and Halifax Bank of Scotland. Problems in all these areas and businesses were the result of silence.

There were people in these organisations who knew of the issues but they either kept silent or had their voices quashed at an early stage. In some cases there was a complicity in this silence. This could have been due to a lack of understanding of the significance of what they knew or being under a psychological constraint of 'not wanting to rock the boat' or pressure to be 'a team player'. Those that received the information declined to hear it or delayed acting for a wide variety of reasons, including a refusal to stand up and to be accountable. It is likely that the compliance function, with others, was part of this complicitous silence.[29] They may not have known of the issues or, if they did know, did not understand their significance. They, either alone or with others, simply kept their heads down.

With sufficient 'authority' and firmness of purpose, this need not be the case. Many people and institutions rely on compliance to do its job and speak up clearly, strongly and at the right time – and if not heeded, then swifly to take firm and effective action.

Another perception of compliance: a new conceptual framework

It is important not to become too focused on the purely operational aspects of compliance. There is a need to stand back and consider the wider perspective. This starts with the need to explain both the purpose of the regulated firm and how best the compliance function can assist in meeting this objective. This form of conceptual approach envisages compliance from a holistic perspective. It starts with first determining the purpose of the regulated entities within a community. A regulated entity can be widely defined but it rests on the firm acting sustainably and working together to provide 'the services and products expected and needed by the community, enabling it to achieve its objectives, to prosper, and to provide sustainable wealth and wellbeing to all its members fairly'.[30] This, in many ways complements Ebenezer Howard's 'community' focused corporation with its purpose of raising the 'standards of health and comfort' of all workers in a 'natural and economic' garden city.[31]

Jackman sees the compliance function as acting as much for society 'as for the regulator and the firm'.[32] Like Howard he sees a community as out of equilibrium 'with a deep conflict between the supposed interests of business and the rest of society.[33] Jackman wants compliance to work more closely towards meeting the needs of everyone.

'Compliance holds a heavy responsibility ... compliance's core job is to ensure, beyond any reasonable doubt, that it understands and makes good the industry's promises to its own wider community. This is vital for the firm's sustainability and the prosperity of the community'.[34] He sees five areas that both the firm and compliance should be concerned about. These are:

1   ensuring socially responsible financial products and services,
2   maintaining proper accountability and reporting to the community,
3   engaging with the community in a deep and inclusive manner to ensure that no significant disadvantaged groups or individuals are neglected,
4   investing in society – including taking responsiblity beyond mere compliance with the rules, providing education and spreading costs and benefit equally,
5   working constantly to prevent harm whether to the environment or in the form of combating bribery and corruption.[35]

Viewed from the vantage point of today, these objectives may be seen as too aspirational. However, there is considerable merit in bearing these points in mind at all times. They may help ensure that the compliance function maintains its 'moral compass' and act as a 'vade mecum' – a guide always at hand with which to judge good from ill.

At the same time there are powerful forces working against all this. 'The intensity of financial regulation is cyclical and dependent on political forces. Good times and fading memories make ample room for lobbying by financial firms to loosen restrictions'.[36] Much rests on the control functions; and in particular, in compliance to assert itself and to defend both the public interest and the business from these siren calls.

Main areas covered in this book

Chapter 2 looks at the need to develop the role of the compliance function to match changing expectations and changes in the business and regulatory environment. This includes having a strategic concept for compliance. Everything centres around compliance being seen as trustworthy by the various stakeholders, including the board of the regulated firm and its regulators. In part this will be built on various 'signals' such as the reporting lines of the compliance officer. The chapter examines in some detail the Wells Fargo debacle. This case study illustrates key senior management failings and their failure of imagination, along with that of the various control functions. The lessons from Wells Fargo demonstrate the need for fundamental change throughout many organisations. Corporate boards and senior management need to take the lead, supported by the regulators.

Chapter 3 considers the importance of whistleblowing as a 'tool' of compliance. It uses an example from outside the financial services industry and reviews the findings of the reports on inadequate management behaviour, over a number of years, at the United Kingdom's Mid Staffordshire National Health Service (NHS) Trust. The chapter goes on to look at the closely related issues of senior management psychology and why things go wrong at many organisations. Finally, the chapter highlights what compliance can do to address these issues. These include the role of compliance in improving internal corporate communications and the flow of information by constructing a 'narrative' to explain what is needed and to improve employee morale; providing those in despair with hope.

Chapter 4 examines the need to develop the regulated firm's relationship with the regulators. All this is with the objective of being a 'trustworthy' organisation. As part of this objective, compliance needs to ensure that business errors and operational failings are reported quickly and as fully as possible to the regulators. It also means, for example, not needlessly exasperating the regulators by claiming legal professional privilege. The chapter highlights the frequent risk of mis-communication between businesses and regulators and the important role of compliance acting as an interlocutor. This all needs to be seen in the context of the ever-widening scope of regulation. This includes (in the United Kingdom) increasing regulatory expectations in relation to fairness in pricing products and services, including maintaining fairness between new and existing customers.

Chapter 5 focuses on the difficult task of finding and selecting the right people for compliance. It also covers issues of leadership and professionalism and how to structure the function, including a critique of the so-called 'three lines of defence' model. There are also sections on the relevant aspects of the United Kingdom's Senior Managers and Certified Persons regulatory requirements. The chapter also considers a number of operational compliance issues, including problems with excessive proceduralism.

Chapter 6 considers some of the fundamental elements of a good compliance function including the importance of complying with the spirit as well as letter of the law and the need to consider all stakeholders and to be customer centric in the function's approach. The chapter then turns to a number operational 'tools' of compliance (e.g. risk and heat maps) as well as operating monitoring arrangements, and compliance's preventative work (e.g. financial promotion sign-off and 'up-stream risks'). The chapter also examines a number of common problems experienced by compliance, and new and developing compliance areas (e.g. artificial intelligence, 'robo-advice'), and increasing expectations around environmental, social and governance, and climate change policies and operations.

Chapter 7 examines business cultures, exploring aspects of organisational structures and business models. It also looks at the psychological perspectives of many senior managers and their views on their own personal accountability and why they may act badly. This is considered using the example of the wide-spread mis-selling, in the United Kingdom, of payment protection insurance. The chapter goes on to look at issues of cultural 'contagion' (e.g. seen in the development and marketing of 'precipice bonds'). Finally, there is a section on how the various cultures within a firm can be measured and problems identified.

Chapter 8 emphasises the importance of training within an organisation, including special arrangements for senior executives, and the need for professionalism. It provides examples of training methods and issues, together with ways to measure the effectiveness of training.

Finally, Chapters 9 and 10 examine regulatory enforcement cases against compliance officers in the United Kingdom and the United States as part of the regulatory policy of increased personal accountability.

Conclusion

This books tries to identify the major issues with compliance as a control function within regulated businesses and to suggest steps that can be taken to ameliorate these problems. These include placing a significant emphasis on the role of compliance and improving aspects pf corporate governance and culture within the firm. Although it is primarily aimed at the financial services industry, the issues and solutions are broad enough to cover most industries and many countries.

This work seeks to engage both the compliance officer and regulator as they reflect on the objectives of the compliance function, its issues and possible approaches to undertaking the role successfully. This book examines the current problems with compliance functions and challenges some of the current concepts often mentioned in texts on compliance, such as the 'three lines of defence'.

In addition, there are a range of structural and psychological conditions in organisations which are likely to result in poor behaviour and which may undermine a sound culture in any business. These need to be recognised and addressed by boards and senior management, as well as compliance and other control functions, to remove – or, at least mitigate – their effects.

Notes

1 Parliamentary Commission on Banking Standards – Minutes of Evidence Session 2013-14, HL Paper 27-VIII/HC 175-VIII, 28 November 2012, https://publications.parliament.uk/pa/jt201314/jtselect/jtpcbs/27/27viii_121128d.htm (accessed 18 February 2020).
2 FT, 'Southern Water hit by £126m penalty for 'serious failures'', 25 June 2019, https://www.ft.com/content/518b21fa-9711-11e9–9573-ee5cbb98ed36 (accessed 25 July 2020).
3 Ibid (Southern Water).

4 Ibid (Southern Water).
5 Ofwat, 'Ofwat's final decision to impose a financial penalty on Southern Water Services', 10 October 2019, https://www.ofwat.gov.uk/wp-content/uploads/2019/06/Ofwat's-final-decision-to-impose-a-financial-penalty-on-Southern-Water-Services-Limited.pdf (accessed 25 July 2020), 54–60.
6 Ibid (Ofwat final decision), 54.
7 Ibid (Ofwat final decision), 54.
8 Basel Committee on Banking Supervision ('Basel Committee'), 'Compliance and the compliance function in banks', April 2005, 11, https://www.bis.org/publ/bcbs113.pdf (accessed 15 April 2020).
9 FCA Rule Book (known as the 'handbook'), SYSC 6.1.1 R, 'Senior arrangements, systems and controls, Chapter 6 compliance, internal audit and financial crime', SYSC 6/12, Release 48, March 2020, https://www.handbook.fca.org.uk/handbook/SYSC/6.pdf (accessed 15 April 2020).
10 FCA Rule Book, SYSC 6.1.2 R.
11 FCA Rule Book SYSC 6.1.3 R.
12 FCA Rule Book SUP 10 C.4.3 R, 'The most senior people ('senior managers') who perform key roles ('senior management functions') will need' regulatory approval 'before starting their roles'. 'Every Senior Manager needs to have a 'statement of responsibilities' that clearly says what they are responsible and accountable for' and the regulators will hold them personally accountable for failings within their areas of responsibility.
13 Securities and Exchange Commission, 'Compliance programs of investment companies and investment advisers' (17 CFR Parts 270, 275, and 279 [Release Nos. IA–2204; IC–26299; File No. S7–03–03] RIN 3235–AI77, Federal Register/Vol. 68, No. 247, 24 December 2003), https://www.sec.gov/rules/final/ia-2204.pdf (accessed 15 April 2020).
14 Federal Reserve letter to all Federal Reserve Boards, staff and regulated firms, 'Compliance risk management programs and oversight at large banking organizations with complex compliance profiles', 16 October 2008, SR 08-8/CA 08–11, https://www.federalreserve.gov/boarddocs/srletters/2008/SR0808.htm (accessed 15 April 2020).
15 Sharon Gilad, 'Institutionalizing fairness in financial markets: mission impossible?' (2011) *Regulation and Governance*, 5(3), 309–332, 315.
16 Ibid (Gilad), 315.
17 Richard Moorhead and Steven Vaughan, 'Legal risk: definition, management and ethics' (2015) *UCL Centre for Ethics and Law*, 19, https://papers.ssrn.com/sol3/papers.cfm?abstract_id=2594228 (accessed 19 April 2020).
18 Robert Baldwin, Martin Cave, and Martin Lodge, *Understanding regulation: theory, strategy, and practice* (Oxford University Press, Oxford, 2012), 303.
19 Andrew Bailey, 'The supervisory approach of the Prudential Regulation Authority', speech on 19 May 2011, 3–4, https://www.bankofengland.co.uk/-/media/boe/files/speech/2011/the-supervisory-approach-of-the-pra-speech-by-andrew-bailey.pdf?la=en&hash=722C36565F17942C503A2F355F0B1251CA689575 (accessed 20 April 2020).
20 Julia Black, 'Forms and paradoxes of principles-based regulation' (2008) *Capital Markets Law Journal*, 3(4), 425–457, 443.
21 Deloitte Touche Tohmatsu, 'The changing role of compliance' (2015), 4, https://www2.deloitte.com/content/dam/Deloitte/gr/Documents/financial-services/gr_fs_the_changing_role_of_compliance_en_noexp.pdf (accessed 20 April 2020).
22 FCA, 'The compliance function in wholesale banks' (November 2017), 22.3,

https://fca.org.uk/publication/research/the-compliance-function-in-wholesale-banks.pdf (accessed 13 May 2019).

23 Stacey English and Susannah Hammond, 'Cost of compliance: global survey' (2018), Thomson Reuters, 28, https://legal.thomsonreuters.com/content/dam/ewp-m/documents/legal/en/pdf/reports/cost-of-compliance-special-report-2018.pdf (accessed 20 April 2020).

24 Banking Standards Board website, 'Statement of principles for strengthening professionalism' (March 2019), https://bankingstandardsboard.org.uk/bsb-statement-of-principles-for-strengthening-professionalism/ (accessed 20 April 2020).

25 Iris H-Y Chiu, *Regulating (from) the inside* (Bloomsbury, London, 2015), 65.

26 Richard Moorhead, 'Mapping the moral compass: the relationships between in-house lawyers' role, professional orientations, team cultures, organisational pressures, ethical infrastructure and ethical inclination' (2016), *UCL Centre for Ethics and Law*, 4–5, https://discovery.ucl.ac.uk/id/eprint/1497048/1/Moorhead%20et%20al%202016%20Mapping%20the%20Moral%20Compass.pdf (accessed 19 April 2020).

27 Ibid (Mapping the moral compass), 4–5.

28 Juliet Norton, 'Interview with Dan Hill, author of emotionomics' (2011) *Strategic Direction*, 27(3), 32–34, 33.

29 Pierre Bourdieu, *Outline of a theory of practice*, Richard Nice (tr) (Cambridge University Press, Cambridge, 1977), 188.

30 David Jackman, *The compliance revolution: how compliance needs to change to survive* (John Wiley, Singapore, 2015), 155.

31 Ebenezer Howard, *Tomorrow a peaceful path to real reform* (Swan Sonnenschein, London, 1898), 13.

32 Supra note 30 (Jackman), 159.

33 Supra note 30 (Jackman), 159.

34 Supra note 30 (Jackman), 159–160.

35 Supra note 30 (Jackman), 159–160.

36 Alexander Dill, 'Banks have learnt their lesson on risk management', *Financial Times*, 16 December 2019.

2

A NEW APPROACH TO COMPLIANCE AND THE LESSONS FROM WELLS FARGO

The need to develop the role of the compliance function in financial services

This chapter looks at how the role of compliance needs to change. The need for change was highlighted by the Wells Fargo debacle. This event is considered in detail in this chapter as a recent case study, illustrating many of the challenges faced by compliance and the other control functions.

Some changes are happening. For example, there is evidence that compliance functions are becoming increasingly independent with a greater involvement in the corporate governance of the business and its strategic committees.[1] This is demonstrated by the changes in compliance reporting lines, with more compliance officers reporting direct to either the firm's CEO or chief risk officer.[2] Additionally, the level of training of compliance staff has increased with a significant focus on new technologies.[3]

Nevertheless, there are still many issue with current compliance arrangements. As mentioned in Chapter 1 these include a lack of 'authority' within the business and a failure to engage with the board and other senior executives. In many instances, compliance has failed to adapt to changing business, and other stakeholder, expectations. In some cases, compliance may be doing the wrong work and its focus may be mis-aligned with what is really important.

A regulatory survey in 2017 of the wholesale banking, found that the compliance function had very limited, and often, vague objectives (e.g. to deliver 'regulatory compliance') with little, or no, emphasis on challenging the business or creating or supporting the right culture within the organisation.[4]

There were also issues found relating to compliance competence and difficulties with compliance recruitment, particularly in finding sufficient compliance staff with the ability to manage and analyse 'big data' and artificial intelligence (AI). There were also difficulties in recruiting individuals who had good interpersonal skills and who could convey sufficient credibility to influence others.[5] IT skills, and in particular those relating to AI, were for example necessary for devising programmes which would capture all trade transactions and voice and messaging communications within the firm. This

16

information would be used to look for patterns of behaviour which might indicate some possible market abuse. Similarly, there might be opportunities to employ data analytics on client due diligence and staff recruitment. This could include social media analysis and various databases looking for linked associates, name transliteration and so on.[6] These aspects are considered in more detail in Chapter 6. However, to undertake this work and to provide value, the board, senior management and compliance needs to take a broader perspective and recruit from a wider pool for competencies and experience.

Strategic compliance

Compliance needs to broaden its perspectives. There is a tendency for compliance officers to focus on the near horizon, not looking out much beyond the period of the next annual compliance plan and report. Compliance needs to think much more strategically, working in parallel with the strategic plans for the business. This will include taking account of likely market developments and the business reaction to these; the direction of regulatory change, including possible areas of political focus (e.g. concern about social exclusion, tax avoidance and high net-worth individuals etc.); how technology may change and its implications. The time-horizon should at least match that of the strategic plan for the business.

The context behind this planning is the need for continual reflection on the questions of what compliance is seeking to achieve and what outcomes are desired. These strategic plans will need to be reviewed if there are significant business changes (e.g. the acquisition or disposal of a business area), major regulatory changes (including new legislative proposals) and a change in the political context (e.g. a revolution in the one of the jurisdictions in which the business operates).

The purpose of this planning is to ensure, to the greatest extent possible, that compliance remains relevant and best positioned. The planning may include a long-term investment programme in new technology such as AI (as mentioned earlier'), new staff training requirements and the acquisition of new compliance staff with new skills. This process of reflection may indicate that compliance needs to think more broadly about its role, including determining its social purpose, its style of engagement with the regulators, the role of compliance in changing and developing the right culture and individual ethics in the business. This rethinking will include a need to consider areas of increasing risk such as threats to the reputation of the business and the mechanics of developing trust both within the firm and with the regulators.

Compliance and developing trust

There is a growing interest in reputational risk. Since, for example, banking is wholly based on trust preserving the reputation of a bank as a safe place to deposit money is crucial to the continuing existence of the business. But trust, as an aspect of reputation, goes further. Trust needs to be earned so as the organisation merits being trustworthy. The issues of trust and trustworthiness are constant themes throughout this work.

'Signalling' forms part of this process of developing trust. The business needs to signal that it takes compliance seriously and that its fine words mean something. This requires compliance, as a function, to have a high status in the firm's decision-making process with its views listened to and acted upon. Signalling requires that compliance has sufficient authority in the bank, a subject considered in more detail later. Where compliance figures in the firm's hierarchy is an aspect of this process of signalling.

Reporting lines

Compliance has traditionally been a 'second or third tier' unit. Because, generally, the role of compliance was not fully understood it was not clear where the compliance function should be located in a bank's structure. Following the US model, compliance was often placed under the legal division. Other firms had the function as part of operations or risk. However, more recently, there is some evidence that compliance reporting lines are moving away from heads of legal and chief operating officer to the CEO and chief risk officer.[7] At the same time compliance operations are being re-aligned to global and functional divisions away from regional sections and some compliance functions are being merged with that of operational risk.[8]

The senior management, including the non-executive directors, are responsible for ensuring that the strategy and business model reinforces the firm's general and specific legal duties. They also need to check that the strategy is not mis-interpreted by the organisation's staff and that the right conduct prevails. The compliance function should have a major role in this.

However, business management has tended to regard the compliance function as a technical unit called upon, from time to time, to provide advice. This tendency may be seen in the compliance officer's lack of authority within the organisation. Compliance, along with the other control functions such as internal audit and risk management, may have little or no input into business strategy, product development and the firm's operations. This approach may be one of a number of reasons for various corporate failings in recent years. The lack of input in financial services has been particularly evident with the debacle of Wells Fargo in the United States, Coop Bank in the United Kingdom and in the various banks that collapsed in the 2007–2009 financial crisis. The lack of any, or any adequate, compliance function may also have been a factor in the problems, for example, of large international outsourcers and construction firms such as Interserve and Carillion.

As a second- or third-tier function compliance has not, with some exceptions, been at the heart of business decision-making and the compliance officer has not been a member of the bank's executive committee ('exco'). In parallel, normally the CEO and chief financial officer have been the only executive board members. Change is required so that the chief risk officer becomes an executive board member and the compliance officer a member of exco. However, such change is possible only if the compliance officer takes a broader perspective of their role and engages at a senior level with the business as a whole with full exercise of their authority.

As mentioned, compliance, along with the other control functions, needs to be closely involved with the board and its strategic decision-making. However, compliance officers have usually hesitated to undertake this role, viewing themselves as technicians working in the bowels of the organisation. This tendency has reinforced the senior management perception of compliance mentioned earlier. In part, this may be because compliance officers lack sufficient 'authority' within the business. Consequently, this self-perception and general reticence may be one reason why compliance may be ignored or seen merely as an after-thought, called upon only to 'rubber-stamp' decisions already taken.

There is also a parallel tendency – equally strong – among compliance staff to focus on the details of regulation. This over-focus can result in the simulacrum of compliance while the business goes on very much as before. This approach is sometimes described a 'box-ticking' but encompasses something much deeper and more worrying. It is the abdication of responsibility and the antithesis of establishing and demonstrating 'authority'.

It is worth examining a recent example of the challenges faced by compliance, and other control functions, in relation to corporate strategy and management. It is also an example of the compliance function's self-inflicted failings.

Wells Fargo Bank, compliance and corporate governance

Why the Wells Fargo example is so important

The senior team at Wells Fargo wished to do the right thing. There is nothing to suggest that these senior staff did not believe what they were saying. There is nothing to suggest that their motives were dishonourable. They did not think they were doing anything wrong. It was a straight-forward retail bank. It was not seduced by any 'wicked' investment bankers. For year after year they were supported by their control functions, including compliance. But at its heart was a poisonous self-delusion, made worse by a mixture of arrogance coupled with a lethargy and an over-arching failure of imagination by both the senior management and the control functions.

The cultural and corporate governance issues and their relationship to the compliance function are illustrative of a range of problems that may face a compliance team. These include:

- an outwardly ethical, highly regarded firm which contained a significant canker,
- a senior management team pushing a poisonous strategy,
- a highly defensive culture which tolerated no opposition,
- a culture that neither listened nor understood,
- a series of control functions with no strategic view pursuing highly siloed roles with no broader perspectives,
- a serious failure of imagination and a failure to see the consequences of their actions.

Remedying all of these problems requires a leadership, who exercises 'authority', and who can develop a thinking, assertive and truly ethical compliance function. Hopefully, by analysing what can go wrong it may be possible to learn.

A poisonous strategy but outwardly an ethical bank

The senior executives at Wells Fargo seemed to have been oblivious to the potential effects of their business strategy to expand, significantly cross-selling of retail banking products. Many banks seek to increase product cross-selling. However, Wells Fargo had highly ambitious plans which it pushed aggressively. Neither the board nor the various control functions challenged this strategy, even when the consequences started to come to light.

What is odd is that Wells Fargo was not known as a bank with a pre-datory reputation. It had fared the 2007–2009 financial crisis well and was viewed as generally a 'good citizen'. The bank's board had a Corporate Responsibility Committee (CRC) with 'primary oversight for the company's policies, programs, and strategies' including: 'community development and reinvestment activities and performance, fair and responsible lending, policies and programs related to environmental sustainability... human rights'.[9] The CRC monitored the bank's 'reputation and relationships with external stakeholders' and the CRC also advised the board 'and management on strategies that affect the company's role and reputation as a socially responsible organization'.[10] The bank's 'Vision and Values' code of principles was derived from Norwest bank when it merged with Wells Fargo in 1998.[11] The film's key 'vision' was 'to satisfy all our customers' financial needs and help them succeed financially'.[12]

The then chairman and CEO at Wells Fargo, John Stumpf, in an interview in 2008, said he felt 'badly anytime anyone from our industry does something that does not put the customer at the center of everything that they do ... We feel what our customers feel ... so when our customers grow and benefit and succeed, we grow and benefit and succeed. So if anybody that doesn't do that ... as the primary motivation of their business model, I think is not serving our industry well and is not serving customers well'.[13]

Stumpf is quoted as saying that Wells Fargo believes 'in values lived, not phrases memorized. If you want to find out how strong a company's ethics are, do not listen to what its people say. Watch what they do'.[14] Stumpf saw the bank's culture as protecting the firm. In particular, Stumpf linked 'the vision to its corporate strategy of cross-selling products to its customers; as customers thrive, and have a good experience', and it placed Wells Fargo in a good 'position to provide them yet more products and services'.[15]

A central part of the bank's retail strategy was for each customer to have eight Wells Fargo products. The bank was known for being a leader in cross-selling to customers and in a 2010 letter to shareholders, the CEO 'wrote that Wells Fargo's goal was eight products per customer because eight 'rhymed with great'.[16] However, other large banks generally 'average fewer than three accounts per customer'.[17] Cross selling is seen as important in retail banking since 'to remain competitive in a largely saturated market where revenue opportunities from new customers tend to be limited, deepening relationships with existing customers will likely remain critical to increasing banks' top-line growth. One important way this might be achieved is through more refined strategies and targeted execution of cross selling programs'.[18]

Scale of the issue

In 2013 the Los Angeles Times reported of Wells Fargo branch staff 'to meet quotas, employees have opened unneeded accounts for customers, ordered credit cards without customers' permission and forged client signatures on paperwork. Some employees begged family members to open ghost accounts'.[19] 'One former branch manager ... described her dismay at discovering that employees had talked a homeless woman into opening six checking and savings accounts with fees totaling $39 a month'.[20] Daily cross-selling quotas were set and 'results were reviewed at day's end on a conference call with managers from across the region ...'. If you do not make your goal, you are severely chastised and embarrassed in front of 60-plus managers in your area by the community banking president', the former branch manager said'.[21] 'Then came the threats: Anyone falling short after 2 months would be fired ...'. We were constantly told we would end up working for McDonald's', said Murillo, who later resigned. 'If we did not make the sales quotas ... we had to stay for what felt like after-school detention, or report to a call session on Saturdays'. [22]

Staff bonuses at branch level were not an issue since they could earn only about 3% in incentive pay based on a mixture of sales and customer service. A standard branch position (a 'teller') earned approximately, $26,000 (£20,000) per annum. The pressure was generated by the stick rather than the carrot.

This is similar to the findings of a New City Agenda and Cass Business School review of UK bank culture where, for example, a Halifax bank branch employee recorded that:

All sellers and managers sit at a table with the customer information that is in each seller's diary for that day. Each seller is grilled about which products customers can be cross-sold. Either that or they are referred to another seller to sell them something. That leaves people so disheartened and demotivated it's untrue.[23]

An independent review of Wells Fargo by PwC, an accountancy and consultancy firm, identified 1.5 million deposit accounts and 565,000 credit card accounts that 'may have been unauthorized' ... of the approximately 2.1 million accounts identified, PwC determined that approximately 115,000 accounts were charged a fee, averaging less than $25 per account and totaling $2.66 million in revenue to Wells Fargo'.[24]

Wells Fargo had a policy of firing employees who manipulated or gamed the cross-selling system and some 5,300 staff had their contracts terminated between 2011 and 2015, or approximately one thousand each year.[25]

Mis-leading key risk indicators which all showed 'green'

Neither the senior management nor the board of Wells Fargo was concerned about this strategy. In fact they appeared proud. Stumpf said that 'it's not about I, me, and mine; it's about we, us, and ours. We say 'team members' and not 'employees' because we view our team members as resources to be invested in, not expenses to be managed. It's why we train our leaders to coach and inspire team members and work together—as One Wells Fargo—to achieve our vision. I keep my 41-page Vision & Values booklet close by, and I know many of our team members do as well. But it's not the words in the document that are important. It's how we embody these words in all that we do—for fellow team members, customers, communities, and shareholders'.[26] In part, this lack of concern was influenced by the high regard expressed by both customers and staff generally. For example, the bank saw its customer service scores rising with 'almost eight of every ten of our Regional Banking customers said they're 'extremely satisfied' with their recent call or visit with our banking stores or contact centers. For the second year in a row, we ranked #1 among large banks, according to the American Customer Satisfaction Index'.[27]

The chairman and CEO, was named 'the 2013 Banker of the Year' by the American Banker.[28] In 2015 the bank was voted the seventh most respected company in the world just behind Google and Johnson and Johnson.[29] Carrie Tolstedt, the head of the retail banking division of Wells Fargo, was named one of the twenty-five most powerful woman in banking in 2010.[30] In 2007 Wells Fargo's retail banking arm was one of a dozen firms to win the Gallup Great Workplace Award based on high levels of staff engagement.[31] This recognised 'excellent companies for their extraordinary ability to create an engaged workplace culture'.[32] It won the same award again in both 2014 and 2015.[33]

A mis-leading corporate reputation

Wells Fargo was very conscious of the need to protect its reputation. It had come out well from the 2007–2009 financial crisis and this may have augmented its inherent corporate hubris. At a 2010 investors conference, Pat Callahan, an executive vice-president at the bank and chief administrative officer, expressed clearly 'certainly 2 years ago, while we thought about reputation risk, we didn't think about it as frequently, we didn't think about managing it as intensely as we need to do today … the most important thing that we talk about inside the company right now is that the lever that we have to manage our reputation is to stick to our vision and values. If we are doing things for our customers that are the right things, then the company is going to be in very good shape … and we always consider the reputational impact of the things that we do'.[34] She went onto emphasise that no single manager is 'responsible for reputation risk. All of our business managers in all of our lines of business are responsible'.[35] This philosophy echoes the phrase used by the then head of group compliance at Barclays mentioned at the beginning of Chapter 1. Although 'everyone' in the bank was responsible for compliance, no one was to be held accountable.

All these awards, coupled with statements by senior managers such as Pat Callahan, indicate a company wishing to do the right thing by all its stakeholders. There is nothing to suggest that these senior staff did not believe what they were saying. They did not think they were doing anything wrong. There was, however, a lack of thinking and introspection. All managers may have been responsible for preserving the bank's reputation but none of the senior management thought through their acts of commission or omission. Moreover, as a large responsible firm, Wells Fargo had constructed a panoply of controls and a number of important monitoring and reporting units to ensure that it behaved responsibly. Like the senior team, this edifice proved to be a weak structure.

A compromised and distrusted 'ethics line'

Wells Fargo had a confidential ethics line which employees could call. However, for good reason, it was not trusted by staff. A Wells Fargo Texas-based employee said 'I don't feel … comfortable calling the ethics line … The employee said she was troubled that a branch manager whom she reported to the ethics line this summer seemed to know from which part of the branch the complaint came …' He would make comments saying, 'I know somebody's calling the ethics line,'. That's why I don't feel comfortable reporting anything,' she said. 'If you submit a complaint or a violation of ethics, why should the person who's being reported know where it's coming from? That opens the door for retaliation'.[36]

The regulators took action and in 2017 Wells Fargo was ordered by the US Department of Labor's Occupational Safety and Health Administration to pay compensation of $5.4m and to reinstate an employee.[37] In this instance, in 2010, a bank manager had been fired after reporting suspected fraudulent behaviour to superiors and a bank ethics hotline.[38]

Use of euphemisms to disguise hard selling

Boards, senior management, control functions and regulators need to look out for marketing euphemisms which may conceal what, in reality, are bad practices and poor cultural behaviours. For example, beginning in 2003, Wells Fargo had an annual sales campaign known as 'Jump into January'. The bank recognised that December was generally a poor month for bank product sales due to the holidays and the aim was start the new year with a high level of sales and to avoid a slow sales wind-up in January following the new year break. These campaigns often drove poor sales cultures. Staff would 'stock-pile' sales leads in December and activate them in January. 'Bank staff recalled that bankers were encouraged to make prospect lists of friends and family members who were potential Jump into January sales targets'.[39] The diseased culture can be seen in the example found in one region where district managers had to 'running the gauntlet'.[40] They dressed in various costumes according to a set theme and formed a gauntlet and each manager had to 'run down the line to a whiteboard and report the number of sales they achieved'.[41] This evoked shades of the corrupting sales culture highlighted by David Mamet in his play 'Glengarry Glen Ross'.[42] Such an atmosphere was reinforced by the fact that 'promotion was based on sales levels. To many employees, the route to success was selling more'.[43]

In the face of growing internal concerns within the retail bank Tolstedt ended the 'Jump into January' program but she was worried that ending the January campaign would harm sales figures. In 2013 it was replaced by the 'Accelerate' sales programme aimed at first quarter results.[44] However, Tolstedt need not have worried. 'Accelerate' appears to have been merely a change of name – the underlying toxic sales culture remained.

Senior management at Wells Fargo

The independent board report considered that Tolstedt had failed 'to appreciate both the negative impact on customers and the grave risk to Wells Fargo's brand and reputation. There is no evidence that Tolstedt showed serious concern about the effects of improper sales practices on Wells Fargo's customers or that she initiated efforts to evaluate or remediate customer harm'.[45] She saw cross-selling as the engine for the bank's rate of growth and was reluctant to change the strategy even in the face of negative comments on the effects of pursuing this approach. Instead, she reinforced the high-pressure sales culture. For example, she praised high-pressure tactics and held these up 'as a model for others to emulate'.[46] 'Despite the universal criticism of the 'Jump into January' program as an incubator of low-quality sales and bad sales practices, Tolstedt was 'scared to death' that changing it could hurt sales figures for the entire year and opted instead for only incremental changes'.[47]

Tolstedt and other senior management suffered from a form of 'belief perseverance' - 'the tendency to cling to one's initial belief even after receiving new information that contradicts or disconfirms the basis of that belief'.[48] The evidence suggests that individuals rarely seek out disconfirmatory evidence in naturalistic settings.[49] They will ignore strong arguments opposing their beliefs.[50] Moreover, 'receptiveness to evidence may be further reduced if the evidence is 'inconclusive, or misrepresented'.[51]

Tolstedt compounded this highly blinkered approach with an obsession with control which excluded negative information, coupled with an extreme reluctance 'to make changes'.[52] This approach was enforced by 'an 'inner circle' of staff that supported her, reinforced her views and protected her' and augmented the 'insular culture' she had 'fostered' among the senior management of the retail bank.[53] It is also evident that 'Tolstedt actively discouraged providing information to people outside the [retail bank]'.[54]

The effect of operating a 'fortress' retail bank inhibited the ability of the control functions to operate effectively and many people within Well Fargo 'referred to, and documents confirmed, the difficulties in getting information from her senior leadership team'.[55]

Senior management remuneration

Senior management remuneration was determined by a sub-committee of the Wells Fargo board: Human Resources Committee, chaired by Lloyd Dean, a non-executive director.[56] The 'senior management incentive system had protections consistent with best practices for minimizing risk, including bonuses tied to instilling the company's vision and values in its culture, bonuses tied to risk management' and so on.[57]

For example, Stumpf's bonus was awarded, as recorded in the 2016 SEC filings, for his 'strong and effective leadership reflected by his success in instilling and reinforcing our Vision and Values and risk culture and our progress in achieving key long-term company strategic goals including 'communicating the Company's mission, strategic vision, and values to our team members, investors, communities, and other stakeholders'.[58]

It seems clear that the board sub-committee did not pay much regard to staff complaints nor to the *Los Angeles Times* 2013 article and related media concerns.

Failure 'to join the dots' – a failure of imagination

Stumpf was pleased in 2013 when he was told 'that approximately 1,000 (or approximately 1%) of Community Bank [the retail bank] employees were being terminated for sales integrity violations each year. Stumpf reacted positively to the 1% number; in his view, the fact that only 1% of Wells Fargo employees were terminated meant that 99% of employees were doing their jobs correctly'.[59] Part of the problem was in the way issues were 'framed'. If senior management viewed the strategy and processes as sound then any failings were seen as due to a few individuals. Things would be fine if the small number of 'bad apples' were identified and removed. The same perspective applied to the various control functions and, in part, explains their consistent failures. Again, this is all evidence of a lack of imagination with any doubts or introspection left by staff at the bank lobby as they came into work each day.

Senator Brown asked why 'it never occurred to you that you should bring in somebody, without the regulators suggesting it' to find out what was going on? In reply Stumpf said it was 'a good question, and I have thought about that, a lot about why, and it was—it was early in 2015, about the time that we were considering or talked about who we would bring in, that we finally connected a dot. And there is no excuse why we did not connect it before ... It never dawned on us—and, again, no excuses, and we were wrong ... It was the first time that light bulb went on'.[60] This lack of insight was reflected in comments by the then bank's chief financial officer and subsequent chairman and CEO, Tim Sloan, who said that he was 'not aware of any overbearing sales culture'.[61] These are clear examples of failure of Arendtian 'imagination': 'the capacity to represent the perspectives of other people in our own mind'.[62]

Senior management also ignored another problem indicator. Staff turnover in the retail bank was over 40% in the twelve months to October 2012 and average around 30% annually between 2011 and the end of 2015.[63] This was higher than other financial services firms but significantly lower than other retail businesses but 'Tolstedt's view ... was that there were always people willing to work in Wells Fargo branches'.[64] 'The result was the many of the branch staff were very inexperienced and lacked training'.[65]

The non-executive members of the bank board also lacked expertise in retail banking which forced them to depend too much on senior management. They also were dependent on the control functions being effective. As discussed later, these were weak reeds and were unable to bear the weight of the responsibilities placed on them. Coupled with all this was an overly defensive mind-set. There was no effective action by the board, or by any other part of the bank, in response to the *Los Angeles Times* 2013 article and the non-executive directors' reaction in 2016 was to engage a Washington PR firm to defend Wells Fargo (and possibly themselves).[66]

In 2017 the board tried to increase its level of oversight by creating a new Office of Ethics, Oversight, and Integrity reporting to the board's Risk Committee.[67] The board's Corporate Responsibility Committee's now requires reports on customer complaints and allegations from other sources, such as the Ethics Line.[68] However, the board is responsible for setting the strategic direction of the bank as well as monitoring its behaviour. It is not clear how the board had addressed this critical element of its role. There may also be a need to give a 'voice' to both customers and the most junior employees. How this may be best effected falls outside the scope of this work.

Additionally, the role of regulatory compliance has been 'broadened to include the company's compliance culture' with a view to clarifying the board's 'oversight of conduct risk'.[69] This is a step in the right direction but it is not clear how the role of the control functions has been strengthened and how their perspectives have been changed and developed in practice.

All the risk control arrangements failed

The bank spent lavishly on compliance resources. In 2015 the bank 'had over 10,000 employees dedicated to organizational risk and compliance, with plans to grow its headcount and budget another 16 percent in the coming year'.[70] This followed a McKinsey report in 2013 on risk management practices.[71]

The retail banking operation developed its own 'Sales Integrity Task Force' which, among other things, developed 'training materials for managers and employees, including appropriate and inappropriate sales activity and consequences of misconduct'.[72] There was also an in-house legal team which specialised in looking at aspects of staff fraud; an extensive risk management series of controls and monitoring and reporting; a high-powered, diverse, board of directors, a fraud investigation team; a customer complaints assessment and reporting unit and a confidential 'ethics line'. All of these units failed.

There is nothing to suggest that the bank was a corrupt organisation. Generally, the board and employees wanted to do the right thing. However, all the controls and compliance arrangements went wrong. All the information need to identify the problems existed but the information was not reported, or it was mis-reported, or the data was looked at from the wrong perspective.

The control functions within the retail bank

The bank operated the so-called 'three lines of defence' model discussed in more detail in Chapter 5. At the apex was the Internal Audit function.

Internal audit

As a 'third line of defence' Internal Audit saw its role as 'testing the operation of specific processes and the processes' effectiveness at managing the risks they were designed to control, but that they did not generally investigate root causes of risks ... that task rests with the business'.[73] Its reports on sales practices raised no 'red flags'.

There was also a general lassitude in Internal Audit's approach. It displaying no sense of urgency and there was little evidence of any attempts to follow-up on issues. There is similar criticism of the other control functions within Wells Fargo where, for example, the group function planned to review sales processes in 2013 'but these initiatives did not start to be implemented until 2015'.[74] Further, Internal Audit had a very narrow view of its responsibilities. The function recorded that the sales practices were 'effective' since 'sales integrity violations were identified, investigated and, when violations were confirmed, responsible employees were terminated'.[75]

There was also confusion over who was responsible for what under the so-called 'lines of defence' model operated by the bank. For example, in 2012 Internal Audit reviewed bank compensation and reach a satisfactory conclusion based solely on compensation plan documented actions. No staff were questioned to see how things operated in practice since Internal Audit saw this as the role of the first and second lines of defence.[76] Internal Audit restricted their role to assessing process controls and did not investigate 'root causes of risks' since 'that task rests with the business' because the latter had 'greater familiarity with the risk environment, better access to operational data and both proximity to and responsibility for its employees' actions'.[77] This is compounded by the lack evidence that the 'three lines' worked together, and they did not coordinated their work.

Internal Audit's judgement continued to be questionable. For example, even after there was evidence of customer and staff concerns over product selling practices, it continued with its monitoring the retail bank's sales processes and found these to be satisfactory. Its review of the bank's remuneration policies concluded that these 'did not promote unethical behavior'.[78] Some issues were identified in its 2015 audit, almost 2 years after the Los Angeles Times article. These included the need for 'improvement' in recognition of enhancements needed to become 'fully effective relative to heightened regulatory expectations' but overall the culture of the retail bank was found to be satisfactory.[79]

Risk

The head of risk at the retail bank at the time was Claudia Russ Anderson. She appears to have seen her role as 'a team player' and consider that an internal adverse report 'made the problem sound 'so much worse than it is'.[80] She seems to have seen it as her job to protect Tolstedt and the retail banking

28

operations from criticism. She was described as being an advocate for the bank and was not independent or objective 'when dealing with regulators on sales practice issues'.[81] When discussing a draft risk report Russ Anderson wrote to another manager that she was 'worried about putting something like that into a deck [a slide presentation]. I'd rather we did that verbally because this deck is subject to the regulators [sic] review'.[82] Clearly, these statements and actions are not those of a responsible individual in a control function. However, this defensive frame of mind is not that unusual in other banks and organisations and it is critical that it is resisted.

In addition, the chief operational risk officer ("CORO") did not see sales practice issues as falling within her remit. In her view, this area was the responsibility of the line business and other control functions (i.e. Legal, Human resources, Audit and the Investigations team). 'She viewed sales gaming as a known problem that was well-managed, contained and small'.[83]

There was a clear tension between the group risk function and the individual business risk units. This not unusual and is found in many organisations. It manifests itself in a lack of trust, and in local business units taking a defensive stand against the 'centre', and is often buttressed by regional and business loyalties and cultural affiliations. It makes it very difficult for the group functions to get accurate and timely information. The central functions are seen as remote, out of touch and ineffectual with a 'chateau' or 'grand lamasery' mentality.[84] The centre considers the local units to be difficult and uncooperative and lacking a wider perspective. The latter see the centre as interfering, unjustifiably privileged and adding little value. There is a spectrum of solutions; from a highly centralised set of control functions, to a looser federation but with strong reporting lines to the centre with the latter having control over appointments, promotions, budgets and so forth. There is probably no one right answer. Much will rest on personalities and individual relationships, and levels of trust. Wells Fargo never devised a workable arrangement during the period in question and through 2016 and 2017 it began a process of changing the business risk reporting line to the group function. Again, there was no obvious urgency.[85]

The in-house law department

There were two in-house legal sections involved in the scandal: one covering employment law and the other responsible for litigation issues. The former were 'generally focused on the litigation costs of sales integrity cases in the event of lawsuits by terminated employees'.[86] In addition, from 2002, the legal teams were conscious of the risk of damage to the bank's reputation. However, 'notwithstanding the growing awareness of the reputational risk associated with [widespread staff] terminations, and the fact that many of these incidents involved unauthorized products or accounts, the perception persisted in the Law Department that sales integrity issues involved 'gaming' the [retail bank's] incentive programs and not conduct affecting customers'.[87]

The in-house teams provided legal advice throughout the period but appears that none of this went to the heart of the issues and the various sections making up the in-house legal team appeared to be have been content to stay in their purely 'advisory' mode and did not wish to 'rock the boat'. 'There continued to be a lack of recognition within the Law Department (as in other parts of Wells Fargo) about the significance of the number of sales integrity terminations, and the potential reputational consequences'.[88] In terms of litigation, the aim appeared to be to keep costs down. 'Confident those costs would be relatively modest, the Law Department did not appreciate that sales integrity issues reflected a systemic breakdown in Wells Fargo's culture and values and an ongoing failure to correct the widespread breaches of trust in the misuse of customers' personal data and financial information'.[89]

Internal Investigations

The Internal Investigations unit was focused on investigating employee misconduct. During the period in question it variously reported to Internal Audit, Group Risk and Group Human Resources, at different times. In 2004 the Internal Investigations unit identified the issues regarding poor sales practices and noted that 'the incentive to cheat is based on the fear of losing their jobs for not meeting performance expectations'. The report warned of the reputational risks for Wells Fargo'.[90] This report was widely circulated in 2004 but a subsequent report to the retail bank's senior management lacked data and any 'root cause' analysis.[91]

Compliance

Around 2005, Patricia Callahan set up the Operational Risk Management and Compliance group. However, the scope of compliance was limited to anti-money laundering and compliance with consumer credit and mortgage disclosure, and similar, regulations. The role of compliance was seen as very narrow and conduct of business and sales practices were outside its remit.[92] These latter areas were either not see as significant, or were thought to be well controlled based on Internal Audit's assessments.

It was not until 2015, and later, that the scope of compliance's role was widened to cover aspects of sales practices and culture, but by then it was much too late.

Conclusion to the failures at Wells Fargo

It is tempting to take the comfortable view that the Wells Fargo debacle, and similar failures, were the result of extraordinary greed and incompetence and to see these fiascos as outliers.[93] In practice, what went wrong was the result of common foibles and misconceptions. The consequences of the actions and inactions of managers such as Stumpf and Tolstedt may have been bad but it is unlikely that these individuals were 'wicked'. Paradoxically, this makes them more dangerous. A malicious or psychopathic manager would have been more obvious. But the senior team at Wells Fargo were more likely to be described as 'hard-driving', 'goal-orientated', 'highly competitive' and so forth. These may be described a positive attributes but at the same time they contain the seeds of failure. They lost their faculty of thinking with a consequential failure of imagination.[94] As Tim Sloan said 'we were slow to see the harm ... we either minimized the problem, or we failed to see the problem for what it really was – something bigger than we originally imagined'.[95]

The process of thinking goes beyond simply 'imagining' the perspectives of others. In forming our own judgements 'we must actually talk with others to incorporate their perspectives'.[96] The process of activating thoughts and developing our imagination does not involve, metaphorically, sitting in a dark room. It is an active process of real engagement with others. 'The cultivation of one's moral imagination flourishes in such a culture in which the self-centered perspective of the individual is constantly challenged by the multiplicity and diversity of perspectives'.[97]

The bank had invested heavily in a number of control functions. However, each, in their own way, failed. Even then, from time to time, they did manage to raise a red flag – most notable Internal Investigations in 2004. But often these were countered by contrary, comforting indicators – largely from Internal Audit. Other, potentially important control functions operated with a very limited scope – either as designed or self-imposed. Even as late as 2013 and the *Los Angeles Times* article nothing significant was done. The imagination of the senior team remained dormant. It took regulatory action to finally bring about change from 2015 onwards. The chairman and CEO still denied that there was a significant issue, in practice until he was faced with a Senate hearing in 2016:

> Stumpf: 'Senator, I do not know how—what motivated or why people did this, but we did fire managers and managers of managers, and in one case, an area president. So, again, you know, this 1 percent is way too many. I do not want to minimize it. But I also want to make sure that we recognize that the vast majority of the people did exactly the things we wanted them to do to help deepen customer relationships'.[98]

In part the senior management of Wells Fargo did not see sales misconduct as a 'material' issue.[99] Their view of materiality was aligned to a purely accounting concept reflecting the effect of an issue on balance-sheet valuations. With a significant lack of imagination they failed to see that regulatory compliance, the value of the firm's shares and reputational damage to the business may be interlinked with serious consequences for the business.

The issues go well beyond companies like Wells Fargo

There is evidence that all is not well in many UK companies, including those outside financial services. The collapse of Carillion, BHS, Patisserie Valerie, Monarch Airlines and Thomas Cook are recent examples. There were also major issues with a number of other businesses such as London Capital and Finance and the funds managed by Neil Woodford. In some other companies there is evidence that corporate debt has been piled-up and used to make large dividend and executive remuneration payments even as the business may have faltered.

Some of this may be evidence of poor corporate governance and risk control failures. This has been recognised by the UK's Financial Reporting Council, currently in the process of being revamped. In is 2020 Annual Review of compliance with the UK's Corporate Governance Code it found that 'companies need to improve their governance practices and reporting if they are to demonstrate their positive impact on the economy and wider society'.[100] More generally, the FRC was critical of firms 'concentrating on achieving box-ticking compliance, at the expense of effective governance and reporting'.[101] This was seen as only 'paying lip service to the spirit of the Code and does a disservice to the interests of shareholders and wider stakeholders, including the public'.[102] This focus on mechanical compliance by firms may allow them to convince themselves that they are compliant but it demonstrates that they have 'little insight into governance practices'.[103]

For example, 'The directors should confirm in the annual report that they have carried out a robust assessment of the principal risks facing the company, including those that would threaten its business model, future performance, solvency or liquidity. The directors should describe those risks and explain how they are being managed or mitigated'.[104] While most FTSE 350 companies identified risks there was only limited explanations for changes and any risk mitigations.[105] The FRC Annual Review also noted that almost half these companies 'gave little insight into how they assess long-term viability ... and how these link back to principal risks'.[106] At the very least, this does not meet the spirit of the Code's intentions.

The updated 2018 Code requires that 'the board should establish the company's purpose, values and strategy, and satisfy itself that these and its culture are aligned. All directors must act with integrity, lead by example and promote the desired culture'.[107] However, the FRC 2020 review found some issues with corporate understanding of what was meant by a firms' 'purpose'. There was a tendency by FTSE 100 companies to 'conflate mission and vision with purpose'.[108] A business needs to know why it exists before it can set out what its mission is and how it will seek to carry out its purpose. It is likely that the executive and other staff will not be clear if the board does not know itself. The business model needs to connect with the organisation's purpose. So, for example, the purpose of Disney theme parks might be to 'create the happiest place on Earth'.[109] This needs to be distinguished from its mission statement which sets out, at a high-level, how it intends to achieve its purpose - 'the mission of The Walt Disney Company is to entertain, inform and inspire people around the globe through the power of unparalleled storytelling ... to use creativity, technology and innovation to bring storytelling to new heights'.[110]

Similarly, the FRC found that 'companies substituted what appeared to be a slogan or marketing line for their purpose or restricted it to achieving shareholder returns and profit'.[111] There were also issues about the difficulty in connecting the company's stated purpose with its business model. All of this suggests that boards and senior management and their advisers either do not understand their company's purpose or have little regard for why it may be important. It is also likely that they may have not properly considered the importance of the firm's culture nor how the business relates to its various stakeholders.

In parallel, the boards of some firms apparently delegated issues relating to corporate culture to committees dealing with a variety of miscellaneous issues such as environmental sustainability and health and safety.[112] Similar lack of concern can be seen in the fact that corporate measurement of culture was very limited for number of firms. For example, some used gender diversity as the single culture metric while others focused on the completion rate of the annual employee survey.[113] Again, this demonstrates a corporate failure to understand the importance of culture within the business; the damage that a poor culture can produce and the benefits of a good culture. Only a few of these organisations operate in the field of financial services and many will not have compliance and risk functions. However, it does show what a long way many of the largest firms in the United Kingdom still have to go. It also calls into question the role of their professional advisers, both in-house and external, as well as their statutory auditors.

Conclusion

Wells Fargo and other corporate failures provide a number of lessons. As a result there are several key points to note:

- rarely are individuals conscious that they are doing wrong in a company. In most instances they suffer from self-delusion. This may take the form of hubris and denial but at the heart are a number of psychological factors evidenced by a casting off of responsibility and a failure of imagination,

- the control functions, including compliance, take their lead from these individuals and similarly display a matching sense of loss of imagination and a 'Pflichtversäumnis' or avoidance of responsibility or one's duty towards oneself and others,
- there is a lack of perspective and a failure to think about the role of compliance with no, or little, strategic considerations,
- there is a deficit of professionalism,
- there is a failure to develop the trust of stakeholders, and, in particular, the regulators,
- seeing compliance as a purely technical function, advising the business without asserting its 'agency' is at the centre of the firm's decision-making and operations.

All this means that the compliance staff must speak and operate with authority and this authority must be deserved and recognised. Some in compliance will already be doing all of this but many are not – and this needs to change. The lessons from Wells Fargo demonstrate the need for fundamental change throughout many organisations. Corporate boards and senior management need to take the lead, a lead supported by the regulators.

Notes

1 FCA, 'The compliance function in wholesale banks' (November 2017), 1.3–1.4, https://fca.org.uk/publication/research/the-compliance-function-in-wholesale-banks.pdf (accessed 13 May 2019).
2 Ibid ('The compliance function in wholesale banks'), 6.1.
3 Ibid ('The compliance function in wholesale banks'), 5.1.
4 Ibid ('The compliance function in wholesale banks'), 1.3–1.4.
5 Ibid ('The compliance function in wholesale banks'), 3.1 and 4.4.
6 For example, using the Statistical Analysis System web-site, DataFlux Quality Knowledge Base (QKB), https://support.sas.com/software/products/qkb/index.html (accessed 13 May 2019).
7 Supra note 1 ('The compliance function in wholesale banks'), 2.1.
8 Supra note 1 ('The compliance function in wholesale banks'), 2.1.
9 Wells Fargo, 'Corporate social responsibility report 2013. The right people. The right passion. The right focus - serving communities in the real economy', 18, https://www08.wellsfargomedia.com/assets/pdf/about/corporate-responsibility/2013-social-responsibility-report.pdf (accessed 27 March 2020).
10 Ibid ('CSR report 2013'), 18.
11 Thomas Stanton submission to the Federal Reserve Board, 'Enhanced prudential standards and early remediation requirements for covered companies', 13 February 2012, 33–34, https://www.federalreserve.gov/SECRS/2012/February/20120215/R-1438/R-1438_021312_105398_555068728868_1.pdf (accessed 27 March 2020).
12 Ibid (Stanton submission), 33–34.

13 Marketplace website, 10 June 2008, Interview transcript: Kai Ryssdal interviewing John Stumpf, https://www.marketplace.org/2008/06/10/interview-transcript-john-stumpf/ (accessed 26 March 2020).

14 An examination of Wells Fargo unauthorized accounts and the regulatory response hearing before the Committee on Banking, Housing and Urban Affairs, United States Senate, 114 Congress, Second Session, 20 September 2016, S. HRG. 114–510, Questions from Senator Elizabeth Warren, 27–28, https://www.govinfo.gov/content/pkg/CHRG-114shrg23001/pdf/CHRG-114shrg23001.pdf (accessed 27 March 2020).

15 Supra note 11 (Stanton submission), 33–34.

16 Supra note 14 (Senate Committee hearing), Questions from the Committee Chairman, Richard Shelby, 1.

17 Supra note 14 (Senate Committee hearing), Questions from Senator Warren, 27.

18 Deloitte Center for Financial Services, 'Kicking it up a notch. Taking retail bank cross-selling to the next level' (2013), 15, https://www2.deloitte.com/content/dam/Deloitte/us/Documents/financial-services/us-kickingitupanotch-092614.pdf (accessed 28 March 2020).

19 Los Angeles Times, 'Wells Fargo's pressure-cooker sales culture comes at a cost', 21 December 2013, https://www.latimes.com/business/la-fi-wells-fargo-sale-pressure-20131222-story.html (accessed 29 March 2020).

20 Ibid (Los Angeles Times).

21 Ibid (Los Angeles Times).

22 Ibid (Los Angeles Times).

23 Andre Spicer and others, 'A report on the culture of British retail banking' (2014) *New City Agenda and Cass Business School*, 21, http://newcityagenda.co.uk/wp-content/uploads/2014/11/Online-version.pdf (accessed 31 March 2020).

24 Supra note 14 (Senate Banking Committee hearing), response to written questions of Senator Warren from John G. Stumpf, 162.

25 Supra note 14 (Senate Banking Committee hearing), response to written questions of Senator Sasse from John G. Stumpf, 146.

26 Wells Fargo Annual Report 2013, 'The right people. The right markets. The right model', 8, https://qjubs3y9ggo1neukf3sc81r19vv-wpengine.netdna-ssl.com/assets/pdf/annual-reports/2013-annual-report.pdf (accessed 28 March 2020).

27 Wells Fargo Annual Report 2010, 6, https://qjubs3y9ggo1neukf3sc81r19vv-wpengine.netdna-ssl.com/assets/pdf/annual-reports/2010-annual-report.pdf (accessed 28 March 2020).

28 American Banker magazine website, 13 November 2013, https://www.americanbanker.com/news/wells-fargos-john-stumpf-the-2013-banker-of-the-year (accessed 28 March 2020).

29 Vito Racanelli, 'World's most respected companies', 29 June 2015, *Barron's, New York*, 95(26), 23–24.

30 US Banker (October 2010), 120(10), 32.

31 Gallup Great Workplace Awards website, https://www.gallup.com/events/178865/gallup-great-workplace-award-current-previous-win-ners.aspx (accessed 28 March 2020).

32 Ibid (Gallup Awards).

33 Ibid (Gallup Awards).

34 Pat Callahan, Wells Fargo 2010 investor conference - final (14 May 2010), Fair Disclosure Wire.

35 Ibid (Wells Fargo 2010 investor conference)

36 The Charlotte Observer, 'Some at Wells Fargo say they fear using 'ethics line,' even as bank vows to fix it', 11 November 2016, https://www.charlotteobserver.com/news/business/banking/bank-watch-blog/article114171173.html (accessed 29 March 2020).

37 Occupational Safety and Health Administration (OSHA) website, 'OSHA orders Wells Fargo to reinstate whistleblower, fully restore lost earnings banking industry', 3 April 2017, https://www.dol.gov/newsroom/releases/osha/osha20170403 (accessed 29 March 2020).

38 Ibid (OSHA website).

39 Independent Directors of the Board of Wells Fargo, 'Sales practices investigation report', April 2017, 22, https://www08.wellsfargomedia.com/assets/pdf/about/investor-relations/presentations/2017/board-report.pdf (accessed 29 October 2018).

40 Ibid (Directors Report), 23.

41 Ibid (Directors Report), 23.

42 David Mamet, *Glengarry Glen Ross* (Methuen, London, 1984), 13.

43 Supra note 39 (Directors Report), 28.

44 Supra note 39 (Directors Report), 22.

45 Supra note 39 (Directors Report), 46.

46 Supra note 39 (Directors Report), 46.

47 Supra note 39 (Directors Report), 46.

48 Stephanie Anglin, 'Do beliefs yield to evidence? Examining belief perseverance vs. change in response to congruent empirical findings' (2019) *Journal of Experimental Social Psychology*, 82, 176–199, 176.

49 Asher Koriat, Sarah Lichtenstein, and Baruch Fischhoff, 'Reasons for confidence' (1980) *Journal of Experimental Psychology*, 6, 107–118, 117.

50 Randall Kleinhesselink and Richard Edwards, 'Seeking and avoiding belief-discrepant information as a function of its perceived refutability' (1975) *Journal at Personality and Social Psychology*, 31(5), 787–790, 788.

51 Supra note 48 (Anglin), 198.

52 Supra note 39 (Directors Report), 46.

53 Supra note 39 (Directors Report), 46–47.

54 Supra note 39 (Directors Report), 47.

55 Supra note 39 (Directors Report), 47.

56 Wells Fargo 2016, SEC Proxy Statement, Schedule 14A, 21, https://www.sec.gov/Archives/edgar/data/72971/000119312516506771/d897049ddef14a.htm (accessed 31 March 2020).

57 Brian Tayan, 'The Wells Fargo cross-selling scandal', 8 January 2019, Stanford Closer Look Series, 2, https://www.gsb.stanford.edu/sites/gsb/files/publication-pdf/cgri-closer-look-62-wells-fargo-cross-selling-scandal.pdf (accessed 27 March 2020).

58 Supra note 56 (SEC filings Schedule 14A), 51.

59 Supra note 39 (Directors Report), 55.

60 Supra note 14 (Senate Banking Committee hearing), response to oral questions of Senator Brown from John G. Stumpf, 12.

61 Supra note 19 (Los Angeles Times).

62 Andrew Tyner, 'Action, judgment, and imagination in Hannah Arendt's thought' (2017) *Political Research Quarterly*, 70(3), 523–534, 524, https://www.jstor.org/stable/pdf/26384921.pdf?refreqid=excelsior%3A752f019ddf2b6dca7adbe633807e28d4 (accessed 31 April 2020).

63 Supra note 39 (Directors Report), 27–28.

64 Supra note 39 (Directors Report), 27–28.

65 Supra note 39 (Directors Report), 27–28.

66 Financial Times 'Wells Fargo's independent directors hire lobbying firm', 22 February 2017, https://www.ft.com/content/e27d7446-f921-11e6-bd4e-68d53499ed71 (accessed 6 April 2020).
67 Supra note 39 (Directors Report), 54.
68 Supra note 39 (Directors Report), 54.
69 Supra note 39 (Directors Report), 17–18.
70 Matthew Bedan, 'Compliance culture, culture eats compliance for lunch: behavioral science lessons from the Wells Fargo scandal', 28 November 2018, The Anti-Corruption Report, 7(24), 3, https://www.forensicrisk.com/wp-content/uploads/The-Anti-Corruption-Report-the-definitive-source-of-actionable-intelligence-covering-anti-corruption-laws-around-the-globe-_-Article_-_p_Culture-Eats-Compliance-fo-002.pdf (accessed 28 March 2020).
71 Supra note 39 (Directors Report), 101–102.
72 Supra note 70 ('Compliance culture'), 3.
73 Supra note 39 (Directors Report), 96.
74 Supra note 39 (Directors Report), 63.
75 Supra note 39 (Directors Report), 92.
76 Supra note 39 (Directors Report), 93.
77 Supra note 39 (Directors Report), 96.
78 Supra note 39 (Directors Report), 91.
79 Supra note 39 (Directors Report), 94.
80 Supra note 39 (Directors Report), 50.
81 Supra note 39 (Directors Report), 50.
82 Supra note 39 (Directors Report), 50.
83 Supra note 39 (Directors Report), 61.
84 A description often used to describe British army headquarters in World War One in France which were frequently located in countryside chateaux which operated like a monastic order many miles away from the front. Dan Todman, 'The grand lamasery revisited: general headquarters the Western Front 1914–1918', in Gary Sheffield and Dan Todman (eds.) *Command and control on the Western Front* (Spellmount, Staplehurst, 2004), 39–40.
85 Supra note 39 (Directors Report), 71.
86 Supra note 39 (Directors Report), 72–75.
87 Supra note 39 (Directors Report), 75.
88 Supra note 39 (Directors Report), 78.
89 Supra note 39 (Directors Report), 78.
90 Supra note 39 (Directors Report), 89.
91 Supra note 39 (Directors Report), 90.
92 Supra note 39 (Directors Report), 60.
93 Supra note 70 ('Compliance culture'), 2.
94 Hanna Arendt, *Responsibility and judgement* (Schocken, New York, 2003), 139.
95 Supra note 39 (Directors Report), 59.
96 Seyla Benhabib, 'Judgment and the moral foundations of politics in Arendt's thought' (1988) *Political Theory*, 16(1), 29–51, 47–48.
97 Ibid (Benhabib), 48.
98 Supra note 14 (Senate Banking Committee hearing), response to oral questions of Senator Toomey from John G. Stumpf, 18.
99 Supra note 14 (Senate Banking Committee hearing), response to oral questions of Senator Toomey from John G. Stumpf, 17–18.
100 Financial Reporting Council (FRC) website, FRC's Chief Executive, Sir Jon Thompson, 'Improved governance and reporting required to promote

sustainability and trust in business', 9 January 2020, https://www.frc.org.uk/news/january-2020/improved-governance-and-reporting-required-to-prom (accessed 9 January 2020).

101 Ibid (FRC website).
102 Ibid (FRC website).
103 FRC, Annual Review of the UK Corporate Governance Code, January 2020, 1, https://www.frc.org.uk/getattachment/53799a2d-824e-4e15-9325-33eb6a30f063/Annual-Review-of-the-UK-Corporate-Governance-Code,-Jan-2020_Final.pdf (accessed 10 January 2020).
104 FRC, UK Corporate Governance Code, April 2016, C.2.1, https://www.frc.org.uk/getattachment/ca7e94c4-b9a9–49e2-a824-ad76a322873c/UK-Corporate-Governance-Code-April-2016.pdf (accessed 12 January 2020).
105 Supra note 103 (FRC Annual Review January 2020), 7.
106 Supra note 103 (FRC Annual Review January 2020), 8.
107 UK Corporate Governance Code, July 2018, 4, https://www.frc.org.uk/getattachment/88bd8c45–50ea-4841-95b0-d2f4f48069a2/2018-UK-Corporate-Governance-Code-FINAL.pdf (accessed 12 January 2020).
108 Supra note 103 (FRC Annual Review January 2020), 9.
109 Lauren Newell, 'Happiness at the house of mouse: how Disney negotiates to create the 'happiest place on Earth'' (2012) *Pepperdine Dispute Resolution Law Journal*, 12, 415–528, 419. Available at SSRN: https://ssrn.com/abstract=2109491 (accessed 12 January 2020).
110 Disney websites, https://www.thewaltdisneycompany.com/about/ and https://dpep.disney.com/parks-and-experiences/ (accessed 12 January 2020).
111 Supra note 103 (FRC Annual Review January 2020), 9.
112 Supra note 103 (FRC Annual Review January 2020), 10.
113 Supra note 103 (FRC Annual Review January 2020), 10.

3

COMPLIANCE AND 'WHISTLEBLOWING' AND CORPORATE PSYCHOLOGY

Introductions

This chapter considers the importance of whistleblowing for the firm, its board and senior management and the compliance function. It is possible that staff who raise concerns are the most powerful 'tool' available to the board and compliance since they provide valuable information on what may be happening in the depths of the organisation. As discussed later, the subject also provides a number of valuable insights for regulators. An examination of whistleblowing may also assist senior management who may lack sufficient understanding of what is happening. Consequently, it is important that those in compliance ensure that the pathways for this information are open and they listen to what they hear with an open mind. This requires that there is:

- some form of 'cultural permission' to whistleblow,
- whistleblower training,
- active listening to whistleblowers,
- adequate information provided back to the whistleblower on what has happened to the concerns they raised,
- no vindictive action taken against those that raise concerns,
- evidence that whistleblowing is taken seriously.

However, in some businesses there are countervailing pressures to suppress whistleblowing. These firms live in permanent denial. They are often dominated by a culture of fear and secretiveness. They will frequently employ non-disclosure agreements (NDAs) to hide the truth. NDAs effectively use contractual arrangements to prevent employees and others to speak up. While there are good reasons to use NDAs, all too often lawyers, both in-house and those in professional firms, go along with their abusive use out of misplaced loyalty to their 'client'. At the same time the compliance function may turn a blind eye to their use and claim both a lack of knowledge and interest in this misuse of NDAs.

As mentioned earlier, organisations with a poor culture will always be in a state of denial, claiming that there are no significant issues. They will often distance themselves from any responsibility claiming, for example, that any issues arise from areas outside their remit or factors beyond their control, or that worse abuses can be found elsewhere. They will also frequently, attack the person who raised the concern. All this reveals an organisation in the throes of moral turpitude. It is an enterprise which has fallen into the Slough of Despond and is full of 'many fears, and doubts, and discouraging apprehensions, which all of them get together, and settle in this place'.[1]

This chapter uses the severe failings at the UK's Mid Staffordshire National Health Service (NHS) Foundation Trust to illustrate these points and a culture which was fatal to many of its patients.

All this indicates the need for compliance to understand the psychology and emotions of those working in the organisation and the implications for compliance. Organisations are almost, by nature, defensive with 'the wagons circled' in a 'wagenburg' to repel outsiders. Mistakes and sins of omission and commission are likely to be rationalised and minimised. In parallel, there is also a strong risk that processes and mindless routine will substitute for thought and reflection and many employees will work with their critical faculties numbed, while those that do think may despair.

Regulation, in these circumstances is not sufficient. There is an important role for compliance to counter these potential risks with compliance staff acting as educators. This can done, in part, by improved communications – often based on constructing and communicating a narrative. These may include looking back to lessons from the firm's past. Communication needs to indicate a high degree of humanity in the way staff operate and treat others, including their colleagues, customers, suppliers and so on. It is intrinsically worthy to do so and, additionally, is more likely to result in a business that complies with the regulations with less need for checking and disciplinary actions. This thoughtful approach to regulation, with an appeal to individual emotion, may help develop a culture of compliance and sustain it for the future.

Compliance and 'siloed blindness'

It is likely that someone knew about almost everything that went wrong in recent years at banks and other financial services firms before the regulators became aware of the issues. Often these individuals were in relatively junior roles. Although understanding that there was something awry, they may not have appreciated the full seriousness of the problem. They may have tried to raise their concerns but were metaphorically, 'patted on the head' and told that there was no issue, or that it was known about and that they were not to worry further. They may have been too scared to speak-up, or worried about informing on a colleague or because of some misplaced loyalty to the company. Working in 'silos' they view the actions in another section as 'none of their business' and consequently, a problem for someone else. It may be simply the desire to avoid being made to look foolish if their concern turns out to lack foundation.

The effect of silos on the work of compliance was clearly set out be Baroness Kramer in her questioning of Mike Walters (Group Head of Compliance, Barclays Bank), in relation to the London Inter-bank Offered Rate (Libor) scandal.

'DQ721 Baroness Kramer: I'm beginning to get a grip slowly on the silo culture at [Barclays Bank]. If I understand it correctly, Mr. Walters, who was in charge of compliance ... essentially is facing off against the regulator and what the regulator is responsible for and therefore, in a narrow sense, is expecting to happen in the organisation.

The silo ends there, so when we have a situation such as Libor, which was not a regulated activity and fell outside that narrow competence, there is no one to pick it up because everybody is operating on a silo basis, which, from what I understand from what you said earlier, is a fundamental part of the structure. People work within a narrow silo arrangement'.[2]

Information from a variety of sources is critical to compliance, senior management and the board. Consequently, it is important to understand the reasons why this information may not be forthcoming and what can be done both to access and to act upon this vital intelligence.

Ensuring that the conduit for information is open

As mentioned earlier in this chapter, and also in the previous chapter covering the issues at Wells Fargo, one or more staff knew of the problems. It is important that compliance, other senior management and the board have access to these concerns. Staff need to know that they can freely raise these worries, or in terms of common parlance 'whistleblow', and that they will be listened to, action will be taken on this information, and, at the very least, there will be no vindictive consequences for the employee who did their duty.

Whistleblowing and regulatory insight

Whistleblowing is important for two particular reasons. First, it provides, management, control functions and regulators with an opportunity to see into the depths of the organisation. As discussed elsewhere, both regulators and management face severe difficulties in knowing what is really going on inside an organisation. Consequently, early awareness of issues should be welcomed by managers. Whistleblowing needs to be acknowledged as a tool of management and compliance.

Second, it gives an indication of the culture and ethics of a business. This includes providing an indication of how receptive an organisation is to internal criticism, whether it listens and takes action, and the extent to which managers adopt a more vindictive approach seeking out the person who has raised their concerns, and visiting retribution upon them as a warning to others to keep quiet in the future.

'Whistleblowing' and compliance

Whistleblowing can be defined as 'the disclosure to a person or public body, outside normal channels and management structures, of information concerning unsafe, unethical or illegal practices'.[3] It is difficult to express how important whistleblowing is for regulators, regulated firms and the senior management, board and the various control functions within the firm. If handled properly it can give them all an insight into the bowels of the business. Those who raise concerns are like gold dust and should be treated accordingly. They are likely to be both brave and loyal, imbued with an inner sense that something is not quite right. There will be some whose actions are malicious but, anecdotally (from my own experience), these are few and far between.

It is for compliance to ensure that:

- there is a process for handling whistleblowers within the firm, including a means of protecting the individual from retribution,
- these arrangements include a member of the senior management – which could be the compliance officer – to oversee the policies and their implementation,
- there is a non-executive director who carries out the same role but at a board level,
- all staff, including contractors, are aware of these processes, the protections they afford and who to contact and how best to do so,
- all concerns are followed up appropriately, and the whistleblower kept informed and protected,
- other senior management, control functions, the board and the regulators are informed and updated.

These aspects are addressed in more detail later in this chapter.

Whistleblower guidance

The FCA has issued whistleblowing guidance on its website but it is confused and much less emphatic compared, for example, to the clear statement of the Royal College of Nursing (RCN), on the same subject. The latter is discussed later. The FCA guidance states that 'if you are a deposit-taker (bank, building society or credit union) with over £250m in assets,

PRA-designated investment firm,[or an] insurer subject to the Solvency II directive, then your firm must set up procedures that will urge staff to inform the relevant team about any internal misconduct in regulated activity. The Public Interest Disclosure Act 1998 provides protection for someone if they are harmed or dismissed as a result of 'blowing the whistle' (known as making a disclosure) about a firm or individual'.[4] This is clearly accurate but uninspiring and rather limited as guidance goes. It is also not clear why it does not apply to all FCA-regulated firms.

Few individuals, unfortunately, in financial services belong to professional bodies. Those that do may have access to more helpful guidance. For example, in an area where I have a personal professional interest, the Chartered Banker Institute has issued guidance on its website.[5] 'It is vital for banking professionals – and the wider industry – to have options to understand how to report wrongdoing in the workplace ... [in] supporting the public interest, it's important to ensure that our members have somewhere they can go if they feel they want to discuss whether a professional ethical dilemma should be reported, or to find out how to raise a concern'.[6]

More broadly, the Department of Business, Innovation and Skills, as it was in 2015, issued 'Whistleblowing: Guidance for Employers' which is short, clearly written and should form the basis for producing guidance for all levels of staff within a bank, and more widely. For example, 'recognising workers are valuable ears and eyes: workers are often the first people to witness any type of wrongdoing within an organisation. The information that workers may uncover could prevent wrongdoing, which may damage an organisation's reputation and/or performance, and could even save people from harm or death'.[7]

Whistleblowers and the regulators

As discussed elsewhere, both regulators and management face severe difficulties in knowing what is really going on inside an organisation. On the assumption that almost all problem issues are known about by someone in the firm, raising these issues early on should be welcomed by managers.

Whistleblowing also gives an indication of the culture and ethics of a business. This includes providing an indication of how receptive an organisation is to internal criticism, whether it listens and takes action and the extent to which managers adopt a vindictive approach seeking out the person who has raised their concerns and visiting retribution upon them as a warning to others to keep quiet in future. It is not clear that regulators have fully engaged with the benefits of whistleblowers. As will be seen later, the United States has focused on whistleblowers but largely for other purposes.

It is important that regulators support good whistleblowing systems. It acts as an indicator both to individuals within organisations about the importance of speaking up and it provides a marker to boards and senior executives that they need to focus on this area as well. Finally, contacting the regulators provides an alternative route for the whistleblower if management remains deaf to the issues raised. However, it is not yet clear that much has changed to any significant extent since the Parliamentary Commission on Banking Standards expressed its views in 2013 that the evidence it 'received from whistleblowers demonstrated a lack of confidence in the regulator's willingness and ability to support them and to act upon their concerns'.[8] One whistleblower, based on their experience with the FSA, indicated that regulators may be reluctant to follow up, fully, on information from whistleblowers since it may reveal failures by the regulator itself.[9]

Firms of any size will have a hierarchy of 'reporting lines'. Information tends to flow up and down these conduits. If the flows fail for any reason, then whistleblowing represents a means of communication outside these normal channels. The best option to avoid this happening is to ensure that information moves unimpeded up through the organisation. This may be facilitated by ideally having a 'flat' organisational structure but this is a subject outside the parameters of this book. Another method is to focus on a 'procedural approach' and have, for example, open-ended questions in regular reports from staff (e.g. 'is there anything concerning you that senior management should know about?').[10]

However, this system to get away from the ever-present managerial temptation to 'shoot the messenger' of bad, or unwelcome, news. It is also likely that reports, of all types, will be collated and aggregated and be summarised as they proceed up the management chain. From my own experience, any reports that are distilled up through more than two layers of management become 'sanitised' to such an extent that they are probably not worth having. In addition, any adverse comment is usually, quickly and easily rationalised away (e.g. it is seen as an example of 'sour grapes', 'it is a personal grievance', 'result of a personality clash' etc.).

The advantage of a whistleblower process is that it falls outside the normal reporting channels and it relies on independent investigators who have no position to defend and who will not be fobbed off with management platitudes and facile rationalisations. Further, a process only works if it is supplemented by an investigative mind and the power and authority to take clear and effective action. In addition, as mentioned earlier, there needs to be:

- some form of cultural permission to whistleblow,
- whistleblower training,
- active listening to whistleblowers
- adequate information provided back to the whistleblower on what has happened to the concerns they raised,
- evidence that whistleblowing is taken seriously by the regulators.

These are considered in more detail in the next sections.

An open cultural of 'permission' to raise concerns

Employees working in a firm need to understand that they have 'permission' to raise concerns. This has been a particular issue in very hierarchical institutions such as hospitals. For example, the Royal College of Nursing (RCN) has actively campaigned to encourage nurses to raise concerns. The College's training and leaflets makes it clear that in the UK's National Health Service (NHS) staff must not 'wait for a problem to develop. If you see poor care or feel you are being prevented from providing safe, compassionate care, you should raise your concern as soon as you can. All NHS employees have a contractual right and a duty to raise concerns with their employer that they consider to be in the public interest – including malpractice, patient safety, financial impropriety, or any other serious risks'.[11]

The same standards should apply in financial services, and in other industries, with all staff encouraged to speak freely where they are concerned about issues of malpractice, including bullying and harassment; actual or potential harm to stakeholders, including customers; and serious risks to the business.

Whistleblower training

Whistleblower training is important both for managers and their teams. It not only informs everyone of the processes to be used but also, as mentioned earlier, 'gives permission' to staff to raise their concerns as part of the firm's culture. However, even in a large organisation, such as the United Kingdom's NHS, which has spent an enormous amount of time and effort on training on whistleblowing, as a means of protecting patients, there are still large gaps in understanding and acceptance of what is needed. The 2018 NHS England staff survey found that only some 70% reported that they would 'feel safe raising these concerns' and only 58% reported that they would 'feel confident' that their organisation would address them'.[12]

The position of doctors, from an older survey, appears to be worse. Confidence in whistleblowing procedures 'was very low, with 11% saying they had faith, while 52% of respondents were not even aware of their organisation's policy on whistleblowing. The survey also uncovered signs of inertia when faced with situations that caused concern. Of all respondents, 53% said they had experienced such a situation that they now wish they had done more to address; while 49% said that current whistleblowing processes discouraged efforts because the fear of consequences was too great'.[13]

Whistleblowing and the importance of listening

A significant portion of the benefit from whistleblowing comes from actively listening to the concerns raised and learning from them. It is important to the whistleblowers that they are heard and taken seriously and their concerns understood. As mentioned earlier, they also need to be kept informed of what is being done as a result of their actions. In some circumstances, it may be possible to consult them on what is proposed, since the whistleblower is likely to have a high level of expertise in the subject at issue.

An example of this, outside financial services, was highlighted by the official enquiry and report on the Herald of Free Enterprise Zeebrugge disaster in 1987 in which almost two hundred people lost their lives.[14] The ferry sailed out of the harbour with her bow doors still open and the sea flowed in and capsized the vessel. The doors were not closed due to errors by several of the crew and also the failure by the ferry's captain 'to issue and enforce clear orders. But a full investigation into the circumstances of the disaster leads inexorably to the conclusion that the underlying or cardinal faults lay higher up in the Company. The Board of Directors did not appreciate their responsibility for the safe management of their ships ... the directors did not have any proper comprehension of what their duties were'.[15] Additionally, the ferry captain, on the ship's bridge, could not see the ferry's doors and had no way of knowing whether they were open or closed since there was no alarm or other indicator of the state of the bow doors on the bridge.

Moreover, the investigating judge found that the company's management 'took very little notice of what they were told by their' ship captains. Specifically, the senior managers rarely met the captains and 'did not listen to the complaints or suggestions or wishes of their' captains whose collective voice 'fell on deaf ears' regarding their 'complaints that ships proceeded to sea carrying passengers in excess of the permitted number' and their 'wish to have lights fitted on the bridge to indicate whether the bow and stern doors were open or closed'.[16]

If ship operators can ignore the concerns of their ferry captains, how much more likely are they to avoid listening to more junior employees? Boards, senior executives and control functions all have a duty to engage with the experts in their business no matter their status in the firm's hierarchy. The staff issues and concerns need to be heard and addressed, as publicly as possible.

Information on what has happened with their concern

The key words appear to be 'safety' and 'action'. Theoretical training on its own is insufficient. It needs to be supplemented by evidence that it is actually safe to raise concerns and that action will be taken and the outcome is transparent. This may involve celebrating effective whistleblowing with publicity (assuming that the whistleblower consents) and service awards. The dismissal of managers found at serious fault through the disciplinary processes of the organisation, should also be publicised, including those who resigned while subject to disciplinary action. Some, for example, in the Human Resources department may object. However, it is important that everyone, including all stakeholders, are aware of the consequences of bad behaviour, and that they will be found out, and that there will be personal consequences.

It is also important that those that raise concerns are kept informed of what action is being taken and that they have not been ignored. Clearly there is a balance to be struck between the confidentiality of an investigation and staff disciplinary action, and the provision of information to the whistleblower. However, regular updates and reassurance are important.

Evidence that whistleblowing is taken seriously by the regulators

As already mentioned, there remains a concern that the regulators do not value whistleblowers in financial services. This may be changing but the written evidence by Martin Woods, a former whistleblower to the Financial Services Authority (FSA) is not encouraging: 'I believe that one of the difficulties of blowing the whistle in a bank is that in parallel, the individual doing so is also blowing the whistle against the FSA. It is important to understand the role of the FSA and the connection to regulated firms and banks. The FSA supervises banks and therefore, when there is a big failure within the bank, it commonly follows, there has been a failure in the supervisory process'.[17] It is possible that what he said may still be true. In a recent Parliamentary debate on whistleblowing one MP remarked that the financial services regulators appear to 'stricken with lethargy when it comes to responding to whistleblowers' (Stephen Kerr MP – Conservative) while another commented that 'the sense one gets from the FCA is that it regards these people as irritants' (Norman Lamb MP – Liberal Democrat).[18]

However, it is also apparent that in recent years UK regulators have started to take the subject of whistleblowing more seriously. The need to focus on culture as well as process is noted by the FCA together with practical steps for action.[19] This increased regulatory attention is evident in the PRA's actions regarding Lloyds of London's failure to operate an adequate whistleblowing system.[20]

The PRA has expressed some concerns around Lloyd's whistleblowing systems and controls following its disclosure to the PRA on 15 February 2019 that the 'only anonymous whistleblowing channel provided for Corporation Staff (as opposed to people working in the Lloyd's market more generally) had not been operational since 1 October 2017'.[21] The firm had advance notice that this channel would cease to work but failed to put in place a suitable alternative anonymous channel until the end of February 2019 (i.e. some 16 months later). Lloyds of London voluntarily disclosed this information to the PRA. However, the situation was exacerbated when, in response to a question from the regulator the firm confirmed to the PRA that it had not, as required by the rules, produced an annual whistleblowers report for its board.[22] As a consequence, the PRA took the highly unusual steps of formally intervening.

As a consequence, Lloyds of London has now to report annually directly to the PRA. These reports need to include information on, for example, staff whistleblower training, whistleblower reports received and actions taken as a result, third-party checks that the notifications systems are working properly and 'the results of any surveys of staff or third party assurance reviews carried out during the preceding year to verify that the [whistleblower] channels remained in operation'.[23] In addition, using the format of an 'attestation letter', the PRA have taken the unusual step of making a senior executive of Lloyds of London and the compliance officer, personally responsible for the adequacy of this reporting process for the next 3 years, until 2022.[24]

It is possible to speculate that the PRA's stance is, in part, due to concerns regarding the staff culture at Lloyds of London. This may be evidenced by the 'allegations that sexual harassment was rife at the [Lloyds] market, a lack of diversity and an enduring reputation for 'laddishness' [which] have made Lloyd's appear out of step with much of the rest of the City. A survey published in September found almost 500 people at the market, equivalent to one in 12 of the respondents, had witnessed sexual harassment in the previous 12 months'.[25]

In another example, in foreign currency trading markets in London it was reported that 'the dangers of the overwhelmingly male culture in trading rooms have been exposed by the global probe into improper practices in currency markets, which focused on chat rooms with revealing names such as 'Semi Grumpy Old Men'. None of the chat rooms had female members' and all the alleged wrongdoing was undertaken by men.[26]

Challenges to an open culture which supports raising concerns

Poor quality organisations often demonstrate similar problematic issues. These include poor staff morale, high levels of denial that there are any issues or insistence among staff that they are personally not responsibly for any issues and that the problems are the fault of the complainants. For example, see the issues surrounding the German firm, Wirecard AG.[27]

Additionally, these troubled firms may have misaligned incentives, and they also tend to be highly secretive and inwardly focused. They also may have inadequate leadership, who often rule by fear to make up for their own failings. The result is that 'numerous surveys across different professional groups highlight a disconnect between whistleblowing policies in theory and how such arrangements work in practice'.[28]

These key issues can summarised as:

- organisational fear,
- the psychological fear of taking action,
- poor staff morale and disengagement,
- secretive and inward focused organisations,
- management operating in denial of the problems.

These issues are considered in the next sections.

Organisational fear of 'disloyal' insiders who tell the truth

Many organisations 'fear the insider, who armed with their insider knowledge tells the truth'.[29] As a consequence, 'organizations are afraid of men and women who remember that they are first of all citizens who belong to an entity larger than the organization'.[30] The result is that firms need to consider to whom they are accountable. This includes all stakeholders not just shareholders. 'As citizens, their first responsibility is to patients, tax-payers, the affected public'.[31]

If an organisation has the wrong culture, it will seek to ensure that 'every act, practice, and ritual' promotes loyalty in 'an attempt to persuade its members to think of themselves as first and foremost citizens of the organization'.[32] This is clear from, for example, the Wells Fargo debacle considered in the previous chapter. This type of culture is a strong warning indicator for non-executive board members, regulators and compliance, and other control functions.

The psychological fear of taking action

Often, an individual may not have raised their voice due to a psychological fear of taking action. Speaking up will draw attention to the speaker and is likely to have consequences, many of which may not be good. It is simpler to stay quiet and to let events take their course. Passivity may not only be rational but it can be rationalised to oneself. Like Joseph Conrad's Jim, the individual believes that they have no agency and can do nothing. They have a simple desire for a quiet life which leads to a state of paralysis.[33] Jim wants to act but he is overwhelmed by his surroundings and the events happening before him – he can only stand still.[34]

At the same time, not speaking up or acting gnaws away and may undermine the individual's self-belief. But they have taken the first steps in thinking. They may decide to deaden their thought by, for example, with alcohol. Or they may, like Sartre's Delarue, find that the act of taking action is 'cleansing' and provides a form of freedom from indecision.[35]

Senior management, including the compliance team, need to understand these worries. These concerns need to be acknowledged in the staff training and in the implementation of a whistleblower scheme within the firm. 'False positives' should be encouraged since there may be issues which help future learnings. For example, someone raising concerns about a staff event with a free bar may indicate a deeper problem with the role of management, how they incentivise their team and the implications for staff safety and the firm's reputation.

The FCA has published its own guidance on the 'psychological safety' of staff at regulated firms.[36] In particular, the FCA is concerned that managers may not understand how all powerful they appear to staff. Their status and the 'shadow they cast' may intimidate employees sufficiently to deter them from speaking up. A key part of a manager's role is to create 'psychological safety', which encourages staff to say what they think.[37]

Poor staff morale and disengagement

It is a cliché to say that staff need to feel valued. However, it is true that employees that feel disengaged from the organisation are less likely to raise concerns. 'The overwhelming majority of people respond positively to being appreciated for what they do'.[38] However, normally as a result of poor leadership and management, their morale declines, sickness absences rise and 'more stress is placed on the diminishing number of well-motivated staff'.[39] It requires the leadership of organisations to ensure that their workforce do not feel taken for granted'.[40]

Organisations which are secretive and inward focused

Organisations with a poor culture will often be highly secretive and the management inwardly focused. Although in a different field than financial services, the inquiries between 2008 and 2013 into the Mid Staffordshire NHS Foundation Trust provide many examples of bad management practices and institutional deafness to whistleblowers. The very poor management of the hospital trust resulted in a high number of patient deaths and sub-standard care and worse. It is claimed that, for example, some patients were left to drink water from flower vases and 'hospital receptionists [to] assess emergency cases' while 'patients needing pain relief either got it late or not at all, leaving them crying out for help, and there were cases where food and drinks were left out of reach'.[41] The hospital trust used non-disclosure agreements (NDAs) to silence dissent and one whistleblower in particular, Julie Bailey, a former nurse, who used to work in the hospital's accident and emergency (A&E) department was ostracised.[42] The issue of NDAs and the role of compliance is considered later in this chapter.

50

The issue of secrecy and keeping failings hidden is central to the management failings at the hospital trust. For example, a senior manager at the Mid Staffordshire NHS Foundation Trust gave evidence to the public inquiry of the gap that existed then between management and staff 'the executive team at that time was very much inward looking. I mean, it was a small cabal who ran things but didn't get out and about much and meet the people ... there was a feeling that management held everybody at arm's length'.[43]

Poor culture and denial

When concerns are raised, an organisation with a poor culture invariably responds with one or more of the three responses:

- denial that there is any issue,
- denial of responsibility,
- attacking the accuser.

These approaches, which are not mutually exclusive, reflect some of the reactions experienced by the employees themselves.[44]

Denial that there is any issue

As already mentioned, denial comes in many forms. There may be defensive comments, denying that there is an issue. 'One of the things I learnt through ten-plus years of dealing with people who didn't like what we were telling them about their heart surgery results is your first response is to say, 'The data's wrong'. Your second response is to say, 'Okay, the data's right but your analysis is wrong'.[45] In financial services there were similar issues with the sale of payment protection insurance. This is covered in more detail in Chapter 7. It can be seen in the legalistic arguments put forward by the British Bankers Association (BBA), the former trade body for UK banks, when it challenged in court the regulator's review of the sale of PPI in 2011.[46]

Denial of responsibility

A culture which fails in a culture to encourage 'ownership' of issues can result in all problems be blamed on outsiders and the 'other' – things that cannot be controlled. This may result in 'numbing' staff into believing nothing can ever be done and lapsing into 'fatalistic acquiescence'. It may also involve the excuse of 'acting on orders'.[47] In the Mid Staffordshire NHS Foundation Trust Inquiry the former chair of the Trust gave evidence saying that the bad publicity attracted by the public inquiry exaggerated the problem and that there was, in fact, no serious issue.[48] 'The reality is that once a trust is publicised as having killed up to 1,200 people, however mistakenly, then that ... stigma advertises it so much that all sorts of things start to surface which wouldn't in a normal hospital ... I am genuinely, not defending bad care. I am really not ... It could be that we are worse than most. I seriously hope that is not the case but it could be. But there are often two sides to quite a lot of stories'.[49] The Inquiry Report commented that: 'regrettably the impression left by [the former chair's] evidence is that, while she genuinely regrets that such incidents of poor care have occurred, she has been unable to accept the enormity of the problems that engulfed the hospital and ... did not appear to accept the Board's responsibility for what went wrong. Such a position, held in the teeth of external adverse opinion, suggests an entrenched attitude of denial and dissociation from the issues that beset the hospital and its patients'.[50]

Another senior manager who gave evidence to the Inquiry describes that first there was 'an overwhelming sense of denial in the organisation, characterised by 'It's not our fault, it is somebody else's', it is the PCT [Primary Care Trust] or the department or the Healthcare Commission or whoever else was around that you could blame for how awful it is. Then the second overwhelming impression that everywhere else is probably the same but they just have never been caught'.[51] The Trust's new medical director attended a board meeting in 2009 as an observer since he had yet to start in his new role and described an organisation in denial – there 'was the overwhelming feeling of denial, that there wasn't acknowledgement that things were going wrong ... clinical matters were left right at the end, like a serious event that was discussed right at the end of a three and a half hour meeting and all the other agenda items were nothing to do with patient care'.[52]

Attacking the accuser

Frequently, managers will attempt to refute allegations by attacking the whistleblower. An example of this is cited in the Francis Report on the Mid Staffordshire Foundation Trust. Nurses at a mental health hospital when challenged about their poor care of patients responded in writing that they, the nurses, were 'defenceless against, and wide open to, unfair criticism from people who are inexperienced in the care of subnormal people, and who are also hypersensitive and prone to exaggeration'.[53] These types of comments and the phrasing used tell a story of their own.

Wrong targets

As seen in the previous chapter setting the wrong targets can easily undermine an organisation's culture. This may be exacerbated by the climate of fear generated by the targets. For example, at the Mid Staffordshire NHS Foundation Trust one witness mentioned that a 'high priority was placed on the achievement of targets, and in particular the A&E waiting time target. The pressure to meet this generated a fear, whether justified or not, that failure to meet targets could lead to the sack'.[54]

Whistleblowing: the danger of focusing on process

While it is important to have whistleblower processes, it is even more important to create the right environment to encourage staff in the business to raise concerns. 'Our organisations are still stuck in the era of, 'What processes can I put in place in order to manage you to do your job?' We need to think about what values to put in place'.[55] As Martin Woods has said 'ultimately it is all about culture, a culture which promotes the rights morals and values'.[56] In addition, there is a tendency for whistleblowing policies to be written by lawyers. Public Concern at Work (now called 'Protect'), a charity to support whistleblowers, has stated that in the course of its work it sees 'a great number of whistleblowing policies ... many policies are too legalistic, [and] complicated ... do not provide adequate (or any) assurances to the individual, [and] place the duty of fidelity above all else, and contain contradictory and/or poor reassurances on confidentiality'.[57]

Raising concerns and the temptation to use non-disclosure agreements

Non-disclosure agreements (NDAs) are often used by employers. They may be useful for legitimate purposes to protect the firm from improper disclosures. However, NDAs may be misused 'to silence and remove a problem from an organisation rather than face up to it. In this way, NDAs can be seen as a means of stifling proper governance and scrutiny of those organisations'.[58]

The UK government propose 'to outlaw the use of NDAs that silence healthcare workers who raise safety concerns or make complaints of harassment or workplace bullying'.[59] In addition the government has proposed to limit the use of NDAs more widely. These include measures to ensure that:

- no provision in an employment contract or settlement agreement can prevent someone from making any kind of disclosure to the police, in order to report a suspected crime,
- NDA clauses in an agreement are 'properly highlighted, can be easily understood by an individual and prevent exploitation',
- employees receive independent legal advice before signing a settlement agreement.[60]

A full discussion on the uses of NDAs is beyond the scope of this work but compliance, within a firm, needs to consider whether NDAs are appropriate and whether they are being misused.

The US perspective on whistleblowing

The Dodd-Frank Act amended the Securities Exchange Act 1934 to permit payments to be made to whistleblowers.[61] Specifically, Section 21F of the Securities Exchange Act of 1934 (15 U.S.C. 78u-6), entitled 'Securities Whistleblower Incentives and Protection', requires the Securities and Exchange Commission (SEC) to pay awards ... to whistleblowers who provide the SEC with original information about violations of the federal securities laws.[62] The information must be provided voluntarily and leads to a successful SEC actions resulting in monetary sanctions over $1 million and successful related actions.[63] Any award must be equal to between 10–30% of any monetary sanctions collected.[64] 'Since the beginning of the whistleblower program, the Commission has awarded approximately $387 million to 67 individuals'.[65]

The SEC acknowledges, as every compliance officer should know, that inside information provided by a whistleblower 'can be among the most powerful weapons in the law enforcement arsenal'.[66] It is acknowledged that not only has this programme been responsible for the recovery of many billions of dollars lost, for example, as a result of fraud and false accounting but it has encouraged whistleblowers who may never work again.[67] It is also a powerful deterrent for those who might consider defrauding the taxpayer since an 'insider' has a strong incentive to tip off the SEC.

The UK's Parliamentary Banking Commission on Banking Standards considered introducing a similar incentive in banking. However, the FSA, at the time persuaded the Commission not to go down this route; in its view there was an 'associated 'moral hazard' [and] it argued that the prospect of already highly-paid individuals receiving a 'reward' for doing what was arguably their duty could lead to public disquiet'.[68]

In written evidence to the Commission, Public Concern at Work (now known as 'Protect') also expressed its opposition to providing monetary rewards for whistleblowers since 'there will be a risk that individuals will have an incentive to sit on information until it becomes 'serious' enough to be eligible for reward, limiting the ability of organisations and regulators to detect malpractice early'.[69] Currently, there is no move to reward whistleblowers from funds recovered in the United Kingdom. However, there is nothing to prevent firms providing incentives, monetary to otherwise, for those who raise valid and serious concerns. This would not only reward individuals who come forward but would also publicly recognise that speaking up is an important and acceptable action. The risk of one of their members of staff speaking up might also deter managers from attempting to intimidate and bully their staff.

The psychology of those working in organisations and the implications for compliance

All of this has implications for compliance's role. It is important that compliance understand the psychology and emotions of those working in organisations and the implications for compliance. Aspects of this are considered in the next sections.

Organisational defensiveness

Some may see whistleblowing as 'proof of management failure' since 'usually several managers directly above the whistleblower' will know of the complaint and will have failed, in the opinion of the whistleblower, to have addressed the issues satisfactorily.[70] This failure is likely to reflect badly on them since they have failed to 'keep control', with the result, in many cases, that they will have to employ much of their time to writing reports and dealing with various questions.[71]

Adopting a highly defensive role in organisations can be deeply embedded. It is often seen in a culture of blame-shifting, accountability avoidance, meaningless routine, team insularity and high levels of operational rigidity.[72] All these are danger signs for boards, senior executives, regulators and control functions. In another area, it is exemplified, for example, by the French army in 1940 whose doctrine 'demanded a rigid, centralised command and control structure, with little scope for initiative at divisional level or below' exercised via fixed line telephones and dispatch riders – radios, along with individual initiative, were not trusted.[73] Similarly, the French army in 1920s and 30s had great difficulty incorporating innovation into its doctrine due to, largely, complex organisational structures which fought to keep change to the minimum.[74]

It is also possible for managers to divert concerns (and other pressures) using a variety of 'defences'. These 'defences' include individual responses (e.g. 'I would like to make the changes you suggest but my hands are tied or the decision is above my pay grade') and those with structural connotations. The latter may include faux collective decision-making, where an informal group or committee is used to endorse a pre-agreed course of action legitimating it and preventing further discussion.[75]

Rationalisation

When things are not going well there is invariably a general move for the main actors to distance themselves from the problems. This can take many forms, including blaming others and attempting to justify their past decisions through continued commitment to the failing strategy. They may seek to justify themselves by portraying themselves as rational.[76] There is also evidence of the 'ill effects of egocentric bias' where the response to negative news is to increase the commitment to the embedded view or strategy.[77] A belief in one's own expertise can also lead to contrary information being discounted and, again, the belief in the correctness of the chosen path reinforced.[78]

Set routines within organisations

All organisations have a number of set operating routines which are normally undocumented but simply reflect the way things are done within the entity. They have been called 'scripts'.[79] They exist for a variety of reasons. These include 'control' by setting out a structure for processing activities (e.g. a board meeting agenda), and legitimating a procedure (e.g. deferring discussion on an issue: for example, 'we will take discussion of the problem 'off-line'), organising actions by, for example, structuring a reaction and so on.[80]

More specifically, for the purposes of this section, they may be used to 'regulate both the process and contents of decision making'.[81] They may result in the organisation taking irrational decisions since, for example, they frame the concerns in such a way as to 'blinker perceptions' so that individuals will interpret any issue from the perspective of their own area. Consequently, a manager with a background in, for example, marketing or trading will tend to use their 'functional experience to narrow their cognitive processing'.[82] If the operations director, for example, takes on responsibility for solving an issue their response is likely to focus on an operational analysis and solution. A legal team will frame issues in legal terms and so on. These biases need to be countered by ensuring that a broad number of departments and functions are employed in addressing an issue lead by someone who can see the full canvas and is aware of the issue of sectoral framing.

Feelings of despair and helplessness

It is possible that many of the issues in an organisation stem from feelings of helplessness, coupled with intense despair as a result of individual powerlessness. The result is low morale, dysfunctional behaviour and high levels of sickness and staff turnover.[83] Employees express the view that they 'do not have enough power to make any real changes', combined with a general lassitude and defensiveness.[84] The consequence is that there is likelihood that bad conduct will be tolerated and not challenged.

The effective use of emotion in companies and compliance

Companies are legal constructs, often driven by the hard logic of financial and production numbers. Nevertheless, people working in these firms are still subject to all the normal human emotions. All too often it is these emotions that determine what the company actually does. These may include greed and fear but more often the emotions of those working in the organisation will be influenced by those working around them, their immediate managers and how they see themselves within the firm and its operations. There is a continuing dialogue within the work group between colleagues, strongly influenced by the local manager. There is also an 'interior' dialogue within the individual. Stories have an important role in all of this. Our self-view may be, in part, the result of the stories told within the company and the narrative we associate with ourselves – 'I work for the biggest company in [wherever]', 'I am proud to be part of an ethical partnership' and so on. In practice, most companies of any size operate under a self-created image powered by emotion and reinforced by salient stories.

Further, prospects of change and uncertainty can produce their own emotional responses. For example, major technological change is often associated with 'peculiar beliefs and magical thinking' as the power of emotion takes control.[85] The 'dot-com' bubble is a recent example of the power of engaged emotion with stories of 'company founders transforming a clumsy geek into an industrial titan, ritually showering the public with heroic rags-to-riches stories'.[86] As we saw with, for example, Wells Fargo, emotion and delusion are closely linked. However, emotion is such a powerful force, even in the corporate world, that it is a tool that can be employed for compliance purposes.

An appeal to emotional strength and purpose can be used to explain how rooted the business is in society, its core purpose and its 'creation story'. This helps to encourage longer term thinking. It reminds everyone of the need to protect the firm's reputation and, to each individual, in Kantian terms, their own self-respect. An individual will respect themselves when they have a sense of their own self-worth and this can apply more generally.

Any appeal to emotion must be based on integrity. It is important that the management of the organisation demonstrate both integrity and unselfishness since these qualities always permeate good leadership.[87] This reflects the need for trustworthiness – a theme throughout this work. Being worthy of trust includes taking the risk of bringing all staff into your confidence. If you trust them, and explain this, this trust is likely to be repaid.[88]

Human Resources departments, in firms, may speak of 'dignity at work' but its meaning and importance is much great than this. It means operating at work, or elsewhere, to a high standard of morality, particularly in how individuals approach and treat others, including colleagues, customers, suppliers and other stakeholders in the business. The capacity for moral behaviour gives 'humanity dignity' and 'being moral (e.g. keeping promises and principled benevolence) has intrinsic worth and gives man dignity'. [89] Stories also work in anthropological terms by conferring 'membership' of a group.[90] It allows individuals to self-identify with the organisation and their colleagues. Even those new to the business are inducted by the narration of the history of the firm and its origins myth into sharing its values and culture.

The challenge for any firm is to change high-flown words into every-day speech which resonates and which can be used in practice. Setting a narrative is part of this process. 'Promoting the power and place of stories and storytelling in organisations, and as learning, communication and socialisation devices, are well established'.[91] In terms of psychological analysis people 'think, perceive, imagine and make moral choices according to narrative structure'.[92] Abstract discussion, raw data and the like tend not to resonate. 'A useful rule of thumb is to avoid making ... generalizations and to concentrate on the event ... focus[ing] on the event's emotional ... qualities'.[93] Formal processes, may be 'insufficient to meet the needs of problems that arise in the real world. In such circumstances, the tacit, experience-based knowledge built on practice comes to the fore instead. 'Stories about the work convey such tacit knowledge in a more manageable and absorbable fashion'.[94]

The compliance officers will need to spend much of their time on this process of education. They will be trying to reframe regulatory requirements in terms that mean something to, say, front line staff and managers. Simply regurgitating the rules will not work. Regulations need to be explained in terms that others will understand. **Consequently, compliance staff need to be educators – a role often based on constructing and communicating a narrative.**

Compliance: using narratives to communicate and educate

There are a number of approaches available to the compliance officer seeking to communicate with line staff and managers. Use of short stories or narratives can be very powerful. 'Humans are storytelling organisms who, individually and socially, lead storied lives. Thus, the study of narrative is the study of the ways humans experience the world'.[95] In the context of business, stories embody peoples' understandings about work on both an organisational and an individual basis.[96] Some use can be made of the organisation's history which can provide 'a map for navigating the terrain of the current cycle'.[97] For example, the importance of values and ethics can be found in the Quaker origins of Barclays bank.[98] Stories can also be used to demonstrate a rejection of 'short-termism' and can be used to ground individuals in the history and continuum of the business and to encourage them to think of the firm's long term future.[99] These can be drawn from regulatory enforcement cases and this book contains a number of examples of this.

In a medical context it has been found that allowing patients to tell their story and experience is a well tested method of improving clinical care.[100] In the financial services the personal experience of those who have been defrauded, or suffered the effects of corruption or simply received poor service can be powerful reminders of why regulations exist and what they are seeking to prevent.

Providing a narrative and telling stories is a means of creating an identity for the organisation, division, team and so on. 'Organizations that lack a 'story' lack an identity, a culture, core values that can be articulated and drawn on to motivate'.[101] Often these stories include one or more points where choices have to be made and the narrative illustrates the consequences of these choices for good or ill. These are sometimes called 'moments of truth' and are points where the individual or organisation 'faced a challenge, made a choice, experienced an outcome, and learned a moral'.[102] From my personal experience, one of a number of superb senior managers I used to work for would often gather a few thousand of his staff in an auditorium and speaking without notes, and with no PowerPoint slides or lectern, with all the lights up, would hold us spellbound as he told stories to make his points. Some were personal stories while others were about the bank. He would almost always recite a short poem to reinforce his stories, for example, Robert Burns' 'A Man's a Man for a' That'.[103]

He aimed, using stories and poetry, to convey the norms and values of the business division and the need for everyone to have an independent mind and not, as per Burns, to be seduced by the sight of those with titles and baubles who were but conceited ('birkie'), prating blockheads ('coof'). This approach broadened the perspective of his audience giving us bedrock foundations and helping to embed the values of the unit.

The stories (and poems) provide an opportunity to show who should be celebrated and why. They illustrate that, for example, that the bank's relationship with the customer is not transactional but is based on service. For example, a retail bank customer ordered some Japanese Yen for their business trip and arrived at their branch to find out that the bank has made a mistake and the Yen would only arrive the next day. Unfortunately, the customer was flying out later that same day so the currency would come too late. Thankfully, a member of staff took some cash from the till and went out to other branches of rival banks to buy the Yen and after visiting a few banks came back in time to help the customer. It is these types of true stories that help to meet compliance objectives and are worth more than a raft of regulatory rules.

Stories also demonstrate how a business is vulnerable to its employees and how much trust is placed in each one. They can be used to show that staff are empowered to act; whether this be to take cash from a bank till to help a customer or to raise a concern. It can clearly show that ensuring that the organisation is compliant with both the spirit and the letter of the regulations rests with each person and cannot be shrugged off as someone else's responsibility.

Stories tap into ancient traditions and roots common to all cultures. People have experienced them from early childhood and through books, film, magazines, on-line and so on. They engage our 'emotions and get to deep meaning, because stories are in their nature about the irregularities ... and hence arouse our curiosity'.[104] 'Stories of the unexpected prompt emotional responses because they suggest the potential threat of not being in control of our lives, but simultaneously offer a way of understanding and responding to our futures. This emotional response makes knowledge 'sticky' and easy to recall'.[105] They work in a communal setting and help form and reinforce bonds between teller and audience and between listeners. As a form of 'poetics' the narrative helps create an identity indicating a past worthy of pride and also acts as a guide to future conduct.[106]

Conclusion

It is important to remember that regulations, 'registers', 'letters of office ... and instructions' and so on, 'do not hold together ... the mysterious whole'.[107] An organisation is complex and how it really works may well be a mystery. What is certain is that the emotion and psychology of the individuals involved play central parts in its functioning. Regulators, boards, senior management and control functions will get glimpses of what is happening but they will need many routes for communications to flow in order to have any hope of knowing what is going on and to understand the drivers and forces at work.

Whistleblowers who raise concerns are one of these important conduits. They should be valued and not persecuted and suppressed. It is of critical importance that boards and senior managers create the environment to allow those that want to speak up to flourish. They need to be heard and heeded. A confident organisation will welcome criticism which allows it to learn and improve. Only a weak manager, operating in a body with a poor culture, will abjure responsibility and work in a state of denial. This is clear from many examples and in particular the example, in this chapter, of the Mid Staffordshire NHS Foundation Trust.

Thoughtlessness and the failures of imagination are themes throughout this work. Coupled with these weaknesses is the effect of mind-numbing process which may destroy the humanity of thought, reflection and compassion.

The compliance function, and others, need to understand emotion and psychology within an organisation and help individuals rise above despair, if this be so. It is only then that there is a chance for regulation to work as it should. This means that it is important that those working in compliance see themselves as communicators and educators. Communicating a narrative is part of the role of compliance. It emphasises the need for humanity in the way people, both inside and outside the firm, are treated. It is intrinsically right to do so and it may help to develop and reinforce a culture of compliance.

All of this serves as a test of an organisation's true purpose, as well as the trustworthiness of the board and senior managers and the resilience and authority of compliance; subjects this work will consider further.

Notes

1 John Bunyan, *The pilgrim's progress*, Part 1 (originally published in 1678, Wordsworth Edition, Ware, Hertfordshire, 1996), 14.
2 Parliamentary Commission on Banking Standards – Minutes of Evidence Session 2013–14, HL Paper 27-VIII/HC 175-VIII, 28 November 2012, https://publications.parliament.uk/pa/jt201314/jtselect/jtpcbs/27/27viii_121128d.htm (accessed 18 February 2020).
3 Russell Mannion and Huw Davies, 'Cultures of silence and cultures of voice: the role of whistleblowing in healthcare organisations' (2015) *International Journal of Health Policy and Management*, 4(8), 503–505, 505.
4 FCA website, 'Whistleblowing', https://www.fca.org.uk/firms/whistleblowing (accessed 1 January 2020).
5 Chartered Banker Institute (CBI) website, 'Speak out', https://www.charteredbanker.com/member-homepage/speak-out.html (accessed 1 January 2020).
6 Ibid ('Speak out').
7 Department of Business, Innovation and Skills, 'Whistleblowing, guidance for employers and code of practice' (2015), 3, https://assets.publishing.service.gov.uk/government/uploads/system/uploads/attachment_data/file/415175/bis-15–200-whistleblowing-guidance-for-employers-and-code-of-practice.pdf (accessed 1 January 2020).
8 Parliamentary Commission for Banking Standards, 'Changing banking for good report' HL Paper 27-I HC 175-I, June 2013, 373, https://www.parliament.uk/documents/banking-commission/Banking-final-report-volume-i.pdf (accessed 8 May 2020).
9 Parliamentary Banking Commission of Banking Standards, written evidence from Martin Woods, 14 February 2013, para 22–24, https://publications.parliament.uk/pa/jt201314/jtselect/jtpcbs/27/27v_we107.htm (accessed 27 April 2020).
10 Michael Davis, 'Avoiding the tragedy of whistleblowing' (Winter 1989) *Business and Professional Ethics Journal*, 8(4), 3–19, 10–11.
11 Royal College of Nursing (RCN) website, 'Raising concerns: guidance for RCN members', https://www.rcn.org.uk/employment-and-pay/raising-concerns/guidance-for-rcn-members (accessed 1 January 2020).
12 NHS England, NHS Staff Survey 2018 National results briefing, February 2019, 32, https://www.nhsstaffsurveys.com/Caches/Files/ST18_National%20briefing_FINAL_20190225.pdf (accessed 31 December 2019).
13 Medical Practitioners Society website, 'An inconvenient truth', 29 August 2017, https://www.medicalprotection.org/uk/articles/an-inconvenient-truth (accessed 31 December 2019).

14 Herald of Free Enterprise Report of Court No. 8074 Formal Investigation (HMSO, 1987), Mr Justice Sheen, Wreck Commissioner, 1, https://assets. publishing.service.gov.uk/media/54c1704ce5274a15b6000025/ FormalInvestigation_HeraldofFreeEnterprise-MSA1894.pdf (accessed 1 January 2020).

15 Ibid (Sheen J's Report), 14.

16 Ibid (Sheen J's Report), 17.

17 Supra note 9 (Written evidence from Martin Woods), para 24.

18 Hansard, Debate on whistleblowing, 3 July 2019, Vol 662, columns 1280 and 1281, https://hansard.parliament.uk/commons/2019-07-03/debates/ AA9B34FC-1CA3-4A24-9EEB-E37F6DE8EBF2/Whistleblowing (accessed 27 April 2020).

19 FCA website, 'Retail and wholesale banking: review of firms' whistleblowing arrangements', 14 November 2018, https://www.fca.org.uk/publications/ multi-firm-reviews/retail-and-wholesale-banking-review-firms- whistleblowing-arrangements (accessed 27 April 2020).

20 PRA's Written Notice, 'Application for imposition of new requirements pursuant to s55M(5) of FSMA 2000', 23 December 2019, https://www.bankofengland.co. uk/-/media/boe/files/prudential-regulation/regulatory-action/written-notice-from- the-pra-to-the-society-of-lloyds.pdf?la=en&hash=825F21DB1C8FB24BD5854BB 8E374E0DFF63C5E3C (accessed 23 December 2019).

21 Ibid (PRA Written Notice), 6.

22 Ibid (PRA Written Notice), 7.

23 Ibid (PRA Written Notice), 2–3.

24 Ibid (PRA Written Notice), 8.

25 Financial Times, 'Lloyd's lapse draws tighter BoE scrutiny of whistleblower systems', 23 December 2019, https://www.ft.com/content/8eabd3fe-2578- 11ea-9305-4234e74b0ef3 (accessed 23 December 2019).

26 Financial Times, 'Trading floor culture remains a barrier for senior female staff', 9 August 2019, https://www.ft.com/content/16cbf8da- b9d7–11e9–96bd-8e884d3ea203 (accessed 23 December 2019).

27 Financial Times, 'Why was Frankfurt so blind for so long about Wirecard?', 21 June 2020. The case raises a disturbing question for Frankfurt's financial community. Why did so many institutions fail to take into account what the Financial Times had reported might be going on there? One reason sticks out. Many saw the reports as an invented, or at least co-sponsored, by shady Anglo- Saxon speculators and 'locusts'..

28 Supra note 3 (Mannion and Davies), 503.

29 Charles Frederick Alford, 'What makes whistleblowers so threatening? Comment on 'Cultures of silence and cultures of voice: the role of whistle- blowing in healthcare organisations' (2015) International Journal of Health Policy and Management, 5(1), 71–73, 72, https://www.ncbi.nlm.nih.gov/pmc/ articles/PMC4676977/pdf/IJHPM-5-71.pdf (accessed 8 January 2020).

30 Ibid (Alford), 72.

31 Ibid (Alford), 72.

32 Ibid (Alford), 72.

33 George Panichas, 'The moral sense in Joseph Conrad's Lord Jim' (2000) Humanitas, 13(1), 10–30, 12.

34 Joseph Conrad, Lord Jim (first published 1900, Penguin Classics, London, 1957), 12.

35 Jean-Paul Sartre, Iron in the soul, Gerald Hopkins (trs) (first published 1949, Penguin, London, 1967), 225.

36 FCA website, 'Psychological safety', 18 February 2019, https://www.fca.org.uk/culture-and-governance/psychological-safety (accessed 23 January 2020).

37 Ibid ('Psychological safety').

38 Report of the Mid Staffordshire NHS Foundation Trust Public Inquiry ('Robert Francis's Report'), (HMSO, London 2013), HC 898-III, Vol 3, 1381, https://webarchive.nationalarchives.gov.uk/20150407084231/http://www.midstaffspublicinquiry.com/report (accessed 8 January 2020).

39 Ibid ('Robert Francis's Report'), 1381.

40 Ibid ('Robert Francis's Report'), 1381.

41 BBC News web-site, 'Mid Staffs: Helene Donnelly and Julie Bailey honoured', 30 December 2013, https://www.bbc.co.uk/news/health-25549054 (accessed 28 April 2020).

42 The Guardian, 'Mid Staffs whistleblower Julie Bailey: 'I don't go out here on my own any more'. She faced threats, abuse and her mother's grave was vandalised, forcing her to leave her home. But the Mid Staffs whistleblower who exposed neglect at the town's hospital is determined to continue her campaign for a better NHS', 27 October 2013, https://www.theguardian.com/society/2013/oct/27/julie-bailey-mid-staffordshire-nhs-whistleblower (accessed 28 April 2020). Nursing Times, 'Whistleblowing Mid Staffs nurse too scared to walk to car after shift', 17 October 2011, 'A whistleblowing nurse from Mid Staffordshire Foundation Trust has told how she was physically threatened by colleagues after raising concerns about standards in the accident and emergency department', https://www.nursingtimes.net/clinical-archive/accident-and-emergency/whistleblowing-mid-staffs-nurse-too-scared-to-walk-to-car-after-shift-17-10-2011/ (accessed 18 April 2020).

43 Independent inquiry into care provided by Mid Staffordshire NHS Foundation Trust (January 2005–March 2009), HC375-I, Vol 1, 168, https://assets.publishing.service.gov.uk/government/uploads/system/uploads/attachment_data/file/279109/0375_i.pdf (accessed 27 April 2020).

44 Anelia Larsen and others, 'Psychopathology, defence mechanisms, and the psychosocial work environment' (2010) International Journal of Social Psychiatry, 56(6), 563–577.

45 Supra note 38 ('Robert Francis's Report'), 1362.

46 R (British Bankers Association) v FSA and others [2011] EWHC 999 (Admin), 20 April 2011, para 8, https://www.bailii.org/ew/cases/EWHC/Admin/2011/999.html (accessed 27 April 2020).

47 Supra note 38 ('Robert Francis's Report'), 1369.

48 Supra note 43 ('Mid Staffordshire NHS Foundation Trust'), 181.

49 Supra note 43 ('Mid Staffordshire NHS Foundation Trust'), 181.

50 Supra note 43 ('Mid Staffordshire NHS Foundation Trust'), 182.

51 Supra note 43 ('Mid Staffordshire NHS Foundation Trust'), 182.

52 Supra note 43 ('Mid Staffordshire NHS Foundation Trust'), 182.

53 Supra note 38 ('Robert Francis's Report'), 1369.

54 Supra note 43 ('Mid Staffordshire NHS Foundation Trust'), 16.

55 Parliamentary Commission on Banking Standards (sub-committee D, Panel on corporate governance below board level, 1 November 2012), oral evidence of Ali Parsa in answer to Q7 from Baroness Kramer, https://publications.parliament.uk/pa/jt201213/jtselect/jtpcbs/uc706/uc70601.htm (accessed 27 April 2020).

56 Supra note 9 (Written evidence of Martin Woods), para 93.

57 Parliamentary Banking Commission of Banking Standards, written evidence from

Public Concern at Work, 24 June 2013, para 10, https://publications.parliament. uk/pa/jt201314/jtselect/jtpcbs/27/27v_we27.htm (accessed 27 April 2020).

58 Richard Moorhead, 'Ethics and NDAs' (April 2018) *UCL Centre for Ethics and Law*, 6–7, https://www.ucl.ac.uk/laws/sites/laws/files/ethics_and_ndas.pdf (accessed 28 April 2020).

59 People Management, 'NHS to be banned from using NDAs to gag whistleblowers', 23 April 2019, https://www.peoplemanagement.co.uk/news/articles/nhs-to-be-banned-using-ndas-gag-whistleblowers (accessed 28 April 2020).

60 Department of Business, Energy and Industrial Strategy, 'Confidentiality clauses: response to the government consultation on proposals to prevent misuse in situations of workplace harassment or discrimination', July 2019, 6–7, https:// assets.publishing.service.gov.uk/government/uploads/system/uploads/attachment_data/file/818324/confidentiality-clause-consultation-govt-response.pdf (accessed 28 April 2020).

61 Dodd–Frank Wall Street Reform and Consumer Protection Act, Public law No. 111–203, § 922(a) amended Securities Exchange Act of 1934, 124 Stat. 1841 (2010).

62 15 U.S.C.§ 78u-6.

63 'Related actions' is defined at 15 U.S.C.§ 78u-6(a)(5) and 17C.F.R.§ 240.21F-3(b).

64 15 U.S.C.§ 78u-6(b)(1).

65 SEC Whistleblower Programe, Annual Report to Congress (2019), 1, https:// www.sec.gov/files/sec-2019-annual%20report-whistleblower%20program.pdf (accessed 28 April 2020).

66 SEC Officer of the Whistleblower website, https://www.sec.gov/whistleblower (accessed 28 April 2020). The Office of the Whistleblower was established to administer the SEC's whistleblower program.

67 Forbes website, Erika Kelton, 'Seven ingredients for a successful whistleblower program', 21 March 2012, https://www.forbes.com/sites/erikakelton/2012/03/21/seven-ingredients-for-a-successful-whistleblower-program/#4cd7ad9b390c (accessed 28 April 2020).

68 Parliamentary Banking Commission of Banking Standards, Written evidence from the Financial Services Authority, 11 December 2012, para 21, https:// publications.parliament.uk/pa/jt201314/jtselect/jtpcbs/27/27v_we78.htm (accessed 28 April 2020).

69 Parliamentary Banking Commission of Banking Standards, 'Written evidence from Public Concern at Work', 7 September 2012, para 18, https:// publications.parliament.uk/pa/jt201314/jtselect/jtpcbs/27/27v_we27.htm (accessed 28 April 2020).

70 Michael Davis, 'Avoiding the tragedy of whistleblowing' (Winter 1989) *Business and Professional Ethics Journal*, 8(4), 3–19, 7.

71 Ibid (Davis), 7.

72 Blake Ashforth and Raymond Lee, 'Defensive behavior in organizations: a preliminary model' (1990) *Human Relations*, 43(7), 642.

73 R. J. M. Porter, 'Higher command and staff course staff ride paper: as the experience of the French and German armies in 1940 demonstrates, doctrine not equipment is the key to success in modern warfare. Discuss' (2003) *Defence Studies*, 3(1), 138.

74 Robert Doughty, *The seeds of disaster, the development of French Army doctrine 1919–1939* (Stackpole Books, Mechanicsburg, PA, 1985), 129–140.

75 Rivka Bar-Yosef and E.O. Schild, 'Pressures and defenses in bureaucratic roles' (1966) *American Journal of Sociology*, 75, 665–673, 670.

76 David Caldwell and Charles O'Reilly, 'Responses to failure: the effects of choice and responsibility on impression management' (1982) *Academy of Management Journal*, 25(1), 121–136, 122.

77 Bradley Staats, Diwas Singh KC, and Francesca Gino, 'Maintaining beliefs in the face of negative news: the moderating role of experience' (2018) *Management Science*, 64(2), 804–824, 821.

78 Ibid (Staats, Singh, and Gino), 821.

79 Blake Ashforth and Yitzhak Fried, 'The mindlessness of organizational behaviors' (1988) *Human Relations*, 41, 305–329, 307.

80 Ibid (Ashforth and Fried), 309.

81 Ibid (Ashforth and Fried), 317.

82 Janice Beyer and others, 'The selective perception of managers revisited' (June 1997), *Academy of Management Journal; Briarcliff Manor*, 40(3), 716–737, 730.

83 B. E. Ashforth, 'The organizationally induced helplessness syndrome: a preliminary model' (1990) *Canadian Journal of Administrative Sciences*, 7(3), 30–36, 35.

84 Ibid (Ashforth), 33.

85 Howard Berenbaum, M. Tyler Boden, and John Baker, 'Emotional salience, emotional awareness, peculiar beliefs, and magical thinking' (2009), *Emotion*, 9(2), 197–205, 203.

86 G. Thomas Goodnight and Sandy Green, 'Rhetoric, risk, and markets: the dotcom bubble' (2010) *Quarterly Journal of Speech*, 96(2), 115–140, 126.

87 William Slim, 'Leadership in management' (2003) *Australian Army Journal*, 1(1), 143–148.

88 Ibid (Slim).

89 Stephen Massey, 'Kant on self-respect' (1983) *Journal of the History of Philosophy*, 21(1), 57–73, 59.

90 Marian McCollom, 'Organisational stories in a family-owned business' (Spring 1992) *Family Business Review*, 5(1), 3–24, 6–7.

91 Terry Quong, Allan Walker, and Peter Bodycott, 'Exploring and interpreting leadership stories' (1999) *School Leadership and Management*, 19(4), 441–453, 442.

92 Theodore Sarbin, 'The narrative as a root metaphor for psychology' in Theordore Sarbin (ed.) *Narrative psychology: the storied nature of human conduct* (Praeger, New York, 1986), 8.

93 Michael Connelly and Jean Clandinin, 'Stories of experience and narrative inquiry' (1990) *Educational Researcher*, 19(5), 2–14, 11.

94 Deborah Sole and Daniel Wilson, 'The power and traps of using stories to share knowledge in organizations' (2002) Learning Innovations Laboratories, Harvard Graduate School of Education, Cambridge, 1–12, 4, https://www.researchgate.net/publication/242189756_Storytelling_in_Organizations_The_power_and_traps_of_using_stories_to_share_knowledge_in_organizations (accessed 29 April 2020).

95 Supra note 93 (Connelly and Clandinin), 1.

96 Supra note 94 (Sole and Wilson), 1.

97 David Fleming, 'Narrative leadership: using the power of stories' (2001) *Strategy and Leadership*, 29(4), 34–36, 36.

98 New Statesman, 'We should look at the Quakers who founded Barclays for an example of banking with values', 20 December 2013, https://www.newstatesman.com/business/2013/12/we-should-look-quakers-who-founded-barclays-example-banking-values (accessed 29 April 2020).

 99 James Cuno, 'Telling stories: rhetoric and leadership, a case study' (2005) *Leadership*, 1(2), 205–213, 212.
100 Rhian Last, 'Using patient stories to shape better services' (2012), *Practice Nurse*, 42(13), 33–37, 2.
101 Marshall Ganz, 'Public narrative, collective action, and power', in Sina Odugbemi and Taeku Lee (eds.) *Accountability through public opinion: from inertia to public action* (The World Bank, Washington DC, 2011) 273–289, 285.
102 Ibid (Ganz), 283.
103 Robert Burns, 'A man's a man for a' that' (1795) Scottish Poetry Library, https://www.scottishpoetrylibrary.org.uk/poem/mans-man-0/ (accessed 29 April 2020).
104 Stephen Denning, 'Using stories to spark organizational change' (2002) Storytelling Foundation International, http://providersedge.com/docs/km_articles/Using_Stories_to_Spark_Organizational_Change.pdf (accessed 30 April 2020).
105 Supra note 94 (Sole and Wilson), 4.
106 Theodore Sarbin, 'The poetics of identity' (1997) *Theory and Psychology*, 7(1), 67–82, 67.
107 Edmund Burke, *Speeches on America. On conciliation with America,* Arthur Innes (ed.) (first published 1775, Cambridge University Press, Cambridge, 1906), 160.

4

COMPLIANCE AND THE REGULATORS

Introduction – the importance of trust and being trustworthy

The last chapter looked at trust between the firm's management and its staff and its importance for compliance. This chapter is focused on the relationship, and the trust, between the business and its regulators. Trust is central to this relationship. It may appear obvious but anecdotal information indicates that while this may be understood, as a concept, it is often forgotten in the course of day-to-day operations within regulated firms. Trust is essential since regulators rely on all levels within the business to act compliantly and to be open and honest in their dealing with their supervisors.

This is for the obvious reason that the regulators will not know all aspects of a firm's business. They have only limited resources available to supervise regulated firms and they cannot always be present on-site. Consequently, they rely on the firm's board, senior management and the control functions to work and act in their stead. This trust is particularly important for the compliance function since it is the primary contact point between the firm and the regulators.

For regulatory trust to exist it requires the firm to be trustworthy and this is based on a number of factors. These include how a firm addresses a series of key tests. These provide evidence of a firm's culture and trustworthiness and its ability, and capacity, to demonstrate that the compliance function is active and engaged. It helps to show a bond of trust between the various elements of the business, including the board and the regulator. Examples would be the extent to which the regulator can rely on the following:

- the quality and completeness of information being sent to it, often daily,
- the reporting of significant issues, within the firm, to the senior executive team and to the board – quickly,
- the regulator's confidence that they will also be notified quickly and these reports will be fully honest and open,

- the efficiency and effectiveness of internal regular communication processes within the firm,
- the regulator's ability to trust the business to carry out a thorough 'root-cause' analysis and quickly to provide an unvarnished report on problems and their resolution. The business should take the initiative and propose a remediation plan, including the 'root-cause' analysis mentioned in earlier chapters. Depending on the significance of the issues, this work may need to be independently assessed and verified with regular reports to both the board and the regulator. These will be factors for the regulator in deciding whether to appoint a 'skilled person review' and whether to refer the matter for enforcement action,
- good customer communication arrangements which take a customer-centric perspective. These include explaining the process clearly to customers at the outset, asking for information without using jargon, updating customers throughout the process and providing helplines staffed by real, well trained and motivated people and not voice-activated responses systems. The importance of ensuring that complaints systems work well can be seen, for example, in the FCA enforcement action against Liberty Mutual Insurance Europe.[1] Here the firm delegated both the handling of mobile phone insurance claims and customer complaints handling to two separate outsource firms. The board also 'delegated compliance oversight to a function that lacked the resources and expertise to understand the nature of the risks and what would be needed to mitigate them'.[2] The insurance company was fined over £5m due to its failure to oversee these outsourced operations properly.[3]
- the openness and effectiveness of the firm's process for employees to raise concerns. This is another important indicator of a firm's compliance culture and requires board oversight and sound staff training and follow-through of issues. This subject was covered in detail in the previous chapter.

Encompassing everything is the regulators' confidence that the regulated firm, at all levels, will be open and honest in its approach and dealings with the regulators at all times. All these points are developed further and in more detail in the following sections.

At the heart of all this has been the frequent abuse of customer trust by many firms. 'Trust' is not just a firm-specific thing. It is fragile and ethereal and can only be built up over time; but trust can be lost through gradual erosion, or suddenly with one significant event'.[4] 'A keystone of any sustainable business model and strategy must be customers' trust' in the firm.[5] Each element of the financial services industry is interdependent and each part of a firm depends on others. Trust is not fractional but mutually binding and supportive. What may be seen as sharp practice will gradually undermine trust and make its re-building more difficult.

This chapter considers aspects of ensuring that the regulated firm is seen as trustworthy, as well as the important role compliance in interpreting and communicating the views of the regulators to the firm's board, senior management and other areas within the business.

Compliance: the wider perspective

As already mentioned, compliance is much more than compliance with the letter of the regulations. This is evident in the FCA's Business Plan 2019/20 where the focus is on examining:

- the regulated firm's assessment of their 'purpose',
- the firm's remuneration and incentive structures,
- the firm's own assessment of its culture.[6]

The regulator sees a possible causal link 'between healthy cultures and business models and healthy outcomes for consumers, markets and firms'.[7] Issues relating to compliance and the firm's culture and purpose are considered in separate chapters but the point here is to note the widening breath of compliance and the increase in regulatory expectations. The latter continue to expand.

The FCA is currently developing its expectations to include:

- aspects of fairness in pricing and product value,
- ensuring fair treatment of both existing and new customers,
- the use of automated decisioning systems covering, for example, investment advice, medical underwriting and so forth.

Fairness in pricing and product value, and ensuring fair treatment of both existing and new customers are considered later in this chapter. Automation and regulation, including the increasing use of artificial intelligence and 'big data' by firms, is examined in Chapter 6.

There are a number of other factors used by the regulators to assess to what extent the business can be trusted. These are considered next.

Additional information published by the FCA on its approach to supervision

The FCA has described a number of key factors which determine their attitude to compliance risk within a business. These are focused around the firm's business model, its culture and the related area of senior management personal accountability.[8] These are key factors that compliance functions, among others, need to concentrate upon. They include the consequences of the firm's purpose, governance and its leadership in reducing the potential for harm arising from the business model.[9] At the same time the firm needs to assess how effective are it systems of control and its oversight arrangements. Together with its people policies, these are all relevant in mitigating the potential for harm.[10]

Similarly, the regulator will look at whether the business model drives excessive risks to harm customers and threaten the firm's financial position. This could be due to high-growth strategies, low or rapidly declining profitability, cross-subsidies and potential conflicts of interest and the competitive market context.[11] These inherent and external factors may help determine whether a business is capable of having a long-term future. How firms address these issues may be influenced by how senior management and the board perceive their own levels of personal accountability.

Consequently, the FCA's approach is to prevail upon firms to consider their business model and strategy and how these may harm consumers and undermine trust. The elements which may determine a firm's culture include the 'the impact of incentives and rewards on individual's behaviours, such as driving inappropriate sales' and 'budget pressures on critical functions such as risk, compliance and human resources'.[12] Aspects of these areas are considered in later sections.

However, regulatory expectations are often not clearly communicated to, or understood by, the regulated firm. The fault may lie with the regulator, or it may be due to poor communication of the message within the business, by the compliance function, or both.

Disjunct between business and regulatory understanding

There is a high propensity for misunderstanding between regulators and regulated firms. There are many occasions during which this may occur. For example, new regulations or forms of regulatory guidance are often drafted in broad non-specific terms. A randomly-selected example might be the Money Laundering Regulations 2007 where regulation 5 requires that the firm undertake client due diligence to obtain 'information on the purpose and intended nature of the business relationship'.[13] The business, in implementing these requirements, often starts from the premise that it already complies with this regulation. This frequently held perspective is considered in more detail in Chapter 8 on business culture and 'hubris'.

It may take a regulatory enforcement case to crystallise the specific standard expected. An example of this can be seen in the FCA's Enforcement Notice for Standard Chartered Bank in 2019 relating to the requirement that firms 'know their customer' (KYC) as part of the anti-money laundering rules. This case made it clear that this KYC regulation is risk-based and a higher standard of due diligence on bank customers is expected when, for example, the 'customer exported a dual use good with civil or potential military applications to over 75 countries, including to two jurisdictions where armed conflict was taking place or was likely to be taking place'.[14]

Consequently, compliance needs to pay close attention to this type of information provided by the regulators in speeches, enforcement notices and in various guidance documents. Compliance also need to be closely attune to *how* the regulators communicate, and to assist the board, other senior management and other elements of the firm to understand *what* is being said and *their implications*.

Regulatory messages 'cloaked' in civility, pleasantries and coded texts

Similarly, messages conveyed face-to-face by the regulator to the business are often, from my own experience, misinterpreted. Frequently, this is due to a misalignment of cultures. The regulator thinks that it is issuing a tough message, but the regulated firm hears something much milder. In part, this is due to business conventions – friendly greetings and handshakes, the offer of refreshments and the exchange of day-to-day pleasantries.

It may also be due to the coded wording of regulatory messages; especially when provided orally, particularly in the United Kingdom, using diplomatic phraseology (e.g. 'we were disappointed in ..., you need to consider ..., you may want to reflect upon ... etc.'). Many in business are more used to hard-hitting, straight language within the firm and will judge what the regulator says accordingly. This confusion may also be the result of the inherent optimism which goes with the territory of sales and marketing and deal negotiation.[15] Many in these areas are attuned to seeing and hearing the positive elements of a message and will often 'tune-out' ambiguity. It is not just salesmen: independent board directors often fail to fully comprehend regulatory presentations. A message stating that the firm is, for example, an 'outlier' may be seen as a positive: the business is special and is ploughing its own course with the rest of the industry failing. For example, Halifax Bank of Scotland (HBOS) prior to its collapse, possessed a brashness which was 'underpinned by a belief that the growing market share was due to a special set of skills which HBOS possessed and which its competitors lacked. The effects of the culture were all the more corrosive when coupled with a lack of corporate self-knowledge at the top of the organisation, enabling the bank's leaders to persist in the belief, in some cases to this day, that HBOS was a conservative institution when in fact it was the very opposite'.[16]

As discussed elsewhere, it is often for the compliance officer and their team to clarify what the regulator means in terms that resonate with the line business functions. To do this, they need to stay as close as possible to the regulators.

Getting close to your regulatory supervisor

All but the smallest regulated firms need to get as close as possible to their regulators and, if possible, their allocated supervisor – if they have one. This requires time and effort by both compliance and other senior management and board members. This can involve attending regulatory events such as seminars and 'town hall' meetings, responding in a measured and constructive manner to consultations, and reinforcing this relationship by seeking out meetings with the regulators at regular intervals.

As mentioned earlier, various reasons for being close to your regulator include:

- helping to understand current regulatory concerns,
- demonstrating that your firm is a 'good citizen'. This is very important when the regulator is deciding against which firms to take action,
- building a general rapport and trust with the policymakers and supervisors.

If things go wrong – and they often do, it is too late to try and build a relationship. You need to start early and to invest in developing this nexus. This process of relationship-building has been described as taking place over a number of stages.[17]

The first stage is when things are quiet. Regulators are often deeply involved in meeting their objectives and delivering key internal projects. At the same time they are concerned – or should be – about what is going on in 'their' part of the financial services industry. They will have lots of data available to them – maybe too much. They will also have their own background knowledge and that of their colleagues if they have previously worked in regulated firms. They will have been on training courses and may have attended industry conferences and round tables. Nevertheless, they are likely to feel isolated and vulnerable.

They are aware of these risks and, in part, in order to address this issue, will have regular meetings with lobby groups and firms of consultants all of whom can and do provide some information. Regulators will also have meetings with other stakeholders, including consumer groups, academics, politicians and civil servants. However, they really appreciate time with regulated firms who 'just tell them things' – such as what is happening in the markets, general issues which concern them and industry gossip. All of this is 'gold-dust' for the regulators if they can understand and consolidate and analyse what they are being told. Additionally, one former SEC regulator pointed out that 'several times when stakeholders came in to complain about a rule after it was adopted. When I asked them if they had commented on the proposed rule before it was adopted, they often said they had not'.[18]

The regulators are also conscious that these discussions may provide information through a form of a distorting mirror. Consultants and lobbyists are likely to have their own specific agendas and any information they provide may will be skewed towards these objectives. Similarly, regulated firms may be burdened by fear of the regulators and limit what they disclose so as not to draw too much regulatory attention. They want to avoid being 'too interesting' so as not to prompt further enquiries.

Counter-poised to this may be the fear, by the regulators, that any substantive interaction with outsiders may compromise their independence and result in 'regulatory capture' and charges in the media and by politicians of bias. Regulated firms need to be aware of these concerns when approaching regulators. This means, at the very least, no offers of gifts, lunches or any special invitations.

Regulated firm board and senior executive routine contact with regulators

Some boards and senior executives of regulated firms do not see the need to have routine meetings with the regulators. Some take the view that keeping their distance from the regulators is a sound policy – the less engagement the better. Some see meeting the supervisory team as a distraction from their role as board chairman or CEO. They consider that this is a job that can be delegated to the compliance function. However, this would be a mistake. Keeping in close contact with the regulators is all part of their role and important for building trust. It also helps the regulated firm's senior management to better understand regulatory thinking and, hence, to avoid surprises. A former SEC Divisional Director advised that firms simply meet with their supervisor to provide some 'observations of your business and the competitive landscape'.[19] These provide valuable insights for the regulator.

Depending on the size of the firm there should be regular and frequent routine meetings between the regulator and the senior business executives, including the CEO, chief finance, compliance and risk officers, as well as the board chairman and sub-committee chairs.

These meetings may present challenges and may need careful preparation by the compliance officer. Problematically, many senior executives will lack a detailed knowledge of parts of their business and may have an inaccurate view of how regulations operate in practice. Other executives may believe that regulators share their own business objectives. For example, I recall one CEO of a life insurance company believing that if regulators understood the business pressures on him and the tightness of profit margins they would loosen the application of the regulations. He seemed surprised that this was not also the regulators' view. Nevertheless, all these meetings and discussions permit the regulators to gain a balanced view – if they take the opportunities to engage widely.

These meetings should not be with just the supervisory team but also the senior regulatory staff including policymakers. The aim should be not just to build a relationship – itself an important objective – but also to provide information valuable to the regulators. As mentioned, this could include insights on markets, and innovations in technology and processes and the like. It could also include key pieces of business data which the regulators may not have or will only obtain in a few months' time such as information on, say, sharply rising or falling margins in particular business areas.

As part of keeping a close, constructive relationship with the regulators, it is critical that any significant issues are reported immediately. This should reinforce the trust that has already been established.

Developing the relationship when conditions are 'quiet'

It is important to develop the relationship with the regulators when there is no crisis. Even at the best of times, if there is a significant issue at the bank the supervisory team will not be pleased. They will have to report the problem internally within the regulator and the issue may not reflect well on the supervisory team itself as they have to explain the problem and their own role to those higher up in their own organisation. Matters may be a bit easier for them if they can provide additional information based on their past interaction with the regulated firm, demonstrating that they have a grip on the issues.

A close relationship may be useful if, and when, there are subsequent problems. 'If your regulator knows who you are and what you are trying to do with regard to compliance, you may get the benefit of the doubt when something does go wrong. I am not saying that you will escape a serious violation of the rules but you may get a lighter punishment. If the infraction is minor, you may get off with a warning. It is just human nature, if the regulators know who you are and have seen you trying to devote resources to compliance and act in good faith, they will have more understanding if something goes wrong'.[20] However, if the supervisory team has only a limited perspective on the firm, it may be difficult in the heat of the crisis to convince them 'that you are a responsible firm with a good compliance program. That is much more difficult if something has already gone wrong'.[21]

It is also important to explain to the regulators how the compliance, and other control functions, operate within the bank. This needs to include how they are integrated into the firm's corporate governance and the status and 'authority' they command within the organisation. Details should be provided of the adequacy of their resourcing and also evidence of potential problems they have detected and prevented. Case studies are useful as examples of where compliance rejected a proposals from the business and what happened as a consequence. Again, a former senior member of the SEC explained that the SEC are encouraged when they see chief compliance officers 'that are well-integrated with management and understand both current business issues that might result in compliance questions but also understand where the business is going so that they can anticipate future compliance needs'.[22]

Volunteering errors and wrong-doing

There are many instances of regulators giving credit to those firms they trust and punishing those they do not trust. A positive example, can be seen in the United States, in November 2017, when the then US Deputy Attorney General, Rod Rosenstein, formalised a pilot programme to give firms an incentive to cooperate under the Foreign Corrupt Practices Act 1977.[23] The US Department of Justice (DOJ) can now issue a public 'declination' to a firm closing the DOJ's investigation in certain circumstances. The latter includes:

- a prompt voluntary disclosure of the matter to the regulators,
- a thorough investigation by the company,
- 'fulsome cooperation with the regulators including cooperation with any investigation of individuals involved',
- timely and appropriate remediation. This may include developing and implementing an enhanced compliance programme, terminating the employment of all the employees concerned with the wrong-doing, paying compensation and so on,
- honesty – for example, the SEC expects that compliance monitoring reviews of the business will highlight errors. 'Compliance is a human endeavor. By definition, human endeavors make mistakes. The SEC is not going to believe it if your program uncovers no mistakes ... you are better off admitting a shortcoming ... than having it discovered by examiners'.[24] Such an outcome may indicate a less than honest approach to regulation and compliance.

An example, of this type of incentive and the benefits for the regulated firm, can be seen in the US DOJ's letter to Nortek closing its inquiry as part of the 2016 pilot.[25]

The creation and maintenance of trust with the regulators is crucial and central is the need for the regulated firm to be open and honest – at all times. The doctrine of legal professional privilege, although wholly in alignment with the law, may undermine this relationship. This is considered next.

Claiming legal professional privilege

Having an adversarial approach to the regulator is likely to be detrimental to the firm in the long run. John Walsh, SEC Chief Counsel, Office of Compliance Inspections and Examinations said that if a firm was 'uncooperative and hostile with examiners, examiners would assume that the firm was concealing wrongdoing and act accordingly ... showing them respect and they will reciprocate'.[26]

Regulatory investigations, paradoxically, provide another opportunity to reinforce the existing relationship with the regulators. This is even more important if the investigation is undertaken by a unit separate from the normal supervisory team. The regulated firm must be fully cooperative and open at every level. It must not be antagonistic and difficult and, although lawyers may need to be involved, it must be made clear to them that the process is not adversarial. Input from the usual supervisory team is important and even more so if the team can verify that the regulated firm has a good track record of being helpful, open and honest.

If at all possible, the allegations should be defended but this needs to be done in an open and non-confrontational way. Full, documented information should be freely provided. If there has been a regulatory failure, then this information should be volunteered at an early stage. Hopefully, it may be possible to demonstrate that the problem was, for example, a technical breach with no harm done; that it was reported to the regulator very quickly and any remedial work was undertaken very quickly; that these actions were independently checked and reported to the supervisory team; and that a wider 'root-cause' analysis has been undertaken. This information may influence the investigation. While such information might provide an easy 'regulatory scalp', there would be little 'kudos' in this for the regulator. With limitations on their own resources, the regulators may decide to pursue a more substantial case against another bank.

When challenged by the regulators there is a temptation to claim legal professional privilege for certain documents requested as part of the enquiry. There may be siren legal voices advocating this course of action. However, this approach is likely to be a mistake. It is a natural response to a regulatory challenge to take a defensive posture and claiming legal professional privilege may be legally correct. However, The key element is again 'trust' and refusing to assist the regulator is a sure route to undermining this asset.

Consequently, it may be possible to win the legal argument but to lose sight of the bigger picture and the need to reinforce the bond of trust. Compliance needs to explain the position very clearly within a firm since objecting to a potential claim of legal professional privilege may result in other executives and in-house lawyers questioning whose 'side' compliance is on. These doubts need to be rejected and the 'authority' of compliance asserted to act in the best interests of the company and its stakeholders, even if this threatens the position of individuals within the firm.

The Director of the UK's Serious Fraud Office has said that:

> when a company calls in a team of lawyers and then throws the blanket of legal professional privilege over all the material they have gathered ... That is not cooperation: courts do not like it, it does not help law enforcement ... companies can waive that privilege if they wish to cooperate with the Serious Fraud Office. And waiving privilege over that initial investigative material will be a strong indicator of cooperation and an important factor that I will take into account ...[27]

It is likely that financial services regulators will take a similar view. 'If you have been uncooperative and hostile and the examiners find something, I promise you they will take a less charitable view of any explanation that you give'.[28]

The next sections examine a number of specific areas where in the United Kingdom there is a current and increasing regulatory focus. These include fair product pricing and value and fairness between existing and new customers. These may become totemic of the culture within a firm and may influence the relationship with the regulator. It is on issues such as these that compliance needs to be highly attuned to regulatory develops and attitudes.

Fairness in pricing and product value

As already mentioned, there is increasing regulatory interest in aspects of fairness in pricing and product value, and also in ensuring fair treatment of both existing and new customers. There is further evidence in the FCA's Discussion Paper on 'Fair pricing in financial services' that compliance needs to move from 'black-letter law' towards a more holistic regulatory approach.[29]

The FCA, using its powers to promote competition, sees two possible approaches to the issue of fair pricing. The first group focus on 'demand-side remedies' which 'try helping consumers make better decisions'.[30] These measures could include reducing the time it takes to search for better deals, and making the information more comparable and easier to understand. Essentially, the FCA believes that if the market is to work it must reduce the level of customer inertia.

The FCA is also concerned that firms engage in 'front and back book' manipulation. This is common in banking, asset management and insurance businesses and relies on customer inertia and a mis-placed sense of loyalty to the firm. This form of pricing strategy may take a number of forms but includes offering higher rates of return and lower fees to new customers to encourage them to deposit their funds or to invest. It may also, for example, deter customers from switching insurance provider. The new customers are, in effect, cross-subsidised by the existing or 'loyal' customers. This is 'sometimes referred to as 'loyalty pricing' or 'inertia pricing',[31] a topic considered further in the next section.

The second group are known as 'supply-side remedies'.[32] These focus on firms and can involve restricting the way firms design, market and price products. They may include price regulation and product structure restrictions.[33] These restrictions can be draconian such as price caps – which limit price differentials between long-standing and new customers – and other pricing strategies which adversely affect customers who loyally renew products.

Clearly, these pricing strategies are not peculiar to financial services and can be found in a number of industries. However, regulators in the United Kingdom in financial services have both the statutory objectives and the legal powers to regulate fair pricing and competition and are increasingly active in these areas.

Fairness between current and prospective customers

As mentioned in the section above, the FCA has widened its perspective to include pricing strategies which may result in unfairness between existing and new customers.[34] Existing customers may be charged more and offered less.[35] Firms may also carry out price testing to see how sensitive different customer groups are to price changes. This can result in differential pricing for the same, or largely similar, products. Current remedies primarily relate to improved information for customers but this may change and require businesses to be more proactive.

It is not certain in what direction regulation will go but it is likely to be another area meriting compliance attention, where, for example, business strategies target vulnerable customers.[36] The FCA has said in this important aspect that:

> assessing whether a particular pricing practice is unfair can be complex and the issues can vary from market to market. So, there is no simple formula that determines whether a practice is unfair and we will use our judgment to balance the considerations in specific context. This implies that prescriptive rules are unlikely to be sufficient to incorporate our thinking into a regulatory approach. We consider at this stage that a principles-based approach may be more effective in driving appropriate outcomes.[37]

It is probable that the FCA will focus on what information firms provide to both current and prospective customers to see if it enables customers to judge the products and services fairly and whether the information and supporting processes enable customers to opt for the best products for themselves. The FCA may also look at whether fees and charges reflect actual costs and to what extend they disincentivise customers from switching produces and services and suppliers. It is likely that the FCA will focus on business strategies which rely on 'sludge tactics' (making it more difficult for customers to exit the product) and 'price-walking' (where the customer is enticed to invest or buy the product based on low introductory rates or charges and which are subsequently lifted excessively).[38]

Conclusion

The centrality of trust as the foundation of financial services regulation cannot be overstated. It is founded on concepts of trustworthiness and fairness. These are themes found throughout this book. Although the 'black letter' law of regulation remains important, the relationship between a regulated firm and its regulators forms a bond of mutual understanding and community of interest. Even if this may not appear to be the case from the day-to-day perspective of regulation, boards, senior management, control functions and regulatory supervisory teams need to appreciate the underlying concepts on which the edifice of regulation is based. Consequently, compliance, as mentioned in the previous chapters, needs to take a strategic approach. There is, of course, an imbalance in the relationship between the regulator and the regulated firm but it is not as great as it appears. The regulatory supervisors have their own internal reporting lines and their own drivers of success and are bound by both limited resources and their own attention spans. The regulator relies on the firm, its board, senior management and the control functions to work and act in their stead. For example, claiming legal professional privilege can quickly destroy all the positive work building this relationship founded on trust. It is all based on there being a good understanding of the regulatory objectives by the business, and a sound culture within the regulated firm.

The relationship of trust is, for the most part, mediated by the compliance function. However, there is also an important role for the board and other senior executives. All need to ensure that the key indicators of trustworthiness exist and operate. These include being proactive and open and cooperative with a customer-centric perspective.

As mentioned in the previous chapter, trust needs also to permeate the regulated firm so that customers can safely rely on the firm and its staff can feel free to make known their concerns on the understanding that they will be listened to, action will be taken and they themselves will not suffer retribution.

The centrality of the compliance function in helping to keep the firm open and honest and meriting the trust of stakeholders depends, to a large part, on the recruitment, training and management of the compliance team. This is the subject of the next chapter.

Notes

1 FCA, Final Notice, Liberty Mutual Insurance Europe, 29 October 2018, https://www.fca.org.uk/publication/final-notices/liberty-mutual-insurance-europe-se-2018.pdf (accessed 21 November 2019).
2 Ibid (Final Notice, Liberty), 5.
3 Ibid (Final Notice, Liberty), 1–2.
4 Karina McTeague, FCA, Director of General Insurance and Conduct Specialists Supervision, speech on 'Leading the Way on Regulation', 16 May 2019, https://www.fca.org.uk/news/speeches/leading-way-regulation (accessed 19 May 2019).
5 Ibid (McTeague speech).
6 FCA, Business plan 2019/20, April 2019, 14, https://www.fca.org.uk/publication/business-plans/business-plan-2019-20.pdf (accessed 22 April 2019).
7 Ibid (Business Plan), 14.
8 FCA's Mission, 'Approach to supervision', April 2019, 8–9, https://www.fca.org.uk/publication/corporate/our-approach-supervision.pdf (accessed 29 April 2019).
9 Ibid ('Approach to supervision'), 32.
10 Ibid ('Approach to supervision'), 32.
11 Ibid ('Approach to supervision'), 10–11.
12 Supra note 4 (McTeague speech).
13 Money Laundering Regulations 2007.
14 FCA, Final Notice, Standard Chartered Bank, 5 February 2019, 10, https://www.fca.org.uk/publication/decision-notices/standard-chartered-bank-2019.pdf (accessed 21 November 2019).
15 'For a salesman, there is no rock bottom ... He's a man way out there in the blue, riding on a smile and a shoeshine ... a salesman is got to dream, boys; it comes with the territory', in Arthur Miller (ed.) *Death of a salesman: certain private conversations in two acts and a requiem* (first published 1949, Penguin Modern Classics, 2000), Requiem, 111.
16 Parliamentary Commission on Banking Standards, 'An accident waiting to happen': the failure of HBOS', Fourth Report of Session 2012-13, Volume I: Report, together with formal minutes, HL Paper 144 HC 705 (published on 4 April 2013), 8–9, https://publications.parliament.uk/pa/jt201213/jtselect/jtpcbs/144/144.pdf (accessed 21 November 2019).
17 Norm Champ, 'Building effective relationships with regulators', Harvard Law School forum on Corporate Governance website, 22 October 2015, https://corpgov.law.harvard.edu/2015/10/22/building-effective-relationships-with-regulators/ (accessed 19 February 2020).
18 Ibid (Champ).
19 Ibid (Champ).
20 Ibid (Champ).
21 Ibid (Champ).
22 Ibid (Champ).
23 15 U.S.C.§ 78dd-1 and 9-47.000 – Policy Concerning Criminal Investigations and Prosecutions of the Foreign Corrupt Practices Act, https://www.justice.gov/jm/jm-9–47000-foreign-corrupt-practices-act-1977 (accessed 10 December 2019).
24 Supra note 17 (Champ).
25 US Department of Justice letter to Nortek Inc., 3 June 2016, https://www.justice.gov/criminal-fraud/file/865406/download (accessed 11 December 2019).
26 Supra note 17 (Champ).
27 Serious Fraud Office Lisa Osofsky, Director, 'Fighting fraud and corruption in a shrinking world', speaking at the Royal United Services Institute in London on 3

April 2019, https://www.sfo.gov.uk/2019/04/03/fighting-fraud-and-corruption-in-a-shrinking-world/ (accessed 5 April 2019).

28 Supra note 17 (Champ).
29 FCA, Fair pricing in financial services – discussion paper 18/9, October 2018, https://www.fca.org.uk/publication/discussion/dp18-09.pdf (accessed 22 April 2019).
30 Ibid (FCA's paper on fair pricing), 28.
31 Ibid (FCA's paper on fair pricing), 3.
32 Ibid (FCA's paper on fair pricing), 32.
33 Ibid (FCA's paper on fair pricing), 28.
34 FCA, 'Fair pricing in financial services: summary of responses and next steps Feedback Statement', FS19/04, July 2019, 14 and 20, https://www.fca.org.uk/publication/feedback/fs19-04.pdf (accessed 4 May 2020).
35 FCA, Price discrimination in the cash savings market Discussion Paper, DP18/6, July 2018, 3, https://www.fca.org.uk/publication/discussion/dp18-06.pdf (accessed 21 November 2019).
36 Ibid (FCA Feedback Statement), 5.
37 Ibid (FCA Feedback Statement), 7.
38 Ibid (FCA Feedback Statement), 6 and 16.

5

FINDING THE RIGHT PEOPLE AND THE KEY FUNCTIONS OF THE COMPLIANCE ORGANIZATION

Introduction

This chapter looks at two important aspects of the compliance function: finding the right people and the key organisational elements of a compliance function including issues such as where the function is located within the organisation's structure and whether it should be centralised or devolved. There is also an analysis of the so-called 'three lines of defence' model commonly adopted by many regulated firms.

Finding and selecting the right people

The importance of finding the right people cannot be overstated. Selecting the right people for a role has a long history. Gideon took the candidates to join him in defeating the host of the Midianites to the water near the well of Harod and gave them all a task to do to find the brightest and the most alert and watchful:

> Every one that lappeth of the water with his tongue, as a dog lappeth, him shalt thou set by himself; likewise every one that boweth down upon his knees to drink. And the number of them that lapped, putting their hand to their mouth, were three hundred men: but all the rest of the people bowed down upon their knees to drink water.[1]

In the same way compliance needs to select the best. Compliance needs to avoid becoming the repository for individuals who do not fit anywhere else in the organisation. It must recruit and develop the highest quality staff. It should find staff with business and operational experience since they are likely to know the business and its issues. Additionally, compliance will need specialists in areas such as cyber-security and data protection, and increasingly, artificial intelligence and advanced computing.

These individuals need to be inducted and trained accordingly. They must act professionally; and with the support of the business, they should be encouraged to take the appropriate professional qualifications. This will develop their competence and ensure they do not breach any general or specific legal duties through ignorance. Professionalism, and membership of recognised industry professional bodies will provide an authoritative moral reference point above and beyond those required by the business itself, including undertaking to adhere to high standards of conduct supported by ethical codes. Professional bodies also provide access to ethical guidance and confidential mechanisms to raise concerns. I have a personal interest in this as a Fellow of the Chartered Banker Institute, a professional body founded in 1875 for bankers, and I am member of both its Forum and Education Quality and Standards Committee.

Each member of the compliance team should have a training record, noting courses, and other training, undertaken together with their membership of professional organisations and related continuous professional development (CPD).

As a managed process, compliance staff should be encouraged to rejoin the business, hopefully on promotion, after a few years in compliance. The compliance function needs to be outward looking. This can be encouraged by staff attending compliance and other business conferences and actively participating in trade body and professional committees. A small number of staff should be recruited from competitor firms and from the regulators from time to time to ensure that different perspectives are brought to bear.

All the usual management techniques should be employed to help develop a high level of esprit de corps among compliance staff.

Who to recruit as a senior compliance officer

As the Director of Compliance at a couple of major UK banks, I often thought about who I should recruit to senior positions in compliance. My starting point was always to promote internal candidates first. The best of these internal candidates were, of course, experts both in the regulations but also in how the regulators expected these requirements to be applied. Most issues arose from business operational problems and these individuals knew how many of the business systems worked and where the deficiencies could be found.

Besides this level of operational knowledge they had built up a wide number of good contacts throughout the business front-line managers, back-office functions and risk and control units and consequently knew who to contact to get things done. Moreover, they had the trust and confidence of senior management within the business and the supervisory team at the key regulators. However, most importantly, they were excellent team managers to lead and motivate their staff.

Leadership and motivation

Of course, it is almost always good for morale to promote staff internally – assuming that they are competent and well respected. If, for any reason, I could not find the right internal candidate I would look at recruiting someone from one of the key business operations units. Although this is not a book on leadership and motivation, it is worth noting that probably, the best person I every found was the head of mortgage business operations. He joined the compliance team to run a large business review, setting up a two-centre review operation with several hundred staff. He set up process flows for electronically scanned documents each bar-coded. He based the process on the Swedish car production model with each team responsible for each business file review from start to finish supplemented by teams of experts ready to help. Consequently, I learned much about good process design and implementation. He was also a superb leader and motivator.

We celebrated everything we could find. These included outstanding bank customer service measured by what customers actually said, professional exam success, recognition by other teams of inter-team cooperation, long-service anniversaries starting at 5 years' service and progressing in five yearly increments and so on. We had a supply of engraved plaques, and other small, non-monetary gifts which we awarded every week. Colleagues would gather around, and another member of staff would take professional photographs of the small award ceremonies. The photos would be framed and put up on a wall to celebrate the event. No opportunity was missed to recognise the work of individuals and teams.

However, the most important method to encourage the teams was simply to walk around stopping to chat for a minute or two at every few desks. Each desk had the person's name prominently displayed and when I spoke at each bank of desks I addressed each person by name and always ensured that I spoke to each person in the unit at hand with no one left out, no matter how senior or junior they were. Leaving someone out resulted only in fueling their self-doubt and, possibly, building up resentment. It was also important to balance out the teams covered by these walk-arounds so that all units felt included and valued. My aim was to include everyone and to treat each person as an individual who was important in their own right.

The more remote a unit was geographically, the more important it was to specifically include it in these celebrations and opportunities to focus on the individual.

It was vital that all staff were asked individually what they thought the problems were and what should be done. This needed to be genuine and not as some form of 'act'. It was often the case that your staff knew much more about an issue than the senior team. In keeping with this it remains important that team structures are kept flat and that management hierarchies are almost non-existent. My 'rule-of-thumb' is that any report that goes up a management reporting line beyond two layers is not worth having because each level 'sanitises' the information and the main messages get diluted and therefore become meaninglessness.

Research on who becomes a senior compliance officer in the United Kingdom

Research in who becomes a senior compliance officer in the United Kingdom is limited. An assessment on who a financial services firm recruits to a senior post in compliance should provide some insight for regulators and others on how a firm's senior executive team view the compliance role.

A number of regulated firms seek their senior compliance staff from the regulators. It is not clear why they do this. It is possible that the firm's senior team may have a distorted view on the what they consider compliance to be about. They may think that they are buying some form of regulatory protection. They may think that compliance can be 'boxed-off' and it may be evidence of a lack of thought by the business executive.

Consequently, I have undertaken some research on the work backgrounds of senior compliance officers at a number of UK banks. I used a sample of fifty senior compliance staff at UK-authorised major banks and building societies. I used LinkedIn, an Internet network for professional staff, to analyse the working experience of these individuals. Each LinkedIn profile contains a CV. Although not representing an exact search, this does provide a reasonable sample since there are very few senior compliance staff who do not have a presence on LinkedIn. For the few who did not have LinkedIn CVs, I was able to carry out separate Internet searches and found information on their professional backgrounds.

Sample split between investment and retail/commercial banks

Of the 50 individuals in the sample 20 were employed by investment banks and thirty by retail and commercial banks and building societies. Forty percent of the sample were female.

Professional backgrounds

The vast majority of the sample had, predominantly, professional backgrounds in compliance, or in line management in banking or had worked recently at the regulators. There were approximately twelve from each of these three areas. Those working in investment or retail/commercial banking or building societies came evenly from one of these three sectors. A few had worked on more than one of these areas but generally the working experience of each individuals had been centred on one sector.

Further, approximately three each came from working in either consultancy or the law. The remaining seven came from a variety of backgrounds including, risk, business strategy, IT and project management. None of the compliance staff in the sample from the investment banks came from either a legal or consultancy background.

The significant number of senior compliance staff with line business banking backgrounds may reflect the importance of recruiting people who know the business. As mentioned earlier, this is particularly important since many of the regulatory problems over the years have had operational failures at their heart. Consequently, it is not surprising that there has been a heavy recruitment from business line management and other areas with banking operational experience.

The importance of professionalism in compliance

Compliance needs to think of itself as a profession. There are a number of views on what constitutes a profession. In the view of Louis Brandeis a profession has three characteristics. 'First, it is an occupation for which the necessary training is intellectual, involving knowledge and learning as distinguished from skill. Second, it is an occupation pursued largely for others. Third, it is an occupation in which the amount of financial return is not the accepted measure of success'.[2] The expectations of what constitutes a profession are built on these attributes and include: acting in the public interest, with, among other things, high standards as a condition of entry; training and education that continues throughout an individual's lifetime and they operate to ethical standards 'designed for the public benefit, higher than those established by the general law'.[3]

Compliance staff should display these attributes of professionalism. However, it operates in an industry which has been described as being a 'long way' from 'where professional duties to customers, and to the integrity of the profession as a whole, trump an individual's own behavioural incentives'.[4] The need for greater professionalism within banks extends much more widely than in the area of compliance. In UK banking the value of membership of a professional body and the acquiring of professional qualifications has declined over the last twenty-five years 'both as a proportion of what has become a much larger industry and in absolute terms'.[5] There are a number of reasons given for this including an increased focus on more product and service sales, 'increasing career specialism, which has resulted in fewer generalist bankers with all-round experience; greater use of technology, which has reduced the demand (though arguably not the need) for professional judgment; and the search for cost efficiencies, for example by outsourcing activities linked to customer service and outcomes' and a consequential fragmentation into siloed working.[6]

As a consequence, training in banks has focused on the 'technical requirements of the job in hand' and often there has been 'very little emphasis on how that job fits in to the broader activities of the institution, and even less on the broader societal role of banking'.[7]

The UK's Banking Standards Board, an organisation formed by banks and building societies to help improve standards conduct and ethics in the industry, has recommended a number of principles to enhance professionalism. These include firms ensuring 'that every individual is motivated and equipped to act in the interests of customers, clients and wider society'; strengthening 'technical knowledge, ethical judgement and people skills' and fostering 'a culture of openness, honesty, challenge and support'.[8]

The next section examines the structure of the compliance function, including the debate on whether or not to establish the 'three lines of defence' model.

The compliance structure

It is important to keep the main objective of compliance in mind at all times. Combined with the work of the other control functions, the primary purpose of compliance is to give confidence to a range of business stakeholders that the firm manifestly complies with the regulations, both to their letter and spirit. Additionally, the actions of the firm need to be buttressed by a compliant culture bent on doing the right thing.

The following sections consider the key organisational elements of a compliance function including issues such as where the function is located within the organisation's structure and whether it should be centralised or devolved. There is also an analysis of the so-called 'three lines of defence' model commonly adopted by many regulated firms.

The chapter also examines some of the key compliance roles including:

- identifying and communicating 'upstream' and 'downstream' compliance risk,
- engaging with external opinion formers, including government departments, regulators, trade bodies, media, consumer organisations and so forth. This work needs to be coordinated with other parts of the business,
- ensuring that new laws, regulation, speeches by regulators and the like are analysed, interpreted and operational and organisational changes made and managed, as necessary. The key skills in this area are the abilities both to understand the business and to communicate in terms that resonate with those who work in the organisation,
- monitoring compliance with the regulations and internal process requirements. Besides knowledge of the business this requires sound

judgement, clarity of communication, and doggedness – never letting go of an issue until it is quickly and satisfactorily resolved,

- covering specialist units; for example, new product development, marketing, data protection and security, market abuse prevention, recovery and resolution planning and so on,
- identifying potential problem indicators. This could include, for example, reviewing 'whistleblowing' information, customer complaints data, detailed analysis of staff opinion surveys, operational data looking for significant system failures, and the like,
- back-book reviewing and remediation projects to ensure that projects are 'owned' within the business and progressed swiftly, to the right standard, and that regular reports are produced for senior management and the regulators,
- briefing new directors and other senior management and participating in their training and ensuring that the Senior Managers and Certified Persons Regime operates properly, ensuring that they have the right attitude towards compliance, regulation and their responsibilities and will provide corresponding leadership for their staff,
- performing ad hoc tasks such as due diligence assessments, special large regulatory projects.

Locating the compliance function within the organisation

There is some debate where the compliance should be located within a regulated business. Much may depend on the firm's jurisdiction and hence the regulatory approach. For example, studies in the United States found that compliance, as a role, is a sub-set of the legal function and consequently the compliance function reports, either directly or indirectly, to the firm's general counsel.[9] In the United Kingdom and most other parts of Europe, there is no clear 'home' for the compliance function. In some instances compliance reports to the head of legal in other cases it is located within the risk unit.[10] In many large companies there are frequent reorganisations and the compliance function's reporting lines are often changed moving between risk and legal divisions depending on personalities, advice from external consultants, 'spans of control' (the number of direct reports) and the perception of compliance risk.

There are other reporting line variants, and I recall that in one major insurance company, compliance reported to the head of taxation. It is rare for compliance to have its own direct reporting line to the CEO and to form part of the management executive committee ('exco'). In my opinion, in any heavily regulated business, compliance should report to the CEO and be part of the exco. It sends an important message to all stakeholders, but particularly the business units and the regulators, and indicates how seriously compliance is taken within the organisation.

Having compliance report to the general counsel presents its own problems. As discussed throughout this book compliance with the law is a necessary but not a sufficient condition for a regulated firm to succeed. There is a tendency for in-house legal departments to restrict themselves to the narrow requirement of satisfying the law and no more. From my own experience of having been in charge of both legal and compliance teams, this can present conflict between the two since concepts of 'fairness' and simply 'doing the right thing' tend not to resonate with those operating in a purely legal setting.

Further, as already mentioned, much of financial services regulation is expressed in general terms and often as principles. Many lawyers find this a challenge and if the regulations are seen as 'indeterminate, as they so often are (something lawyers are trained early on to spot). The ability 'to get comfortable' with actions proposed by the business in relation to the law grows simply by finding enough argumentative space'.[11]

In many other firms the lawyers are seen as 'facilitators'. For example, the general counsel 'of a fast food company made clear that his employer expected his department to be gatekeepers and team players at the same time'.[12] The general counsel has a range of roles and audiences. They may be seen as a 'tough, relentless advocate, the hard-driving negotiator and the skilful planner who is able to exploit whatever loopholes the law offers. To investors and the public generally, it is the wise statesman with an impeccable reputation for integrity'.[13] Besides the provision of legal advice the in-house lawyers are 'also actors' for and on behalf of their firm, and in doing so may see themselves as co-agents with their in-house business 'client'.[14]

However, the general counsel too often is used as an 'agent' of the company and doing so brings with it 'temptations to 'spin', to over or under-state to try to mitigate the adverse impact on the corporation'.[15] This 'may undermine counsel's gravitas as an internal force for compliance with the law'.[16] Clearly, adopting such a role would be detrimental to the position of the compliance function if it is too closely associated with the in-house legal team. 'Of course, an organization that wants an 'attack dog' for a general counsel is probably not going to generate a strong ethical culture in any event... so that ethics and compliance becomes just so much window dressing' and the over-arching culture of the business.[17]

In summary, the debate about whether the compliance function should be based in one business division or another is not in itself that material. More important is having an independent outlook and a strong 'voice' in the decision-making and operations of the business. It is also important that all of this is signalled to the various stakeholders both within and outside the organisation and how this signalling is done.

Compliance functions and departmental structures

Depending on the nature of a firm and its size there are a number of compliance tasks. These can be broadly divided into those that:

- help set policy,
- check and report on the implementation of these policies
- act as interlocutors between the business and regulation and the regulators
- influence regulatory policy
- work with other control functions
- directly support the board.

In more detail, compliance, as a department within a firm, needs to cover a range of areas. These can be seen, conceptually, as following the life-cycle of a regulatory policy initiative:

- a regulatory affairs team looking 'up-stream' at draft legislation and regulations in preparation. This task includes seeking to influence its development, if appropriate',
- a unit considering potential regulatory risks and preparing and updating the regulatory 'risk maps',
- a group talking to the relevant business areas and preparing policies and guidance for use by the business. This role may also include preparing and updating compliance manuals,
- day-to-day liaison with the various business and support areas and other control functions,
- compliance monitoring and reporting teams,
- operation of an independent compliance investigation unit,
- in the United Kingdom, the operation of the Senior Managers and Certified Persons Regime (SM&CR). This will include the preparation and briefing of those subject to the regime. This is covered in more detail below,
- marketing material review, sign-off and monitoring,
- remuneration schemes and business targets review, sign-off and monitoring,
- special projects (e.g. mergers and acquisition due diligence),
- briefing boards and sub-committees,
- liaison and deconfliction work with other control functions,
- IT programmes, prioritisation and progress monitoring,
- day-to-day liaison with the regulators,
- compliance risk assessment and actions for non-core business areas,
- operational aspects of the compliance function (e.g. compliance staff training and development, promoting diversity, staff rostering, location and accommodation issues, compliance staff opinion surveys etc.),

- compliance specialist areas (data protection, anti-money laundering, market abuse prevention and detection, anti-bribery and corruption prevention and detection, police liaison, etc.),
- the encouragement and facilitation of whistleblowing (covered in detail in Chapter 3)
- customer concerns assessment, 'root cause' analysis, back-book reviews and the like (covered in more detail in Chapter 6).

The key elements of these tasks are covered in this and other chapters.

An example

Probably the best way of looking at a compliance function, and its various roles, is to consider a hypothetical example. Let us assume that a newly appointed UK compliance officer for a medium to large financial services firm has a clean sheet of paper and can create their compliance department from scratch. The first question is assess whether to centralise or de-centralise the function. As mentioned earlier, there is no clear-cut answer to this question. If the firm operates in a number of jurisdictions or has several distinct businesses, then a more de-centralised approach is likely to be appropriate.

The key issues that need to be clearly agreed upon include the following.

- The compliance officer, must be responsible for all recruitment, recognitions and promotion of compliance staff, whether centralised or de-centralised. Similarly, only they must be responsible for the removal or sanctioning of any compliance staff. Business line and local management may have some input into these processes, including taking part in interviewing staff, but the final decision must be that of the compliance officer.
- All compliance staff must have their primary reporting line to the compliance officer and their team. They may also have local 'dotted-line' reporting responsibilities to, for example, the CEO of a local subsidiary.
- In a de-centralised model resourcing and budgets may be operated locally, but it will be the compliance officer's responsibility to ensure that the local compliance function is adequately resourced.
- All compliance-related policy and procedures must, of course, conform with local laws and regulations where there are cross-border operations. However, they must also conform with the central or group-wide policies. This may result in areas of potential conflict, for example in data security and protection. These will need to be resolved.
- The so-called 'three lines of defence' model is, as discussed elsewhere, problematic. It could be described as a 'false-friends' since it is

important that the compliance function is embedded in a range of key operations (e.g. product development, the production of marketing material and increasingly, product and services pricing decisions).

- The control functions need to work closely together and be central to the business strategy and decision-making process, at all stages.
- It is important to consider how the compliance function should be portrayed within the business and to other stakeholders. This includes establishing and maintaining an ethos for the function, internal guidance, 'branding', team building, determining what is celebrated and how, establishing and developing a compliance 'alumni' organisation.
- It is important that any regulatory requirements are implemented in each business division and jurisdiction and all regulatory concerns addressed quickly. There can be no significant areas which are 'off-limits'. There can also be no restrictions on the flow of information. If any of this proves to be an issue, it is possible that the regulators for the group may take personal action against the senior management, including the compliance officer.
- Everything is founded on trust and being trustworthy. This is a theme throughout this book. So the compliance officer and their team must always ask themselves if a particular action, or inaction, will enhance trust or put it at risk.

An example, illustrating many of the issues mentioned in this section, can be seen in the PRA enforcement action taken against The Bank of Tokyo Mitsubishi UFJ Limited (MUFG) and MUFG Securities EMEA (European, Middle East and Africa regions).[18] The two regulated entities were fined a combined total of almost £27m. The UK regulators expect that a regulated firm 'operating across multiple jurisdictions...ensure[s] that it is organised such that, when issues arise concerning its operations in one jurisdiction which may impact other jurisdictions, the regulatory responsibilities of the firm as a whole are appropriately considered'.[19]

In this case the New York based Department of Financial Services (DFS) took action against the New York branch of Bank of Tokyo Mitsubishi (BTM) and entered into settlement negotiations. Under New York State Banking Law these discussions were confidential and could not be disclosed to third parties, including other regulators without permission from DFS. In view of this confidentiality requirement, BTM managers and compliance only proposed to tell the PRA in the United Kingdom about the negotiations with the US regulator once a settlement had been agreed.[20] Shortly after this agreement, in the firm's Tokyo head office, not to inform the PRA BTM compliance in Tokyo contacted their compliance colleagues in London and told them of the negotiations with the DFS and told them not to contact the PRA. The London compliance team objected saying that the

PRA should be informed. Tokyo compliance took external advice which re-affirmed that the PRA should not be approached until the settlement discussions were closer to a conclusion.[21] Unfortunately, the Tokyo staff appeared not to be aware of the regulatory responsibilities of PRA-regulated entitles. It appeared that compliance in London was often not kept informed of group developments which might have been of interest to the PRA and had only limited discretion to act without agreement from Tokyo.[22]

It is clear that these arrangements, both formalised and informal, were untenable. DFS permission to disclose the negotiations to the PRA should have been sought. This would have been granted, as it was when permission was subsequently sought.

Three lines of defence

In this example, there may be some pressure to adopt a so-called 'three lines of defence' model. It has been widely adopted in the financial services in-dustry and external consultants, regulators and the like may question why the compliance officer has not implemented it in their organisation.

In summary, this model divides the roles of ensuring control of risks and compliance into three. The front-line business functions taking primary responsibility for risk management and regulatory compliance; with a second line of control functions, such as the compliance department, checking and reporting on the effectiveness of the first line. This is backed up by the firm's internal audit function providing a third and final line of defence.

This approach does sound conceptually attractive but it is difficult to operate successfully and has been described by the Parliamentary Commission on Banking Standards as providing 'a wholly misplaced sense of security....responsibilities have been blurred, accountability diluted, and officers in risk, compliance and internal audit have lacked the status to challenge front-line staff effectively. Much of the system became a box-ticking exercise whereby processes were followed, but judgement was ab-sent'.[23] The same report stated that the 'three lines of defence' model also promoted the use of an 'accountability firewall' which seems to have de-veloped 'to prevent those in senior positions having a strong sense of per-sonal engagement with and responsibility for failings and misconduct within their line of management'.[24] The report described the model as the 'Maginot line of defence'.[25]

It is for the senior management and the business to operate compliantly. The compliance function should provide expert advice to help the business achieve the goal of compliance. Compliance should also provide in-dependent monitoring and reporting. However, if all else is failing, com-pliance cannot stand aside. It must step in and take ownership and operationally achieve the changes required. This may blur the neat theoretical lines of independence but even worse is the risk of potential harm, for example, to customer, markets, reputation and so forth. An assertive, authoritative compliance function is central to this change of approach.

The three lines of defence model has been described as being at the 'heart of the dysfunctionality of risk and compliance' since it reinforces misjudgements and over-complexity.[26] It may also induce a false sense of security. Those operating the compliance function in the first line of defence may be confused as to their role and suffer conflicts of interest. They are very much part of the line business unit with local reporting lines. This may provide some advantages since they are closer to the issues and may understand both the issues and the business in greater depth than a more centralised function. On the other hand, they are likely to identify too closely with the business and may not approach problems with sufficient criticality and objectivity of mind. At the same time small, locally based compliance units may pose problems of inconsistency and divergent and poor compliance methodologies.

Theoretically, the first line of defence is overseen by the second line. The latter is more likely to be objective and to have the necessary technical expertise but may also lack the local and business knowledge. Moreover, the second line of defence may be too late to identify harm. It will employ a rolling compliance programme used to identify, assess and to report risks but by the time it arrives 'on site' the damage may have already have been done and their role will become one of largely sweeping up the pieces.

This issue became clear in the oral evidence provided by Mike Walters (Group Head of Compliance, Barclays Bank) to the Parliamentary Commission on Banking Standards. Mike Walters described the compliance function in the second line of defence signing off new business products (see Chapter 6 of this work for more on this important area). Walters went on to to say that if the central compliance function 'did not like a product at all and either send it back to the drawing board or, effectively, kill it'.[27] Mark Garnier MP, chairing this hearing rightly said 'does that not make you the first line of defence?' In response Walters stated:

> I don't think so...we are the second line of defence, and we are very clear that we are. The tension, of course, is: what is the best way to operate? One could pull back from having anything to do with the first line of defence and simply seek to quasi-audit them after the event...we are much better off and more likely to be successful as a compliance function and to protect Barclays if we have the ability to put our hand up and to ask our questions when that debate is happening. It is a somewhat sterile exercise and, therefore, has some inherent risks if you seek to do that on a cold review basis after the event.[28]

Internal audit, who form the third line of defence, would have to staff-up with people competent in both regulation and the details in the business. The third line also needs to adapt their standard internal audit methodologies to address these areas. This can all be done but at a further level of costly duplication. The audit function is also likely to be remote from the business areas and their reviews undertaken episodically. The evidence from regulatory enforcement cases, both in the United States and United Kingdom, does not indicate that the internal audit has been particularly effective in their oversight of many areas of regulation. Additionally, the third line of defence, as with the second line mentioned above, 'however independent it might be, is often perceived as intervening too late to be useful in preventing risks crystallising'.[29]

Consequently, it is likely that competence, power and influence rests in the second line of defence while detailed knowledge of the issues remains with potentially confused and conflicted individuals within the business. The situation is muddled by a number of 'work arounds' such as those covering new product development designed to address inherent problems in the conceptual model.

Paul Moore, the former Head of Group Regulatory Risk at Halifax Bank of Scotland (HBOS), who was fired by the HBOS CEO who was, himself, subsequently disgraced, considered that 'the 'three lines of defence' governance model (designed by consultants with little or no practitioner experience) which is commonly in use in large organisations, does not work and is dysfunctional'.[30]

Prevalence of the three lines of defence model

The three lines of defence model is now common in both risk management, as well as compliance structures. For example, The independent report by the law firm Slaughter and May in 2019 into the IT systems transfer failures at TSB recorded that this model was employed both as business as usual for risk management and specifically for this major project.[31] Unfortunately, the first line failed to identify a number of key risks and failed during the courses of the programme to update the risks log sufficiently to reflect the recognition of important changes and risks to the successful execution of the programme.[32] The second and third lines were no better at identifying the significant risks, a number which caused the project to fail with the subsequent resignation of the CEO and several other senior staff.[33]

Compliance and the UK's Senior Managers and Certified Persons Regime (SM&CR)

A lack of personal, individual accountability is seen as being at the heart of the various recent debacles and scandals in the financial services industry.

The SM&CR was introduced in the United Kingdom in 2016, initially, for banks and insurance companies. These regulations were extended to all financial services firms in 2019.

The aim of the new regulations is to ensure 'that senior management and other staff who are in a position to do significant harm to financial firms and their customers will, in future, each have their own documented areas of individual responsibility and will be held accountable, and hence liable to sanction, for regulatory failures within those areas'.[34] Compliance should have an important role in making certain that all the individuals are identified and understand their individual roles and responsibilities, and that the certification process is effective and meets the expectations of the board and the regulators.

This UK regulatory initiative is central to the supervisory approach. However, there is anecdotal information that compliance functions may be too focused on the technical elements of delivering and operating this new regime. There is danger, as identified in a different context by the PCBS, that compliance pursues 'a box-ticking approach to compliance, adhering only to the specifics of their interpretation of the regulator's detailed rules'.[35]

Understanding the business in depth

The challenge for the compliance function is to know the business and the world in which it operates, in depth. Working from the inside outwards, this means understanding:

- the business, this includes its people, entities, governance, finances, profit centres and assets and liabilities, products and services and operations,
- the customers of the business, and their concerns, expectations and perspectives,
- the regulations, codes and regulatory guidance,
- the various regulators and how they think and operate,
- the context in which the business operates. This will include the political environment, the media, societal dynamics and technological developments and business competitors.

Compliance needs to ask a number of fundamental questions covering all these aspects: what is happening, why, and looking ahead, what might happen under a different sets of circumstances?

Measuring success and 'compliance engineering'

The subject of measuring compliance success is difficult. All too often it has resulted in excessive complacency as the measures, reported to the board, all indicate 'green' – everything is fine and there are no issues (see Chapter 2 and Wells Fargo). There are also difficulties in interpreting the measurements. For example, it is difficult to tell whether a high or low number of whistleblowing reports is a good or a bad sign. A small number may indicate no significant problems or that staff are too afraid to speak up. Conversely, a high number may be a sign of major issues or an indicator of a good culture in an organisation where raising concerns is welcomed and followed up and staff, who act in the general interested, are celebrated. The important area of whistleblowing and the role of compliance is covered in depth in Chapter 3. There are similar issues with, for example, customer complaints and regulatory breach recordings.

Some writers recommend 'compliance engineering' with compliance staff undertaking regression analysis.[36] This might be undertaken using multi-variate regression analysis. This relies on testing whether or not it is possible to hold some of the variables constant such as the availability of the whistleblower telephone line and the level and style of response to those who call. It is likely that the design of these types of analytical systems will take time and effort and it is unclear how effective they will be in practice.

Excessive proceduralism

All too often the compliance and internal audit work is too focused on process adherence. The PCBS report remarked that witnesses to the commission 'described adherence to procedure with little regard to judgement throughout the three lines system'.[37] Generally, judgement is lacking. which was acknowledged by Paul Lawrence, Group Head of Internal Audit at HSBC who said it 'is actually very difficult for an audit unit, based on the skill sets it had and where it traditionally was in the organisation, to pass an opinion on judgments or issues of strategy'.[38]

Consequently, no purpose is served by turning to perfunctory or 'tick-box' compliance. I saw one large company which each month required all its staff, in each section, to circulate a large lever-arch file of its policies with a cover-sheet on which each member of staff was required to sign and date their confirmation that they had read the policies for that month. The process was empty – without purpose or rationale – and was a viewed as a curious version of the game 'pass the parcel' to get the tome round each department as fast as possible and the task completed to everyone's mutual and vacuous satisfaction. The process encouraged employees to lie in stating that they had read the policies; a situation compounded by the general understanding and acceptance in the firm that this was an empty process and of no value. However, it persisted year after year.

It is possible, but unlikely, that by signing that they had read the documents the company may have been protecting itself against some form of subsequent litigation. It is also possible that an employee who broke one of the policies exposed themselves to disciplinary action for, at the very least, lying that they had read the policies. This may be useful for a HR department since it makes their life easier but it risks categorising compliance as simply a legal process. As seen here, and elsewhere, this approach may fail stakeholders and undermine key regulatory trust.

In his evidence Joris Luyendijk, an anthropologist and journalist specialising in the banking industry, said that a trader constructing a new product would ensure that it met all the rules. 'He probably went to all his compliance people and ticked all the boxes. Most traders talk about compliance as box ticking, or hurdles. They have externalised ethics... Banks tend to have departments tasked with dealing with regulators, enabling the rest of the company to get on with making money'.[39] Professor John Kay, in his evidence to the Commission, said something similar; that in financial institutions 'regulation is regarded unequivocally as a nuisance, and, secondly, that regulation is largely entrusted to a department whose job it is to deal with regulation, and that department is itself regarded as a nuisance'.[40]

In part, the issue arises from the regulations frequently being focused on procedure with less emphasis on achieving certain outcomes. This is reinforced by many of the regulatory enforcement actions being framed as procedural breaches (see Chapters 9 and 10 for more detail).

Conclusion

The need for high quality compliance staff is paramount. The compliance function needs people who know and understand the various parts of the business and its inherent risks and recognise what a good process looks like. Further, there is a growing need for specialists on, for example, aspects of AI and cyber-security. All these individuals need to be selected carefully and inducted and trained to the highest standards.

All compliance staff must see themselves as professionals and be encouraged to gain professional membership of appropriate professional bodies including studying for and attaining, professional qualifications. It is good to do this for its own sake but it may also help provide a 'moral compass' for the future and act as an independent reference point when the individual is faced with hard choices. I have already declared an interest in professionalism for bankers, and I restate the importance of this approach. It will increase the confidence of compliance staff, aid them in their careers and indicate to other stakeholders how serious the firm takes acting properly. Being a professional requires ongoing learning as part of continuous professional development (CPD). None of this is easy nor is it cost free in terms of time, dedication and expense. However, I believe it is the way forward as part of the strategy of enhancing, and in some cases, restoring trust in the financial services industry. All of this needs to be backed by the usual high standards of leadership, so compliance is seen as the place to be within a firm with many applicants for each post with only the few – the best – being chosen.

The main objective of compliance needs to be kept at the forefront of each individuals' mind. Along with others, the primary purpose of compliance is to give confidence to a range of business stakeholders that the firm manifestly complies with the regulations, both to their letter and spirit. Additionally, the actions of the firm need to be buttressed by a compliant culture bent on doing the right thing.

Based on the centrality of compliance and its direct dealings with customers, compliance is in the best position to be the 'customers' advocate'. 'For example, compliance personnel are in the best position to bring the customer's perspective to the firm's decision-making – such as in assessing the clarity and understandability of [a firm's] disclosures. They are also in the best position to make sure customers with complaints are treated fairly'.[41] Consequently, the recruitment, induction and training of the compliance team is fundamental to the success of the compliance functions and also to the business and its stakeholders. Further, good leadership will buttress, develop and sustain professionalism.

'The practice of compliance is an intellectual challenge that should be met through the exercise of expert judgment. Compliance should make sure the customer's interests, and the customer's perspective', are at the forefront of the firm's approach.[42] The ethos of compliance can be summed up by the following: 'Do not obstruct. Do not cover up. Be alert to what is happening. Be proactive. Be accurate. And be remedial'.[43]

Notes

1 King James's Bible, Judges 7:6–7.
2 Louis Brandeis, former Associate Justice of the Supreme Court of the United States, 'Business: a profession', an address delivered at Brown University Commencement Day, 1912, https://louisville.edu/law/library/special-collections/the-louis-d.-brandeis-collection/business-a-profession-chapter-1 (accessed 7 May 2020).
3 Keyur Patel, *Professional bodies and the financial services sector* (The Centre for the Study of Financial Innovation, London, 2014), https://static1.squarespace.com/static/54d620fce4b049bf4cd5be9b/t/55dde01fe4b02fcd4471b848/1440604191144/Setting+Standards_by+Keyur+Patel.pdf (accessed 7 May 2020).
4 Parliamentary Commission for Banking Standards, 'Changing banking for good report' HL Paper 27-I HC 175-I (June 2013), https://www.parliament.uk/documents/banking-commission/Banking-final-report-volume-i.pdf (accessed 8 May 20 20) para 35, 90.
5 Richard Lambert, 'Banking standards review', May 2014, 23, https://bankingstandardsboard.org.uk/pdf/banking-standards-review.pdf (accessed 7 May 2020).
6 Ibid (Lambert), 23.
7 Ibid (Lambert), 23.
8 Banking Standards Board, 'BSB statement of principles for strengthening professionalism', March 2018, https://bankingstandardsboard.org.uk/bsb-statement-of-principles-for-strengthening-professionalism/ (accessed 6 May 2020).

9 Deborah Demott, 'The stages of scandal and the roles of the general counsel' (2012) *Wisconsin Law Review*, 463–493, 481.

10 Iris H-Y Chiu, *Regulating (from) the inside: the legal framework for internal control in banks and financial institutions* (Bloomsbury, 2015), 51.

11 Donald Langevoort, 'Getting (too) comfortable: in-house lawyers, enterprise risk and the financial crisis' (2011), Georgetown University Law Center, Georgetown Public Law and Legal Theory Research Paper No. 11–135, 7, https://pdfs.semanticscholar.org/998e/3dee456132aa2bfd6bd753db30d-f606aa5c7.pdf?_ga=2.211922004.1127191784.1589123726-894506139.1589123726 (accessed 10 May 2020).

12 Tanina Rostain, 'General counsel in the age of compliance: preliminary findings and new research questions' (2008) *Georgetown Journal of Legal Ethics*, 21, 465–490, 475.

13 John Coffee, *Gatekeepers: the professions and corporate governance* (Oxford University Press, Oxford, 2006), 326.

14 Sung Hui Kim, 'Inside lawyers: friends or gatekeepers?' (2016) *Fordham Law Review*, 84, 1867–1897, 1892.

15 Supra note 9 (Demott), 488.

16 Supra note 9 (Demott), 488.

17 Supra note 11 (Langevoort), 8.

18 PRA Final Notice re the Bank of Tokyo Mitsubishi UFJ Limited and MUFG Securities EMEA, 9 February 2017, https://www.bankofengland.co.uk/-/media/boe/files/prudential-regulation/enforcement-notice/en090217.pdf?la=en&hash=58442B59B07D7F5FB9A14CCD51224BE338BD0CF5 (accessed 14 January 2020).

19 Ibid (Bank of Tokyo Mitsubishi, Final Notice), 4.

20 Ibid (Bank of Tokyo Mitsubishi, Final Notice), 15.

21 bid (Bank of Tokyo Mitsubishi, Final Notice), 16.

22 bid (Bank of Tokyo Mitsubishi, Final Notice), 18.

23 Supra note 4 ('Changing banking for good', Report of the Parliamentary Commission on Banking Standards), Vol I, 18.

24 Supra note 4 ('Changing banking for good', Report of the Parliamentary Commission on Banking Standards), Vol II, 283.

25 Supra note 4 ('Changing banking for good', Report of the Parliamentary Commission on Banking Standards), Vol II, 138. See also Peter Bonisch, website, 'Thinking about strategy and uncertainty', 'Excuse me, how many lines of defence? The new financial Maginot Lines', 18 March 2013, https://paradigmrisk.wordpress.com/2013/03/18/excuse-me-how-many-lines-of-defence-the-new-financial-maginot-lines/ (accessed 10 May 2020).

26 Atul Shah, *The politics of financial risk, audit and regulation: a case study of HBOS* (Routledge, Abingdon, 2017), 39.

27 Parliamentary Commission on Banking Standards – Minutes of Evidence Session 2013-14, HL Paper 27-VIII/HC 175-VIII, 28 November 2012, DQ652, https://publications.parliament.uk/pa/jt201314/jtselect/jtpcbs/27/27viii_121128d.htm (accessed 18 February 2020).

28 Ibid (PCBS hearing 28 November 2012).

29 Howard Davies and Maria Zhivitskaya, 'Three lines of defence: a robust organising framework, or just lines in the sand?' (June 2018) *Global Policy*, 9(Suppl 1), 40, https://onlinelibrary.wiley.com/doi/pdf/10.1111/1758-5899.12568 (accessed 11 May 2020).

30 Parliamentary Commission on Banking Standards, Paul Moore written evidence, 13 May 2013, 3.5, https://publications.parliament.uk/pa/jt201314/jtselect/jtpcbs/27/27v_we94.htm (accessed 24 February 2020).

31 Slaughter and May, 'Independent review of TSB's 2018 migration to a new IT platform', December 2019, 210, https://www.slaughterandmay.com/news-and-recent-work/news/slaughter-and-may-s-independent-review-of-tsb-s-2018-migration-to-a-new-it-platform/ (accessed 25 February 2020).
32 Ibid (Slaughter and May), 211.
33 'TSB loses 16,000 customers after IT meltdown', BBC website (24 October 2018), https://www.bbc.co.uk/news/business-45952283 (accessed 25 February 2020).
34 Alan Brener, 'Developing the senior managers regime', in Costanza Russo, Rosa Lastra, and William Blair (eds.) *Research handbook on law and ethics in banking and finance* (Edward Elgar Publishing, Northampton, 2019), 274.
35 Supra note 4 (PCBS report), Vol II, 94.
36 Hui Chen and Eugene Soltes, 'Why compliance programs fail—and how to fix them' (March/April 2018) *Harvard Business Review*, https://hbr.org/2018/03/why-compliance-programs-fail (accessed 8 April 2020).
37 Supra note 4 ('Changing banking for good', Vol II), 141.
38 Supra note 4 ('Changing banking for good', Vol II), 141.
39 Supra note 4 ('Changing banking for good', Vol II), 141.
40 Supra note 4 ('Changing banking for good', Vol II), 141.
41 John Walsh, Chief Counsel, Office of Compliance Inspections and Examinations, Securities and Exchange Commission, 'What makes compliance a profession?', NRS Symposium on the Compliance Profession, Miami Beach, 11 April 2002, https://www.sec.gov/news/speech/spch558.htm (accessed 4 May 2020).
42 Ibid (Walsh speech).
43 Ibid (Walsh speech).

6

THE OPERATIONAL TOOLS OF COMPLIANCE

Introduction – underlying concepts

Compliance is in the business of risk. This includes detecting, measuring and mitigating risk. It means looking not just at the position today but also looking forward, trying to anticipate future risks, or risks that currently exist but which are not currently manifest.

It is a pessimistic profession. One which continually contemplates failure. This means always asking questions – what could go wrong; what if a control failed; how likely is this and what would be the consequence? Compliance also needs to be optimistic: setting out remedies which can reduce these risks.

The compliance function needs to take a number of practical steps to help ensure that the business complies both with the **spirit as well as the letter of the law**.

This chapter will consider a number of these including 'risk' and 'heat maps', the 'directed telescope', the 'spider's web' approach and also techniques for addressing organisational obstruction and delay.

However, compliance must ensure that the **business considers *all* stakeholders**. Besides customers, the firm needs to take account of the effect of its actions and the consequences of its failures on its staff and suppliers, as well as the long-term interests of its investors and the wider implications for the community. This is fundamental to the success of compliance.

It is also critical that the compliance function **understands the business and its operations** thoroughly. It must also have its own network for obtaining information and influencing outcomes. This is particularly important for IT development which may both enable and undermine regulatory compliance. For example, IT systems limitations may result in a number of significant manual 'work-arounds'. These are often weak points in what might otherwise appear to be a strong operationally-compliant systems.

There are also the more routine but nevertheless important functions of compliance, including **monitoring** work and **financial promotion** development, review and approval.

Further, almost all businesses of any size and duration will have legacy systems and products. It is important that these are subject to detailed, regular review. The firm should have a rigorous risk-based **programme of reviewing those sales** where economic conditions may have changed and regulatory standards and customer expectations may have developed since the original sale to the customer. These reviews should be undertaken against the highest standards and customers recompensed if appropriate.

Again, these reviews should be undertaken in a **customer-centric style**. The information provided to customers subjected to these reviews should not seek to gloss over any of the concerns and risks but should be viewed as a frank conversation with the customer. Dialogue scripts should be piloted to check customer understanding before they are used more widely. There should also be a sample of calls, independently undertaken, to customers again to check their understanding and any issues rectified including re-contacting any customers where there may have been a risk of mis-understanding or mis-sale. Recontacting customers needs to be supervised by competent managers independent of the line business. It is important that the process is not seen as another sales opportunity.

The compliance function should also 'look over the horizon' for **future risks ('up-stream' risks)**. These are risks including proposed primary legis-lation and regulations which are being considered and have not been en-acted. This will allow the business to make preparations in time to meet any new obligations. This is particularly an issue where new IT infrastructure will be required with a considerable lead-time in undertaking the work; often over many years.

This chapter will also cover some of the **common problems experienced by compliance functions**. For example, where a business unit persistently challenges compliance requests for information or is slow to implement required changes. Techniques for addressing these types of issues may in-volve engaging the support of divisional heads and board non-executive directors and forcing recalcitrant executives to appear before these in-dividuals or committees to explain themselves.

Complacency is a major compliance risk. One option to address this is to establish an informal group of compliance officers in a range of businesses to share best practice. It may also be possible to compare information which is not commercially confidential and to come up with 'compliance health' benchmarks such as organisational structures, staffing resources, complaints handling warning indicators and so forth.

The final section considers a number of important areas where com-pliance may need to be involved as the regulators increase their focus and businesses change and develop. These include issues relating to IT systems decommissioning, undertaking back-book business reviews, the risks in-herent in outsourcing of critical organisational functions, data and other aspects of cyber-security, AI and automated ('robo') financial advice and elements of environmental, social and governance (ESG) and climate change risk. Looking both forward, and widely, are important elements of compliance.

The main compliance functions

There are certain roles where it is imperative that compliance is part of the business process. This include reviewing and approving:

- the development of new business products and services,
- new, and material changes, to marketing material, websites and customer communications,
- staff training material including mandatory computer-based training,
- the compliance briefing of new senior management, including board members.

There is also a developing demand for specialist compliance staff able to deal with and analyse 'Big Data', artificial intelligence.[1] These elements are considered later in this chapter.

The next section examines some of the most important aspects of the role of the compliance function.

Policies and procedures

Policy and procedures are clearly important in ensuring compliance but compliance also requires a high level of judgement and intuition. Policies and procedures are good at establishing best practice. However, in practice, what really counts as a key compliance 'output' will be based on how good business units are in complying with these requirements.

The risk, however, is that those operating the systems, and the compliance staff assessing the processes, is that they will cease to think and will instead abjure exercising sound judgement. What is really going on may be missed. For example, at HBOS Group Risk 'conducted its oversight of credit risk on a 'post-approval sample view' basis which tested whether the approval process had been followed by the business. [Group Internal Audit] did not assess the quality of credit decisions because it held the view that the required expertise was in Group Risk or the business. These factors resulted in a fundamental gap in the oversight of credit risk and enabled the deteriorating quality of lending decisions in Corporate and International to go largely unchecked'.[2] This is a clear example of the risks of 'siloed thinking' discussed in Chapter 3. Gaps will appear in the compliance 'net' as different functions, checking various aspects of a process, do so without adequate cooperation and with no overarching perspective.

To some extent, this can be remedied by the active use of 'risk maps'.

Devising and revising 'risk maps'

A compliance 'risk map' is more usefully thought of as an analytical database rather than as a single document. It is constructed by asking a series of questions covering each aspect of the business asking what could go wrong in compliance terms. An indication of whether the possible impact on the business could be high, medium or low is assigned to each question together with an indicator of whether the risk of this is growing, staying the same or declining. The next section, for each question, sets out the main controls which mitigate this risk and an assessment of their strengths or weaknesses, in practice, using 'red', 'amber', 'green' ('RAG' status). The final section is an overall view, against each question, of the risk to the business based on the earlier assessments. In a complex business there may be hundreds, if not thousands of questions. The value of these risk assessments will be informed by compliance monitoring activities which will, in turn, test these judgements and the results factored into constructing the 'map'.

The purpose of this approach is to highlight areas of risk that may not have been considered and to help prioritise action. The process is as important as the result. The review needs to be redone every 6 months or so, or more frequently, if there are major internal or external changes. The process employs both precise data and judgement. Consequently, it needs to be undertaken and reviewed by a range of people coming from different perspectives to avoid 'group-think'.

Risk 'heat' maps

The purpose of the 'heat' map is to convey information in a diagrammatic form and to focus attention on the key areas. Essentially, it is a chart summarising the results of the risk management process. It shows, not only, areas of key risk but also whether these are getting worse ('heating up') or receding as the risk reduces ('cooling down').

Current risk models are 'particularly poor at dealing with human error and decision-making ... however, instructions and written procedures are almost never followed exactly' as those trying to operate them have to contend with a range of pressures.[3] Instead, those trying to operate these systems will find ways around them ('work-arounds') to get their job done as quickly and simply as possible. For example, the systems requirement to change an IT access password every thirty days results in simply adding one to an existing digit in the current password. These 'work-arounds' are often done for practical reasons since sometimes working to the letter of the rules could have the effect of slowing systems sufficiently to bring them to a complete halt.

Another approach is to start by considering actual or hypothetical compliance failures and then looking at:

- the proximate causes (e.g. some unethical behaviour),
- the surrounding conditions what may have been factors in causing the problem (e.g. a change in the incentive scheme),
- the underlying factors that may have produced this result (e.g. the management structure or decision-making process).[4]

Reader and O'Connor do this by examining the Deepwater Horizon disaster highlighting a dozen or more proximate causes for the accident and almost the same number of 'conditional factors' (e.g. flaws in well design, informal risk assessment process, issues with the cement barrier evaluation process etc.).[5] However, there were only five underlying systems failures (e.g. production cost savings pressure, use of third party firms to undertake safety work etc.).[6] This process of analysis results in a wiring diagram of causes for this catastrophe. This approach can also be used to highlight the systemic issues in other areas.[7] Additionally, this form of review may be useful for briefing senior executives and boards. However, it may not be suitable for mapping less dramatic risks. It is a form of analysis which needs to be used judiciously.

In Chapter 3 there is a reference to the Herald of Free Enterprise ferry disaster. The proximate cause was human error in not closing the ferry doors and checking that this had happened. However, these errors were founded on, or were compounded by, poor staff management practices, unsafe ship design and docking procedures, a company policy of routinely over-loading the number of passengers on the ferry and the inherent structural instability caused by the vehicle loading operations.[8] These issues can, in turn be traced back to various management decisions of, or omissions by, the ferry operator.[9] In practice, issues are often caused 'by the interaction of potential side effects of the performance of several decision makers during their normal work'.[10]

Consequently, any belief that creating a series of controls which operate in depth will work is likely to be misplaced. This is because market and competitive pressures, combined with management decisions, may create sufficient tensions that any weakness in controls will be exploited. 'In systems designed according to the defence-in-depth strategy, the defenses are likely to degenerate systematically through time, when pressure toward cost-effectiveness is dominating'.[11]

As a result, it is important that risk maps are not seen as an end-point. They are dynamic and need to be frequently tested and inherent and control weaknesses checked to see if there are more fundamental issues which have not been identified and addressed. It is also important to look for decisions which may over-stress procedures and threaten controls. For example, what might be the effect of targeting a reduction in the duration of telephone calls, or what behavioural responses might be triggered if customer call waiting times are targeted? What is the load capacity of the on-line banking system and how is this determined, how is this tested and who decides all this and why? What is the consequential reserve capacity of the telephony system if the on-line banking system fails or slows down for any reason? Who monitors surges and the underlying reasons and to whom do they report this information and when and what happens next? Who decides this? As can be seen from a few examples the level of complexity is immense and requires careful and extensive mapping and questioning and review.

The risk maps need to be shared and discussed with other control functions both, for information and to gain their inputs and insights. In parallel, the risk 'heat' maps should also be available to the regulators. This will show the working practices of compliance, and will, hopefully, increase both their confidence in the function and their trust in the firm. It is also possible that the regulators will provide helpful guidance.

Finally, in this section, it should be obvious, but sometimes it is not, that the actual monitoring work should reflect the risk assessment. Monitoring needs to reflect risk as determined by the compliance risk maps. Clearly, if an area is high risk it needs to be reviewed more frequently. For example, this was not the case with Standard Chartered Bank's due diligence work on customer account openings of the bank's UAE operations which were known to be inadequate.[12] There were no reviews undertaken of this area for almost 4 years.[13] This left the board and senior executives in the dark about what was happening and what risks the business was running.

The dangers of a risk-based approach

However, a risk-based approach is not without dangers. Following a risk-based approach too closely holds 'out the promise that the challenges and complexities of regulation can be rationalised, ordered, managed, and controlled. But whilst the picture is tempting, risk-based frameworks entail the risk of process-induced myopia'.[14] It may deter other perspectives on risk and encourage a 'herd mentality' with, paradoxically, increased risk. Other risk disciplines work with percentages of possible risks actually occurring, its quantification if the risk if it manifests itself, and the potential consequences expressed in numeric terms. This works well with, for example, credit risk where the risk of default occurring in a portfolio of loans and the cost to the lender can be calculated fairly precisely under a number of economic scenarios. Similarly, risk mitigation has a cost, and will have an effect on these calculations. However, much of regulatory compliance does not operate like this. Many of the risks have a small chance of happening but the consequences can be devastating for stakeholders and the firm itself. Its reputation may irretrievably damaged; the risk may be existential for the careers of the senior management and others; and there may industry-wide consequences if trust is broken (e.g. the Libor scandal).

There are also difficulties employing traditional risk assessment methods since the most serious risks tend to have a very high impact (e.g. the business has to close) with a low probability of them occurring. However, these high-impact but low probability (HILP) risks are faced by many other industries besides financial services. It is increasingly an issue in other important areas such as aspects of climate change, natural disasters such as tsunamis and pandemic illness. A considerable amount of statistical effort has been applied to this subject and it is an area where compliance teams need to employ the services of experienced statisticians.[15] Nevertheless, in many instances, assessing these types of risks comes down to a series of subjective assessments.[16] Moreover, they may be subject to high levels of statistical 'sensitivity' where a small change in an assumption can have a significant effect on the whole calculation. Consequently, it is important to carry out statistical sensitivity analysis to test for these inflection points.

Because failure, however defined, can come from a wide range of sources regulation seeks to cover all, or almost all, bases. Risks are seen to migrate to new areas as each new avenue of risk becomes the subject of regulation. The scope of regulation continues to grow in a way analogous to the geopolitical concept of the 'turbulent frontier'.[17] Here, empires over-extend themselves by allowing their attention to focus on their frontiers – where there is always trouble. The next valley is occupied to suppress the disturbance which in turn becomes manifest in a second valley and so on. Similarly, regulation is drawn towards new frontiers as risk is perceived to spread.

Constrained by limited resources, and with an increasing breadth of regulation, both the regulators and regulated are forced to decide on priorities. Much of this book aims at demonstrating how regulated firms may best determine where to allocate their emphasis. Having already highlighted the difficulties of a risk-based approach, nevertheless, this approach is still the recommended method. Although it requires the boards and senior management of regulated firms to exercise their judgement when assessing possible risks, this process is valuable in its own right.

The centrality of the risk assessment operation results is a complex dance between the regulated firm and the regulator where each follows the other in a pattern of synchronous steps. This is also mirrored in the 'measures and reels' within each business between management functions and various departments. If done properly it can form part of a voiced or unvoiced dialogue. Consequently, it may aid communication and understanding since risk-based regulation provides the basis for 'a common language between regulator and regulated'.[18]

Monitoring risk 'heat' maps

The US Office of Compliance Inspections and Examinations at the SEC has repeatedly said that it will pursue enforcement action where compliance programs are not tailored to individual business practices.[19] Consequently, 'off-the-shelf' compliance reviews will, in all likelihood, fail and the design of review work is a major element in ensuring the success of compliance in an organisation. The starting point is the risk assessment mentioned above and the use of risk 'heat maps'.

Monitoring risk 'heat maps' comes in many forms. These include set-piece monitoring reviewing processes and outcomes, and the continuous monitoring of transactions passing through a process. The latter, in particular, lends itself to automation and artificial intelligence assessments. The use of AI in this area is considered later.

The risk assessment process is inadequate without extensive monitoring work. It provides much of the empirical data which helps populate risk assessments and provides evidence to support the judgements taken. Consequently, undertaking monitoring to assess the extent and depth of any compliance is central to the compliance role. It fulfils a number of functions:

- it enables senior management and the board to gain confidence that systems are operating as they should and that issues are subject to effective remediation,
- it helps the regulators to assess the effectiveness of compliance in the firm,
- it monitors the results, a function fundamental to completing the compliance risk maps for the business,
- it aids the compliance function's engagement with the business and is an overt manifestation of compliance in operation,
- it helps identify issues before they develop,
- it sets a benchmark for business units to measure the compliance risk in areas not currently subject to a monitoring review,
- it provides substantive information to executive and risk committees and to boards,
- it communicates with business units,
- it reveals – if used intelligently – more deep-seated issues with business area management as patterns of problems are revealed,
- it provides a stepping stone for those new to compliance to learn about the both the business and compliance risk and is ideal for training staff.

Monitoring also presents risks. Primarily these are:

- a badly constructed monitoring plan may not cover many of the key risk areas as it develops into an unreflective routine of its own,
- mechanical monitoring may provide false comfort and lead to complacency,
- failure to focus on the core issues may result in a plethora of less important points which may mask the real issues,

- poorly worded monitoring reports may cause alarms to sound, not least amount the regulators, since they may suggest issues which, on closer examination, are of lesser import,
- a lack of rigour in undertaking monitoring may result in vague and unfocused reports which are worthless. For example, reports which lack detail explaining how sampling was undertaken and from what population. This frustrates any robust conclusions being drawn about the total population. An example of this might be a report which states that 'some instances were found which ...'. It lacks statistical precision and fails to say what exactly was done and why, whether the issues found were big or small and what, if anything, can be said about the larger population. Good reports often lend themselves to graphical presentation and interpretation.

A particular problem with compliance monitoring work is what may be termed the 'gotcha syndrome'. This is particularly an issue with those undertaking assessment work operating under poor leadership and management. It is considered below in more detail.

The 'gotcha syndrome'

A tight-knit monitoring team working together month after month, year after year is likely to develop a certain insularity. The work appears routine with a high-level of tedium. The only excitement occurs when problems are found. This given meaning to the job and demonstrates the importance of the team and, particularly, the individual who may become the centre of attention for a time as the person who found the issue. This 'triumphalist' approach is echoed in the infamous 'Gotcha' newspaper headline in the *Sun* in 1982.[20]

Without careful management, identifying failure may become the sole objective of the monitoring teams. There is a corresponding risk that minor issues may be exaggerated to appear of greater importance. This will, clearly, aggravate relations with the business and undermine trust by the board and senior management, and with the regulators, as the cry of 'wolf' is heard.

Monitoring report writing

Monitoring reports need to be wholly factual. Each section needs to explain the risk being assessed, how the assessment was undertaken including any sampling procedure used and the factual finds using neutral wording. From the sampling technique employed it may be possible to say something about the total population. There should be a separate summary of the findings and implications, if any, together with a reappraisal of the risks posed by the area tested and an update of the risk maps.

Remedial work following a monitoring review

Almost all monitoring work will result in remedial tasks. These may require amendments to processes, or sub-routines, within the main systems or steps to remedy some of the outcomes of deficiencies in procedures or their implementation. Remediation work is likely to be a separate task which may, in some cases, be spread over many months and even years. For the compliance function this may require a separate team to agree the work to be undertaken, the timetables, subsequent amendments, progress checking and reassessment and reporting.

Often remediation requires the business to obtain additional resources and budgets and a re-prioritisation of IT development. While all this is the responsibility of the business, it may require compliance to support these actions and to make certain that a less than motivated business unit pursues these actions with sufficient vigour.

Delays may occur where remedial actions straddle a number of functions as each argues about budgets and IT resource. It is important that compliance acts quickly to ensure that responsibility is fix and the right action taken. If there are failures to work quickly or effectively these need rapidly to be escalated by compliance so that senior staff can intervene. For example, in 2018 Santander UK failed to amend its customer bereavement processes quickly due to 'the absence of individual and committee ownership and responsibility for the deceased customer accounts issue ... contributed to the delay in Santander reviewing the probate and bereavement process and working on its improvement'.[21]

For a large organisation, chasing up outstanding actions and pursuing delays with tenacity is likely to require a full-time senior compliance unit, confident of its position, and able and willing to escalate issues quickly. It needs, formally, to agree amendments to remedial programmes and to check the revised processes and outcomes. These should all be reported to senior management and the board, and if necessary, the regulator. However, if, for example, a business unit persistently challenges compliance requests for information or is slow to implement required changes compliance may need to engaging the support of divisional directors and board non-executive directors. They can force recalcitrant executives to appear before an executive or board committee to explain themselves. This approach to making the executive responsible, personally accountable may need to be threatened early on to ensure that the right actions are taken quickly.

Regular remediation progress reports should be submitted to senior management and the board, highlighting work not completed on time or likely to miss its implementation timetable. These reports should include instances where the extent of the work has be reduced below an acceptable level ('de-scoped' in the jargon). These reports should also include formal responses from the business on how they will get back on the agreed track.

Again, in a large, complex organisation this work will often require that the compliance team possesses project management disciplines and skills. There may well be organisational and structural issues which result in delays to completing the remedial work. For example, Standard Chartered Bank failed to implement changes as part of its anti-money laundering remediation programme in 2013 due to 'a failure of governance with initial confusion around which committee or group within [the bank] was responsible for the resolution of this matter. [Even] after the issue was raised before the relevant committee which would ultimately decide to implement the solution in April 2013, ... [the work] continued to lack urgency. In March 2013 a failure to progress resolution ... was put down to the issue having 'fallen between the cracks'.[22]

There is a risk that the importance of the issues found may not be fully understood and, accordingly, the remedial work misclassified. For example, in the UBS rogue trader case, involving Kweku Adoboli, the bank's internal audit function found a:

> lack of effective procedure for delegation by desk supervisors of supervisory responsibility during leave or absence; a failure to ensure desk supervisors always received the necessary reports to perform their role; and an absence of monitoring by Compliance ... in relation to irregular alerts.[23]

However, the bank's Group Internal Audit graded these issues as 'Other', the 'grade below 'Significant', and indicated that they were classed as 'medium risk'. Issues rated as 'Other' were not escalated to the Board Risk and Audit Committees'.[24]

There is also a risk of complacency. Here both the business and compliance become self-satisfied and believe that all material areas in the firm are sound. Monitoring becomes a routine with little purpose. To avoid this risk there needs to be a constant process of challenge. There must be a continuous search for defects and possible errors. It is engendered by a state of mind symbolised by the view that 'the firm is only one phone call away from disaster'. This perspective encapsulates a compliance philosophy believes that serious problems exist but they have yet to be found and that compliance had better find them before someone else does and calls the compliance officer. As already mentioned, it is also important to avoid the risk of complacency by staying close to the regulators and listening carefully to what they are saying. It is also useful to form, or to join, a 'compliance health' benchmarking group to compare non-confidential information relating to compliance practices. However, with such a group it is important not to be lulled into a false sense of safety engender by mutual complacency.

There is also a risk that old, outstanding remedial action may be signed off as completed before the work has been completed. An example of this can be seen in the UBS case where 'issues could be closed by Group Internal Audit on an evidential rather than substantively tested basis'.[25] Control functions such as compliance and internal audit may have targets to close remedial action points. The result may be that there is are personal management performance measurement benefits in showing a rapid closing of outstanding remedial points. On the face of it this is a good practice since it helps avoid the delays evident, for example, in the Santander case mentioned earlier. However, it may also drive short-cuts where issues are closed without adequate evidence or proper testing.

Monitoring report conclusions not justified by the facts

The FCA fined Standard Life almost £31m in 2019 for mis-selling pension annuity products which included the business placing high pressure on its staff to sell its products. This approach was combined 'with poor systems and controls and the complex nature of a product' marketed 'to potentially vulnerable consumers'. This lead to some customers being treated unfairly and it created a significant risk of consumer detriment.[26] The sales calls and training schemes were tested by compliance in 2014 and the two reports concluded that 'the quality of the call handling ... is very high'.[27] However, the actual compliance monitoring data indicated that of the calls tested some 30% failed compliance standards and a further 18% did not compliance with the regulatory 'treating customers fairly' requirements. Consequently, the compliance report's conclusions were not sustained by the data.[28]

The level of monitoring was inadequate (e.g. only 0.2% of sales were checked and in some years there was no testing at all). The level of sampling was not increased in the light of the numerous failures and there was no appreciation by compliance that the staff incentive scheme posed a high risk and that, consequently, this merited increased monitoring.[29]

As a consequence, the insurance company may pay out some £60m to some of the 80,000 customers whose sales were reviewed as a result of FCA's action.[30]

Clearly, the monitoring report's conclusions and judgements must reflect the facts. It is important that the raw monitoring data collected during the course of the work is included in a prominent position in any reports produced so that the conclusions can be tested and verified.

I have found over the years that the wording of monitoring reports to be a constant source of issues. It comes as a result of different interpretations of reports by different audiences, all with their own perspectives. It requires the close attention of the senior compliance team and cannot be delegated since it is important that sound judgements are formed, on the evidence, and properly recorded.

Consequently, having the facts and supporting evidence to hand in the monitoring reports is also important as the report is further assessed by senior managers in the business, the board and their sub-committees and the like. Another risk arises from the natural tendency for report summaries and conclusions to be softened as they are processed through a number of layers of management. It may be better for the raw data, section by section to be reported without any commentary together but with a set of actions (e.g. report issue to regulators, board committee etc., increased level of reviews as a result of the findings, initiate a process of remediation etc.).

Agreeing the monitoring report

One of the key challenges for the compliance monitoring team is to obtain formal agreement from the business to the monitoring report and its consequential actions. It is both a test of the accuracy and expression of the report itself. Assuming that these are sound then it will be a test of the ethics and culture of the organisation. The skill and judgement of the monitoring team will be demonstrated in obtaining business sign-off without the report being substantially watered down. This process needs to be undertaken at the right level of seniority, face-to-face. Again, these discussions require strong negotiation skills and dogged determination not to concede any substantive point.

Escalation of issues – including to the regulator

As already mentioned, significant issues will need to escalated and reported to senior management and the board, as quickly as possible. It may also be the case that the problems are of sufficient concern that they should be reported to the regulators. This was highlighted, for example, in the Santander case, mentioned earlier, where the regulator found that the 'Santander Board Risk Committee was not informed of the issue until October 2015, almost a year after the material risk event escalation. The policy for reporting material risks did not require reporting to the Board'.[31]

The need to inform the regulators of material issues, revealed by compliance monitoring, is a key reason for ensuring that all monitoring reports are detailed and factual with judgemental comments kept to the minimum necessary. Clearly, the information provided to the regulator should mirror that provided to the board or its sub-committees.

It may be good practice, once agreed with the regulatory supervision team, to send all monitoring reports to the regulator as a matter of routine.

Continuous monitoring

As mentioned earlier, monitoring can take a number of forms. For example, there may be automated monitoring systems used, for example, to check for desk-dealing in restricted securities or AI systems looking for transaction patterns which may suggest market abuse. Many of these automated systems may be built into business processes. The latter examples are wide-spread. They can range from those that look at credit application resubmissions to check for attempts to 'game' the credit process to transaction 'break' reports looking for patterns in failed trade settlements.

In practice, compliance should be involved in the design and implementation of these process monitoring systems. Compliance should also be involved in the setting and amendment of system 'tolerances' and in the reporting and follow-up of out of tolerance notifications.

There will be other continuous monitoring arrangements which are designed and operated by compliance. As mentioned, these may relate to detecting market abuse or misuse of the 'know your customer' processes. Much will depend on the systems being operated and whether there is a business 'owner' who can be relied on to appreciate and to follow up, adequately, the information provided by the automated systems. This might be true for aspects of credit monitoring since failures here can have a direct effect on business revenue. There may also be dedicated, specialist units responsible for monitoring, in real-time, important areas such as antimoney laundering or account-opening fraud. The design and strength of these arrangements require the close attention of senior compliance staff.

Use of external assessors

In some specialist areas compliance may need to employ external experts to undertake monitoring work. This might be for highly technical areas such as an actuarial review or to examine IT system algorithms. It might to also be necessary to use external resources to examine aspects of the business in a country where it is important to have local knowledge and language skills.

The consultant's brief needs to be very precise to avoid 'mission creep'. Their work must be closely supervised since the external assessors are unlikely to know the details of the business. A compliance manager needs to be assigned to act as the single point of contact with the consultants. The resulting report needs to follow the same process as for any other compliance report including reported to the business executive and board and regulators if there are material issues.

The approval of financial promotions

The approval of financial promotions is both an important compliance process and a harm prevention arrangement. Under the scope of the latter a good approval process will protect both customers and the business.

It is also a form of compliance monitoring since it provides ready information on the standards and culture of the marketing teams. These can be assessed and formally reported upon as with any other form of compliance monitoring.

The compliance approval of financial promotions is also important in other areas. For example, a 'wholesale' or investment, bank may produce financial products for other firms which are 'white labelled' and branded by the distributing company. It is equally important that both the compliance teams at the 'wholesale' bank and the distributer both assess and approve the financial promotions for these products. Both may do harm to customers and both may come under regulatory scrutiny. The result is that neither can sidestep responsibility.

The FCA takes very seriously compliance approval of marketing material and financial promotions.[32] The regulator has expressed concern that firms are taking insufficient steps to ensure compliance with the FCA's rules on financial promotions and have threatened, as a consequence, that they will exercise their powers and require non-complaint material to be withdrawn and amended and that the sale or distribution of related products or services will be suspended or cancelled with possible limitations 'placed on the activities of the firms' supplemented by 'civil or criminal proceedings'.[33]

The importance attached to this area can be seen in the final paragraph of the 'Dear CEO' letter: 'Furthermore, should we identify concerns with the due diligence performed, you can expect us to examine what governance and oversight failures may have contributed to this and to assess who is responsible. You can also expect us to assess what steps your firm has taken to review financial promotions it has previously approved, and to what extent your firm has self-identified and reported to us issues with such promotions or indeed with promotions it has declined to approve'.[34]

An example of this can be seen in the regulatory enforcement case Standard Life concerning the Standard Life's Pension Sterling Fund. The FSA fined Standard Life almost £2.5m in 2010 due to significant issues with the marketing material for this fund and poor systems of control within the company.[35] In summary, the fund initially invested in a mix of cash and very short dated instruments. From 2005 the investment mix started to change with substantial investments being placed in floating rate notes (FRNs). By 2007 the FRNs represented over 80% of the fund although this had reduced to some 50% by the start of 2009.[36] As a result of the financial crisis at the time the market for FRNs dried up and due to the reduced liquidity of the investment, the insurance company marked down the price of the fund by almost 5%.

The fund had originally been marketed as 'a stable investment suitable for investors who were looking for a temporary home for their money when the outlook for bonds and equities was uncertain. It was also targeted at customers approaching retirement who were looking to protect a tax-free lump sum'.[37] In total over 100,000 investors placed some £2.2Bn in the fund and Standard life had to pay out around £100m to make up losses in the fund.[38]

The life company had a process for creating and updating marketing material. The first line of defence compliance team within the marketing department was responsible for reviewing and approving draft marketing material including ensuring that it was clear, fair and not misleading.[39] However, this compliance unit did not check that fund description actually provided to customers accurately reflected the fund details.[40] A subsequent compliance review of all the material presented to customers 'concluded that customers had not deliberately been misled' but the regulatory review concluded that the compliance assessment 'failed to consider whether customers had been misled, regardless of whether it was deliberate or not'.[41]

There is also a risk that financial promotion material may avoid the checks and controls which should be applied. This is a particular risk when a tweaked, or re-priced, version of an existing investment fund is issued. For example, the 'gate-keep' to the full review process may be a relatively junior employee who may be assured by the products department, working against a tight launch timetable, that the product is merely a re-priced version of an existing product. There may be dozens of these 're-priced' products each month. The overwhelmed individual simply accepts the word of the products team and, consequently, the product avoids proper scrutiny and is launched. It may subsequently turn out that it was significantly different to previous versions and should have been properly examined.

It is possible that something like this happened in the lead up to a Barclays promotion of an Aviva product in 2006. Failures here resulted in a FSA fine of £7.7m and the bank paying, possibly, as much as £60m in restitution to customers.[42] Barclays and Morley Fund Services, a subsidiary of Aviva Life, produced a product to sell to the former's customers which they described as 'balanced'. In fact it consisted 'of approximately 60 percent equities and 40 percent bonds (... up to half of which could be non-investment grade)'.[43]

The Fund was 'not subjected to Barclays' full development and approval process' since it was deemed similar to a previous product.[44] 'This was inconsistent with Barclays' internal policies which mandated a new product sign-off process for all new, or significantly, modified products and services'.[45] In fact the fund was better described as being 'adventurous' under the Barclays' system for identifying fund risk for their investment advisers and customers.

There are a variety of ways of organising the product and product materials sign-off process. The individuals undertaking the assessment and sign-off need to be specialists and dedicated to this area of work. They need to be independent of the product and marketing departments. They need to be able to review and to provide detailed expert comments quickly to assist the marketing department meeting its launch timetable. However, they need to have sufficient authority and independence of mind to stand up to pressure to given approval and to sign off marketing material before they are happy. There needs to be process controls to ensure that all drafts of marketing material are reviewed and that none are allowed to slip by.

Approval decisions need to be made at the right level before allowing a product to bypass the process on the grounds by, for example, claiming that the proposed product only makes minor changes to an existing approved piece of material. Assessments need to be undertakentimeously, but not under such pressure that the bank risk having to carry out an extensive remediation and compensation programme.

In order to relieve the pressure on the compliance unit responsible for signing off marketing material there needs to be a mechanism for them to call on someone to provide what might be called 'a cold light of dawn' perspective. The risk is that, in the intensity of, say, a new product launch the compliance team sees draft after draft of key material. Through a process combining both fatigue and insidious persuasion they start to agree text and layouts which they would not have in calmer times. Consequently, they need the ability to call a form of 'time-out' to seek a third person's view. This might be from another part of the compliance function with sufficient expertise and judgement or from an external law or consultancy firm retained for this very purpose. Clearly, this might upset the marketing timetable but it should provide support for the business, as a whole, where there may be strong doubts about the product and its proposed marketing.

It is also important that there is empirical, independent testing of customer understanding of marketing material messages. The marketing teams will want to do their own customer testing but it is important that the compliance testing is undertaken separately and to a high professional standard. It will probably be undertaken by an independent, expert firm and the testing needs to mirror that done by the marketeers. It is a process which helps to educate both compliance and marketing teams as to what customers really think and read and hear and how the information is interpreted. It can help prevent serious mistakes and protect all those involved. Finally, it is information that can be freely shared with the regulator.

Compliance problems which are often neglected

The next section look at common compliance problems that are often neglected.

Closing down business areas and decommissioning legacy systems

Large businesses will frequently restructure and reorganise. This may involve the disposal or closure of business units and related operations. Depending on the nature of the business concerned it is important that compliance is aware of what is planned and that it is involved in the decision-making and that it influences both the strategy and the process. These aspects are often neglected since it is often much less attractive to work on this task compared to, for example, a business acquisition; and, consequently, this has a lower level of organisational profile and prestige. However, it can have important consequences. For example, if a unit is being sold, working with the lawyers involved, compliance will need to be central to the disclosures made to both the acquirer and the regulators and in any subsequent communications to customers and other stakeholders.

There will be a range of issues which will need to be resolved well ahead of the disposal, including who has responsibility for future claims and complaints, where the relevant records will be stored and on what basis they can be accessed. There may be data archives and there will be issues relating to future retrievability, software licences, cost allocations between the parties and the like. These issues may present problems where data management has been outsourced. There may also be continuing obligations to existing and former customers such as providing tax calculation information. It needs to be clear who is responsible for this and who will communicate what information to the customers.

Over the years staff will come and go and the corporate memory will atrophy. There will need to be a readily accessible archive of what happened and what information is stored and where and how it can be accessed. This may be maintained by an operations section with information available to compliance, and the in-house legal team and the company secretariat. This may become a significant issue in future years under the UK's Senior Managers and Certified Persons Regime where individuals may be held accountable by the regulators for events that may have happened many years ago in parts of the business that have long gone.

Decommissioning legacy IT systems and disposing of old premises and office equipment

There are parallel issues when it comes to decommissioning legacy IT systems. Compliance needs to be involved in the planning since it will need to ensure that the business has continuing ready access to past data and that this information continues to be held securely with regular computer updates to protect the cyber-security of the information. The security and access arrangement will need to be tested from time to time. There may also come a period when data on individuals is no longer required and there will need to be a process for determining this and how this information is disposed of securely. As part of the decommissioning process, there may be a need to ensure that hardware is cleared of personal and other confidential data before it is disposed of.

There are similar issues when old premises and office equipment are disposed of. The old IT equipment needs to be cleaned of data and filing cabinets must be emptied and any confidential files securely destroyed, if appropriate, and not left to be found on waste dumps.

Back-book reviews

There may be a need for back-book reviews where financial service companies have produced and marketed products and services in the past. These reviews are important since there may have been changes in the economy and both regulatory and customer expectations. They should be carried out systematically, probably by a dedicated specialist unit. This needs to be covered by a risk-based programme of systematic review. The process of carrying out these reviews needs to be undertaken, and viewed, from the customer's perspective and compensation paid if there is doubt about how the sale was originally made and the quality of the information, as well as any advice provided.

The aim of these reviews is both to assess if customers have been unfairly disadvantaged by the product and its original sales and marketing and also to ensure that they a fully and clearly informed about the product and understand the risks and issues. Consequently, any new information provided to customers as part of these reviews has to be clear with no attempt at a 'soft-sell'. This means, for example, no imagery which suggest that the product is a 'winner', that having it will provide a life of comfort and ease and also that graphics do not attempt to 'gloss-over' any hard messages. It is important to consider who carries out these customer communications including their selection, leadership, training and remuneration. These reviews should not be undertaken by sales and marketing units.

There will need to be recorded telephone conversations with a sample of customers to check their understanding after they have seen the new information provided as part of the review. These discussion scripts will need to be tested first as part of a pilot. Any issues need to be rectified, including paying customers redress.

It is important that the review process is undertaken properly and not as an exercise in providing comfort to the business that there are no issues. This process needs to be overseen by a committee of the board and the adequacy of the planned work and its implementation checked by the compliance and internal audit functions. These reviews are formal projects and need to be supported using project management disciplines and documentation.

These back-book review programmes are an opportunity for the firm to demonstrate to the regulator that it can be trusted to seek out issues itself and to remedy them to a high standard. It is important to show that the business can also be trusted to produce unvarnished reports to the board and to the regulators which are full, clear and frank. Regulators need to be convinced that there no need for them to impose 'skilled persons' reviews, or other investigators, on the firm to get to the truth.

The regulators need to be briefed on the work and also need to be given an opportunity to comment on the proposed work. If they choose to comment, these views need to be taken in account. The regulators need to be kept informed of progress and any problems found. Ideally, the same reports provided to the board committee should also go to the regulators at the same time as they are submitted to the sub-committee.

Compliance specialist areas

There are many variants in where regulated firms locate in their organisational structure and the more specialised compliance roles. For example, anti-fraud and money laundering are so important in financial services that they often merit their own dedicated functions outside the mainstream compliance roles. This encourages focus and avoids any risk of task-dilution. There is no clear best practice in this area with some evidence in wholesale banking, for example, of financial crime oscillating between compliance and other areas.[46] The position may even more complex with, for example, responsibility for anti-money laundering policy being located within the compliance function but monitoring, implementation and investigation centred within a separate dedicated unit. However, normally it is not crucial where the units are located in the organisational structure. It is possible for a number of variations to work effectively. What is critical is who leads them, how they operate in practice, and their oversight and level of accountability.

Roles which cover areas such as market abuse, corruption prevention and detection and anti-bribery can be located within the legal and company secretariat units equally as well as within compliance. However, responsibility for areas such as data protection probably fits best within the compliance function since it is supervised by two regulators in the United Kingdom: the Information Commissioner and the FCA and, in the normal course of business, it likely to require frequent contact with both regulators. Compliance needs to be directly involved where there is regular and frequent contact with the regulators.

Customer concerns assessment

Any organisation with customers, whether business or personal, is likely to receive complaints. Depending on the numbers involved these will considered by a specialised unit dedicated both to resolving complaints and identifying the root cause of any issues to ensure that they can be remedied. The compliance function needs to be closely engaged in the work of the complaints unit. Customer complaints provide important information on actual and potential issues in the organisation. This can be used to inform the compliance risk assessment and may help direct compliance work and priorities. Nevertheless, it is important to be aware that not all issues will manifest themselves as customer complaints and there may often be a long lag between the events that generate complaints, for example, a product sale, subsequent complaints. Consequently, it is important to consider that just because there have been no complaints there is no issue.

Further, how a firm handles customer complaints is a clear indicator of the culture permeating an organisation. This goes well beyond the letter of the regulations relating to the procedures for handling customer complaints. Compliance with the regulatory requirements is important but it is not sufficient. Compliance with the 'black-letter' regulations may still produce many indications of a poor culture within the complaints handling function and more widely. For example, if the organisation makes it difficult for customers to complain; if customers seeking help are handed off from one department to another; if the attitude of staff is to treat the complainant as a threat or as a nuisance; if the complainant has to fight every step of the way to get their complaint resolved, these are signs of an unhealthy culture within the firm.

Consequently, there needs to be continuous engagement by compliance with the complaints function. In the larger organisations this may require a permanent unit undertaking this work. If there are a large number of complaints this will include reviewing the complaints data for their comprehensiveness, adequacy of the root-cause analysis and speed and comprehensiveness of the follow-up and remedial work. This will need to cover examining the reports produced by the complaints function; where they are sent to and the level and quality of senior staff and board engagement. In the severest instances this may necessitate a large 'back-book' review, mentioned earlier, and a report to the regulators on the issues and actions.

Operational aspects of the compliance function

A long debate has existed on whether, in a large business, to centralise compliance with other group function or whether it is best to de-centralise it by business and country. This issue is often conflated with discussions relating to the 'three lines of defence' concept. This subject is considered separately.

There is an ever-present risk of control functions, including compliance, becoming too close to their respective businesses. This may undermine the independence of the functions and reduce or annul their effectiveness. Short-sightedly, businesses may prefer to have weak and pliant control functions. Countering this requires that local compliance units are accountable to a central compliance function which, among other things, appoints and removes them. This encourages compliance staff to take broader view of their role and to know that they will be supported and that they will not be permitted to be dominated by local management.

There is always a need for local compliance functions since they are best place to understand the business and to know what is going on. However, it is important to ensure that they are independent of the local business management. To determine the level of independence the key tests include considering what are the reporting lines and who decides on the hiring, promotion and removal of compliance staff. Compliance may have a reporting line to the business senior executive and also to the jurisdiction's local managing director. However, it is important that their main reporting line is to the group compliance function which will be responsible for ensuring the quality of their work and the appointment, recognition and removal of all senior compliance staff.

As with any aspect of a business, compliance will need to ensure that its own staff are properly trained and developed. It will need to roster its staff to make certain that its resources are used to best effect and to aid staff development. The compliance team will also need to undertake the usual important management tasks of recruitment, celebrating success, ensuring high levels of staff diversity, promotion, location and accommodation issues, and the implementation of compliance staff opinion surveys and follow up. These issues are considered in more detail in later chapters.

Additionally, as some compliance functions grow in size they become more complex to operate. As a result, there is some evidence in, for example, wholesale banking of compliance units setting up chief administration or operating officer functions.[47] However, my personal view is that compliance structure, like any other function, needs to be kept as simple as possible. This means keeping the organisational hierarchy very 'flat' with very few management 'layers'. Each manager should have no fewer than ten direct reports. There should be very few purely administrative posts. These points are important for two main reasons. First, 'flat' structures, with few purely administrative positions, aids decision making, communications and staff engagement. Second, 'back-office' functions, such as compliance, are often resented in organisations. Consequently, it is important that they do not appear to be complex bureaucracies and that the compliance staff are all engaged directly with business staff and they should not be perceived as being too engaged with the internal workings of the compliance department itself.

Regulatory liaison: day-to-day

It is also important that compliance acts as the single point of contact with the various regulators. This does not mean that other business units are excluded from contact with the regulators. So, for example, the finance function will have regular and frequent interactions with the PRA. However, there should be an agreed list of those permitted to contact the regulators. Compliance should be the custodians of the list and this should be communicated and be understood by all business areas. The regulators should also be aware of who is on the list and how communication with the regulated firm should be effected. This may sound overly bureaucratic and controlling but it helps avoid confusing messages and mis-understandings both within a large and complex organisation and with the regulators.

Compliance and its relationship with the business and other control functions

Post the recent financial crisis there are increased expectations placed on business control functions. Regulated businesses must ensure that that they have competent, well resourced control functions including, internal audit, risk management and compliance units. It is just as important that all these departments have sufficient authority within the organisation. This sends a message within the business and to other stakeholders, including the regulators, that the firm's general and specific legal duties are taken seriously.

The various control functions need to work together to avoid under and overlap in their areas of responsibility. They are all also beset by the broader problem of knowing and understanding what may be happening in large and complex organisations. There are a number of techniques to address this problem. These include employing people who have business and operational experience from within the business, regular meetings between the control functions at all levels to build trust and to exchange information and to agree coordinated actions.

More esoteric approaches can be taken such as embedding control function staff in key business areas tasked with acting as 'directed telescopes' reporting back to the centre on what is happening locally. This is based on a strategy adopted by the Prussian general staff in the later 19th century.[48] The Prussian general staff arranged for officers to be posted among the armies with a remit to find out what was happening and to report back direct to the general staff. This 'directed telescope' saw into the smallest areas and helped control wilful commanders. It is certainly possible for the compliance officer to cultivate individuals in various business unit who can provide insights into what is happening locally and who can alert the control function to developing problems. It is also possible to view this network of 'messengers' as forming part of a 'spiders web'. New material risks or other changes across the organisations will vibrate the web and notify compliance that there is something worth checking.[49]

Areas of developing risk

The next sections consider areas of increasing risk which warrant compliance involvement. Other risk functions may also take a close interest in these potential problem areas.

Business resilience

Threats to business resilience are an example of a potential major area which needs the attention of the board, senior management and the various risk and control functions. These issues can be the result of major problems with the business model (e.g. the liquidity model operated by Northern Rock in the lead up to its collapse in 2007), and inadequate corporate governance and a suspect culture which may threaten a firm's existence (e.g. the failures at Halifax Bank of Scotland prior to 2008). Additionally, there is a sharply increasing trend in IT failings in financial services.[50] These appear to be linked 'to re-platforming and outsourcing failures. The most prominent of these is perhaps TSB's information technology migration' in 2017 but there are many 'outages caused by relatively small changes, usually made on a week day evening'.[51] How both firms and regulators address has been the subject of UK Parliamentary enquiry. The Treasury Select Committee has expressed concern with IT fragility in financial services:

> the current level and frequency of disruption and consumer harm is unacceptable...The Regulators must make plain to financial services firms what their tolerance levels for failure are. It is crucial that the Regulators must not allow firms to set their own tolerance levels for disruption too high.[52]

The regulators are concerned about operational issues which can adversely affect financial stability and 'cause harm to consumers and other market participants in the financial system'.[53] Both the PRA and FCA plan to 'conduct targeted assessments of firms' ... operational infrastructure, activities, decision-making and their supporting data.[54] The regulators will use a number of 'tools' to carry out these assessments including: 'questionnaires, simulations, skilled persons' or experts' reports and wider thematic reviews' and an examination of bank recovery and resolution plans in the light of business resilience planning.[55]

This is not a book which seeks to analyse all business risks and resilience. Nevertheless, set out below is an outline of the main areas where compliance need to be closely involved.

Briefly these include:

- communicating and liaising with the regulators. This is core role for compliance,
- ensuring that there is a business contingence communication plan with customers and that this is adequate and robust. It is important to avoid similar issues experienced by TSB bank when it suffered IT systems failures and its customer contact and communication processes where unable to cope,[56]
- ensuring that the corporate governance processes work and that the board is engaged at the outset and that it is notified of issues quickly,
- assessing the arrangements with outsources in the context of regulatory concerns.

The broader subject of outsourcing compliance risk is considered next.

Outsourcing risks

Firms cannot delegate regulatory responsibilities to an outsourced operation. The regulated firm is wholly responsible at all times for its operations. For example, Linear Investments was fine over £400,000 by the FCA for inappropriately out-sourcing post trade market abuse surveillance to its brokers.[57] Additionally, the regulators have noticed an increasing use by firms of 'cloud' based IT systems 'to gain entry to new markets, lower operating costs, fuel innovation and adapt to the digital economy'.[58] This may aid business resilience but to use this form of outsourcing firms must oversee the provision of 'cloud' 'services effectively and take appropriate steps to protect their applications and data'.[59] Again, this is an area for close compliance involvement.

The increased level of outsourcing by financial firms has increased this area of risk in three key areas:

- cloud-based computing services, particularly since there are so few cloud-based services so there are limited options,
- this is part of a broader issue; 'a large number of firms become dependent on a small number of dominant outsourced or third party service providers who are very difficult or impossible to substitute, this could, over time, give rise to systemic concentration risks. A major disruption, outage or failure at one of these service providers could create a single-point-of-failure with potential adverse consequences for financial stability',[60]
- sub-outsourcing by outsources so that direct management contact with the regulated firm becomes attenuated. These long chains increase complexity and may reduce control and compliance effectiveness. It may mean increased reliance on the compliance functions of the outsourcers.

The increasing complexity of all these arrangements makes it more difficult for senior management and the boards of regulated firms to maintain a grip on what is happening and what risks the business runs. This may be amplified when it comes to the regulators who rely heavily on the abilities of the regulated firm and its control functions.

The issue of outsourcing and the regulatory reaction were highlighted in the Raphael Bank case. The issue revolved around the monthly production of the bank's management accounts. These accounts were meant to be reconciled with the weekly financial data supplied automatically to the regulators.[61] However, for reasons that are not clear, the outsourcing did to work as intended. Consequently, Raphael Bank failed to submit all the required information to the FSA or PRA. In particular, Raphael Bank only reported its loan balances to the Group and not its total exposures to the

Group; for example, inter-company balances were not reported.[62] As a result the regulators 'had an incomplete and erroneous understanding of: the risks that Raphael Bank was exposed to; its capital adequacy; and ultimately the extent to which It complied with the PRA's Threshold Conditions (and, in particular, whether it had adequate financial resources)'.[63]

More worryingly, there are moves to outsource compliance monitoring and surveillance with some of this work being undertaken off-shore.[64] While there may be scope for some very limited out-sourcing, for example, the routine checking of some of the legal obligations in product materials to specialist legal firms, generally this practice should be avoided at all costs.

Cyber-security

In recent years the PRA has increasingly become concerned about cyber-security. This is a highly specialised area but one which needs to engage the attention of compliance. The loss of confidential data may harm customers and other stakeholders and is likely to be the subject of regulatory sanction. Even more damaging will be the threat to the firm's reputation. The regulators see the assessment work undertaken by the firm on its capability to withstand cyber-attacks as an important factor in ensuring financial stability.[65] The business may need to develop and implement a remediation plan depending on the results of a structured review of its cyber-security.[66]

Increasingly compliance is being drawn into the world of cyber-security particularly the protection of customer information. It is an area of growing risk and increasingly of regulatory interest. For example, the PRA has started to work with the financial services industry to develop a new framework, known as CBEST3 to test for cyber vulnerabilities. The PRA, working with Bank of England's Sector Cyber Team, has brought together the 'best available threat intelligence from government and elsewhere, tailored to the business model and operations of individual firms, to be delivered in live 'red team' tests, within a controlled testing environment'.[67]

There are four stages to the CBEST3 process:

- test scope prepared and outsourcing testing providers contracted,
- threat scenario developed with a 'penetration test plan',
- the actual 'penetration testing phase' with an attack against the target systems and services against each critical function with the detection and defensive success reviewed and response capabilities are assessed,
- the 'closure phase' with an appraisal report and remediation plan.[68]

In part, the involvement of compliance is to ensure that the issues are reported to the board and that the specialists dealing with this subject understand the regulatory requirements and are able to interpret what is being said. As always, it is a matter of communication.

In practice, due to the existential importance of this area, cyber-security is likely to be led by a board-level committee bringing together a number of operational and control functions, including compliance. It is important that compliance does not see this as a 'technical' issue best left to the IT function. Compliance needs to have the expertise within the unit so that it can gain the trust of operational units, the board and the specialist teams at the regulator.

Data security: compliance and the board

Issues relating to data security are now clearly of great importance to corporate boards. This is even more the case since regulators are taking an increased level of interest in this area.[69] For example, the US Federal Trade Commission (FTC) wants firms to have annual staff training programmes and access control and monitoring systems.[70] It also want rigorous and accountable independent assessments of the data security arrangements in each firm and clear and detailed senior executive and board focus on this area.[71]

This latter element requires annual presentations to the board on data security and annual certificates presented by a senior executive, under oath, of compliance with the data security requirements.[72] As already mentioned, it is important that the various control functions, including compliance are involved in this since the risks and consequences of a serious data breach are very significant both to stakeholders, including customers, and the firm itself. This is reinforced by the UK's FCA which has also issued guidance stating that IT security and the protection of consumer data are an important part of the roles of senior management and the board.[73]

Regulation, compliance and artificial intelligence (AI)

This is a large and developing area. It is a subject for close compliance and board attention. In summary, this can be stated as the need for ethical behaviour; transparency and explainability and an understanding who is responsible for the development and operation of AI systems.[74] The oversight of AI will require new roles and skills including assessing and taking fine judgements about what is acceptable and what, for example, is 'too creepy'.[75] The decisions of the AI employed need to be 'sufficiently' explainable and the firm cannot simply rely on representing AI as an incomprehensible 'blackbox'.[76] Further, liability for AI decisions may well rest with the regulated firm and the likelihood that AI projects will 'come back to haunt them in entirely unexpected ways'.[77] The FCA have formally stated that as 'algorithmic decision-making becomes more widespread, it needs to be understandable to build public confidence and ensure it is bias-free, well governed and operating in consumers' and markets' interests'.[78]

Close regulatory interest indicates that compliance needs to be involved in the business AI strategy and the development and implementation plans.

In addition, there are the opportunities and threats posed by Open Banking and the Payment Services Directive II.[79] These provide scope for customers to take control of their bank data and encourages new entrants into the payment services industry.[80] The FCA have stated clearly that 'if firms are deploying AI and machine learning they need to ensure they have a solid understanding of the technology and the governance around it ... We want to see boards asking themselves: 'what is the worst thing that can go wrong' and providing mitigations against those risks'.[81]

Using AI as part of a compliance programme

AI can cover a range of current operational, trading and regulatory systems. In the compliance field these have started to develop as 'RegTech' covering aspects of anti-money laundering, assessing potential new customers for possible bribery and corruption issues, assessing market abuse risks and examining customer advice in real time. The Bank of England and FCA have examined AI usage and planning in financial services and found that risk management and compliance, and customer engagement are the most developed AI areas.[82]

There are major risks in using AI. These include opaque models and explainability issues where the rationale for the out-put from the AI system cannot be easily understood and explained. Further, there may be little understood issues with the AI data inputs with the result that machine bias distorts the output. This issue is considered in more detail below. Further, the AI may perform badly, and undetectably, when it first encounters novel information and situations. Firms developing AI have identified issues with how it may be integrated into existing processes and legacy IT systems coupled with the use of 'raw' and unfiltered data.[83]

The current most common method of managing these risks is to embed 'humans in the loop' so that there is some independent assessment of data inputs, process design and the quality of what is produced.[84] There is also the risks posed by dominant AI outsourcers if, as seems likely, largely elements of IA design and operations are contracted out.

Finally, the issue of an unauditable and apparently out of control AI function. This presents a significant challenge to the concept and operation of senior management responsibilities and corporate governance requirements on which much of current financial services regulation increasingly depends. The need for 'explainability' is reinforced by a number of legal cases. For example, the Netherland's District Court of the Hague, found that the Dutch State's use of an artificial intelligence system to identify social security fraud violated European human rights legislation since because the system lacked sufficient transparency and explainability.[85] In particular, the court reviewed the Systeem Risicoindicatie (SyRI) – a legal instrument the Netherlands government uses to prevent and combat fraud in the area of social security and the like. The court considered that 'the legislation does not strike a fair balance, as required under the European Convention on Human Rights, which would warrant a sufficiently justified violation of private life. In that respect, the application of SyRI is insufficiently transparent and verifiable. As such, the SyRI legislation is unlawful, because it violates higher law and, as a result, has been declared as having no binding effect'.[86]

In the United States, there have been a number of legal cases challenging the use of education value-added models (VAMs) which use algorithms for teacher employment decisions.[87] In the most recent case the court in Texas found in favour the teachers on 'due process' grounds.[88] The aim of procedural due process 'is to convey to the individual a feeling that the government has dealt with him fairly, as well as to minimize the risk of mistaken deprivations of protected interests'.[89] The court was particularly concerned to ensure that a teacher facing termination must 'be advised of the cause for his termination in sufficient detail so as to enable him to show any error that may exist' and to do this the teacher would need to see the underlying logic within the algorithm. It was also recognised that there could be coding and input errors. There was an additional issue, that because of the interlocking relationship between individual teacher scores, an amendment or correction of one was likely to have an effect on the scores of all other teachers.[90] This further undermined trust in the use of AI.

There have been some suggestions about the acceptable level of transparency in using AI. These include distinguishing between 'inputs' and 'outputs'.[91] The former includes four 'contextual' factors – who might be using the information and what level of expertise do they have; what level of harm could the algorithm have and what level of explanation would mitigate this potential damage; what is the regulatory and societal context; and finally what is the operational importance of using AI including alternative routes.[92] There will also be technical issues which relate to the inputs including testing for inherent bias in the algorithms. There are many examples of this including AI used to support employee hiring decisions which focus on certain words and phrases in applications which result in unfair and irrational outcomes.[93]

In the United States there are also issues on how AI is developing and its use in, for example, credit decisions in financial firms. 'Modern underwriting is increasingly relying on nontraditional inputs and advanced prediction technologies, challenging existing discrimination doctrine'.[94] For example, with the 'shift away from causality means that we cannot distinguish between an input that is used to form a prediction because it is a proxy for race and an input that is innocuous. For example, the time it takes a person to fill in out online application may be predictive of default risk. Is this because the time it takes to fill out the application is related to a person's education level that relates to creditworthiness?' Or is the length of time it takes to complete the application form due to some other reason? 'Ultimately, we do not know why application time is predictive of default'.[95]

The US Consumer Financial Protection Bureau (CFPB), a Federal consumer protection regulator, is looking at the use of 'alternative data models' and their regulatory implications.[96] This is important because part of its mandate is to protect consumers from unfair discrimination.

There are also 'output' factors to consider when looking at AI transparency and explainability. These include 'saliency maps' which demonstrate key factors determining the outcome, and linked to this 'counter-factual dashboards' testing the population using different factors in a controlled series of tests.[97] This also enables checking what is really important to end-users and why. For example, an AI system may seek to determine which salesmen and women to monitor for compliance purposes. It may seek to correlate certain phrases and words in employment application forms with the subsequent results of independent sales assessment, customer complaints and so on. The AI may highlight, for example, that CVs and covering letters which include words such as 'always meets or exceed sales targets' as a warning indicator. However, this may be a false or unfair correlation and the AI needs to be carefully tested to see if it produces biases against women and minorities or the correlation may be deceptive since, say, it only is true for the sale of one particular product but not for others. There may also be contextual issues where, for example, the bank included this phrase, or something akin to it, in the advert for the role.

There are also dangers in individuals 'gaming' the AI system. This can be countered by varying the population used for the AI assessments and introducing sufficient randomness into the process to render it difficult for outsiders to determine input cause and output effect.

AI presents new opportunities for compliance but there are a number of steps which are necessary to prevent harm and to reduce the compliance and reputational risks to the regulated business. These include:

- preparing corporate policies for the use of AI and ensuring that these are updated as the technologies and their use develop,
- preparing and checking of these policies by the various control functions and the legal team,
- approving the policies at board level with regular and frequent updates on their use to the full board or an appropriate sub-committee. One non-executive director should have overall responsibility for the firm's AI policies and their use and be separately briefed in detail by those operating these policies and the control functions,
- assessing all policies relating to the use of AI by the firm for their

potential effect on stakeholders and an objective consideration of the possible effect on the reputation of the business,

- acting to minimise any potential harm to stakeholders if there is still an intention to employ AI in a particular area. This should include the risk of any abuse of the data and its use and the issues relating to cyber-security,
- Ensuring – by way of a specified personally responsible senior executive – that the AI model, the data feeds, model updates, staff training and the AI's application are in accord with the approved policies. This responsibility also includes assessing and reporting to the other senior executives, control functions and the board how this work is progressing, and any substantive issues found and how these were resolved together with the follow-up checks,
- Ensuring that it is legal to use the AI data and assessing the process to ensure its accuracy and relevance. It is of the highest importance that compliance does this as AI models require accurate and relevant data,
- Justifying the outputs from the AI model. This is important in regulatory terms. For example, if the AI system produces 'robo-advice' (automated investment advice based on the use of AI, considered in more detail later in this chapter) compliance and other senior management and the board have specific responsibilities as part of the regulatory need to protect customers,
- assessing and checking AI for bias. As mentioned earlier, there are many examples of bias in AI and there needs to be extensive assessments and checking to ensure that AI use does not result in unfair discrimination resulting, for example, in bias against vulnerable customers and staff. It has been suggested that unconscious racial bias has been introduced into various AI models due to a clear lack of diversity among programmers,[98]
- Explaining and justifying any potential transparency challenges. Along with issues of potential bias, in many circumstances it may be necessary to explain and justify AI produced decisions. It is likely that regulators and courts will expect a high level of 'explainability' so that AI decisions can be judged and the process assessed. It is unlikely that it will be sufficient to simply say that the computer says 'no',
- Testing and assessing the AI arrangements and outcomes to maintain stakeholder confidence in the AI system, There is a danger that AI systems become self-referencing. The AI is likely to learn from its own decisions. Unchallenged there is a risk that the AI outcomes may evolve away from what is generally considered acceptable,
- Monitoring and setting up a form of 'appeals' by compliance to facilitate the process of challenging the AI system. This may help ensure that the AI does not become all powerful, keeps the business engaged with the technology and ensures that it remains linked to the various stakeholders,
- Being aware of the particular risks with AI and algorithmic trading

(machine-based trading) decisions since these may increase risk significantly, with increased transaction speeds and 'flash crashes' and the move towards 'herd-like' trading behaviours,[99]

- Providing clear and comprehensive documentation, high levels of security and staff training as well as sufficient supervision, upon which AI - like all other forms of technology - depends. All of these factors are important since, over time, unlike a more conventional IT system, the AI will develop itself. Consequently, it may require frequent 're-sets' and to be effective this requires constant over-sight and very good documentation.

The role of compliance in relation to AI continues to develop. It is important that compliance is engaged. It is an area that touches on many aspects of regulation and it presents too many issues to be considered solely a technical problem.

Compliance and robo-advice

The issues surrounding the use of automated investment advice are closely related to those governing the use of AI. By way of background, there has been a marked decline in the number of financial advisers in the United Kingdom from some 40,000 in 2011 to just over 26,000 in 2018.[100] This reduction was largely due to both the increased costs of training and maintaining a force of advisers and the limits placed on the payment of sales commission to these individuals as a result of regulations known as the Retail Distribution Review introduced at the end of 2012.[101] As a consequence, the provision of financial advice has become more expensive and is now 'primarily accessible and affordable only for the more affluent in society'.[102] This has created an 'advice gap' with the vast majority of the population lacking access to investment advice.[103] As a result, there may be a role for automated advice based on AI to address this unmet need.[104]

In the United States, a report in 2017 forecast that 'the number of people using robo-advice ... will increase from roughly 2 million to 17 million by 2021'.[105] However, it is worth noting that a number of investment firms and banks have recently closed their robo-advice businesses due to a lack of consumer demand.[106]

The customer suitability assessment is at the centre of financial advice. It requires an assessment of the customer's circumstances, including their financial objectives, their current income expenditure, assets and liabilities and their attitude to financial risk based on their investment experience and ability to sustain financial losses. The FCA expects 'automated investment services to meet the same regulatory standards as traditional discretionary or advisory services'.[107]

In 2017–2018 the FCA reviewed 'online discretionary investment management' (ODIM) services. The regulator found that firms offering these automated investment advice systems 'did not properly evaluate a client's knowledge and experience, investment objectives and capacity for loss in their suitability assessments. Some firms did not ask clients about their knowledge and experience at all, as they felt their service was suitable for all individuals regardless of their investment knowledge and experience'.[108]

The FCA found that some automated advice systems made personal investment recommendations without finding out sufficient information about the customer. Instead the systems used a number of assumptions and failed to collect adequate information such as the amounts owed by customers as debtors. 'In some cases, auto advice services recommended a different transaction' to the one executed at the end of the advice process.[109] The regulator also saw 'examples where clients could disregard advice given by the automated offering without any safeguards or risk warnings to prevent or challenge this'.[110]

When it came to firms providing ongoing client relationships, the FCA found that most firms sampled 'were unable to show that they had adequate and up to date information about their clients when providing an ongoing service'.[111] Firms also failed to filter out those customers whose needs could not be addressed by the automated service. Similarly, 'there were weaknesses in identifying and supporting vulnerable consumers, with some offerings relying on the client to self-identify as vulnerable'.[112]

Finally, there was little evidence that business considered the adequacy of the outcomes from the automated advice process. There was too much focus on compliance in a very narrow sense without examining the results of these sales and advice processes. 'Firms should consider how they review the outcomes produced by the service. This should include whether adequate testing of the offering has taken place, and the action that should be taken where unsuitable recommendations are identified'.[113]

Based on these findings it seems clear that there is still considerable work to be done on automated advice systems to bring them up to an acceptable regulatory standard. There is also a strong risk that these issues are likely to be systemic and have the potential to require remediation work and compensation across the whole of a firm's client base. This could be an existential threat to the business. It also highlights what appear to be inadequate compliance arrangements in these firms.

Compliance and environmental, social and governance (ESG)

Compliance and environmental, social and governance (ESG) is an area of developing regulatory interest. A full discussion of ESG and financial services falls outside the scope of this work; however, its importance is evident in that a whole chapter is devoted to the risks posed to financial stability by climate change in a report for the Bank of England by a group of experts chaired by Huw van Steenis.[114] The compliance function has an important role in developing a firm's approach to improving its ESG standards. Stakeholders are placing increasing emphasis on high levels of environmental protection and sustainability, as well as good governance and the relationship between the regulated business and society in its broadest sense.

The starting point of much regulatory policy is based on perceived market failures.[115] A major market failure is that businesses frequently omit to take account of negative externalities in their business strategies and operations. In the case of environmental and societal damage this may be due both to the long term nature of the issues which fall well beyond the business planning cycle and also what is known as the 'tragedy of the commons'.[116] For this reason societal and environmental harm may be termed 'negative externalities': the consequence of market failures.

The role of financial services regulation in addressing these areas of concern is still being developed but it will come to fruition over the next few years. Mark Carney, the former Governor of the Bank of England, has termed these areas the 'tragedy of the horizon'. He saw that financial markets were too focused on short term profits and failed to consider the longer-term effect of their actions.[117]

The role of compliance and ESG is also still inchoate. Specific regulations have still to be developed but it is likely that asset managers and their clients may be beginning to take ESG issue seriously. For example, in 2018 Larry Fink, the chairman and CEO of BlackRock, one of the largest global investment management companies, said in an open letter that 'millions of people [have taken] to the streets to demand action on climate change, many of them emphasized the significant and lasting impact that it will have on economic growth and prosperity – a risk that markets to date have been slower to reflect. But awareness is rapidly changing, and I believe we are on the edge of a fundamental reshaping of finance'.[118]

> when a company is not effectively addressing a material issue, its directors should be held accountable. Last year BlackRock voted against or withheld votes from 4,800 directors at 2,700 different companies. Where we feel companies and boards are not producing effective sustainability disclosures or implementing frameworks for managing these issues, we will hold board members accountable ... we will be increasingly disposed to vote against management and board directors when companies are not making sufficient progress on sustainability-related disclosures and the business practices and plans underlying them.[119]

It is likely that regulation will catch-up with market developments to set enforceable standards on ESG policies. The FCA has already consulted on climate change disclosures for listed firms.[120] Compliance, and the other control functions, need to consider what steps they need to take, working with the board, to meet the requirements in this changing world. The FCA assumes that compliance and regulatory analysis staff will be involved in the ESG assessment and reporting process.[121] This work parallels that of the FCA on creating a purposeful company which is aimed at, among other things, in achieving, 'a healthy purposeful culture lead[ing] to better outcomes for consumers and markets, and healthy and sustainable returns for shareholders'.[122]

Consequently, it Is clear that boards, senior management and control functions cannot be reactive and simply wait for new regulations. They need to take the initiative. Set out below are some initial actions.

Compliance has a role in the verification of ESG. A key element of ESG is measurement. A set of these provide the baseline for future ESG work. The measurements need to be valid, relevant and comprehensive and ones that resonate with stakeholders. They must not be measures that show the firm in the best light or be simply a regurgitation of existing data collected for other purposes. Collecting and publishing information which lacks credibility will simply prejudice the firm and its board in the eyes of stakeholders. Consequently, there needs to be an independent, knowledgeable and authoritative view deciding what data is collected, assessed, validated and reported. This process needs to be frequently reviewed and re-assessed. Compliance is likely to have a role in this.

ESG policies must be prepared both at a high-level, setting out the firm's principles, and with more detailed operational policies and procedures aligned to these high-level principles.

There needs to be arrangements for communicating these requirements to all staff, suppliers and outsourcers and also to other stakeholders such as investors and customers. Additionally, other bodies (e.g. the firm's pension trustees, external legal and financial advisers, joint venture partners etc.), need to be aware of these principles and, where relevant, to coordinate their policies and operations to fit.

Staff and suppliers must be trained in the firm's ESG principles and processes and regularly assessed. This training needs to be refreshed at regular intervals. There may be difficulties under existing contracts with suppliers to trace their, and their sub-contractors', compliance with these ESG principles. New contracts will need to allow for this level of intrusion. The level and form of compliance inspection and review will need to be enhanced to meet these new expectations.

It is important that ESG applies across the business and all its aspects. It must not be devolved to a specialist unit as has been the case with much 'corporate social responsibility' (CSR) work. ESG needs to be factored into how the firm markets itself to potential staff recruits, the selection process for these individuals and their induction and training. It needs to form an important part of staff management and remunerations.

Senior executives need to act, and be seen to act, in line with ESG policies and expectations. ESG must be built into everything the firm does. This is likely to include staff and board level diversity, remuneration levels and structures, product development and stakeholder engagement.

ESG needs to be a board level responsibility with a board sub-committee of non-executive directors overseeing its policies and operations. One non-executive director and one senior executive need to be nominated to take personal responsibility for ESG matters. The independent advisors, mentioned earlier, need to assist this sub-committee and the latter need to have direct access to those collecting the data and the control functions assessing the validity and accuracy of the information.

There will also need to be assessments undertaken of both new and current clients to assess whether they meet the new criteria for acceptable ESG practices. This is likely to exceed existing 'know you customer' requirements.

Controls and assessment processes must be employed to consider the accuracy and validity of ESG reported data by business unit. This includes both the underlying information and how it is reported and contextualised. This is of particular importance when ESG material is provided by the firm to various stakeholders including staff, board members, listing exchanges, regulators and the like.

ESG deficiencies need to be identified and reported openly and as early as possible. These reports need to be honest and include remediation steps and their independent verification.

Compliance and climate change

The PRA has specifically stated that they expect regulated firms 'to managing the financial risks from climate change' and that the regulator intends to embed the measurement and monitoring of these expectations in its existing supervisory framework.[123] The assessment and actions required of firms should form part of their business strategy and should be long-term. The PRA expects the board to allocate specific responsibility for all the work relating to climate change to senior individuals over-seen by a board sub-committee and 'to ensure that adequate resources and sufficient skills and expertise are devoted to managing' the risks identified.[124] The regulator places considerable importance on the process of examining these issues. 'Firms should use scenario analysis and stress testing to inform the risk identification process and understand the short- and long-term financial risks to their business model from climate change'.[125]

In addition, the PRA want businesses to develop 'a range of quantitative and qualitative tools and metrics to monitor their exposure to financial risks from climate change'.[126] For example, these could be used to monitor exposures to climate-related risk factors which could result from changes in the concentration of firms' investment or lending portfolios, or to the potential impact of physical risk factors on outsourcing arrangements and supply chains. This information should include the firm's longer-term climate change-related targets and metrics and monitoring and risk mitigation programmes.[127] For example, these should cover the risks to the loan portfolio as well as 'the potential impact of physical risk factors on outsourcing arrangements and supply chains'.[128] The PRA expects all of this to be documented and available for regulatory review.

Work on developing corporate strategies to address the risks of climate change rest on the usual, important roles of corporate governance, with boards, and senior executives, setting targets with appropriate metrics to measure progress within a framework of risk and compliance processes.[129]

Compliance 'engineering'

Compliance, in financial services, is a developing area and merits innovation. Besides the use of technology discussed elsewhere in this work, compliance lends itself to statistical analysis. An example of this is standard regression analysis. This is not a statistics books but statistics may have an important role in aspects of financial services compliance.

For example, statistical regression can be used to:

- explain what is happening in a process or system by demonstrating the cause and effect of one or more factors on an outcome. The use of, for example, regression analysis may indicate a causative relationship rather than a simple random outcome,
- predict future outcome.
- model the consequences of management or regulatory interventions on possible outcomes.[130]

These forms of statistical analysis will be commonly applied, for example, by the marketing department within banks to test customer price sensitivity. There is no reason why similar methods cannot be used to assess, for example, issues of fairness. The statistical method of least-squared regression can be used to look for loan pricing unfairness.[131] Statistical correlation, and many other aspects of statistical analysis, are rarely exact but provide information to a level of acceptable probability.[132]

All this points to the need for compliance to innovate with the need for additional skills. This may come as both a shock and a revelation to more conventional compliance officers and staff. However, if they fail to change they will be failing those that rely on them and the function will drift towards irrelevance.

Conclusion

This chapter emphasises the need for compliance to help ensure that businesses comply both with the spirit as well as the letter of the law. This has been the case in the United Kingdom for many years and, increasingly, in many aspects, it is the direction US regulation has started to take. Linked to the need to follow the spirit of the law, compliance must also ensure that the business considers all stakeholders.

In addition to this broad understanding of compliance, there are a number of operational methodologies relevant to compliance. These include 'risk' and 'heat maps'. To do this successfully, compliance needs to understand the business and its operations, including ensuring that compliance has its own sources of information. This could include the 'directed telescope' methods of over-sight taken from the work of the 19th century's Prussian general staff.

Compliance may also have to deal with issues of complacency both within the compliance function and the business. This issue can best be addressed by establishing and maintaining close relationships with the regulators in order to understand both their thinking and main areas of concern. Informal, compliance 'benchmarking' groups can also help provide that they are sufficiently challenging and that they avoid reinforcing mutual complacency. Additionally, compliance needs to act quickly if it detects delays or obstruction from any business areas. Besides the senior executive team, compliance needs to build up a rapport with the board and the non-executive directors to ensure there is sufficient backing if any elements in the firm appear recalcitrant.

There are also the more routine but nevertheless important functions of compliance, including looking at and analysing what regulatory developments are being considered ('up-stream' risks), monitoring work and financial promotion development, review and approval.

There are also a variety of critical areas that run the risk of being neglected. These include concerns relating to IT systems' decommissioning, undertaking back-book business reviews, the risks inherent in outsourcing of critical organisational functions, and data protection and other aspects of cyber-security. There are also the developing areas of AI and automated ('robo') financial advice and elements of ESG and climate change risk.

As can be seen from the new and developing areas mentioned in this chapter, compliance needs to continue to do what it currently does well. But it also needs to adapt so that it is able to contribute towards protecting all stakeholders.

Notes

1 FCA, 'Review of the compliance function in wholesale banks' (November 2017), 3.1, https://www.fca.org.uk/publication/research/the-compliance-function-in-wholesale-banks.pdf (accessed 26 May 2020).

2 PRA and FCA report on the failure of HBOS Plc (November 2015), 227, https://www.bankofengland.co.uk/-/media/boe/files/prudential-regulation/publication/hbos-complete-report (accessed 20 November 2019).

3 Nancy Leveson, 'Applying systems thinking to analyze and learn from events' (2011) *Safety Science*, 49, 55–64, 61.

4 Ibid (Leveson), 60.

5 Tom Reader and Paul O'Connor, 'The Deepwater Horizon explosion: non-technical skills, safety culture, and system complexity' (2014) *Journal of Risk Research*, 17(3), 405–424, 419–422.

6 Ibid (Reader and O'Connor), 419–422.

7 Ibid (Reader and O'Connor), 419–422.

8 Jens Rasmussen, 'Risk management in a dynamic society: a modelling problem' (1997) *Safety Science*, 27, 183–213, 188.

9 Ibid (Rasmussen), 188.

10 Ibid (Rasmussen), 193.

11 Ibid (Rasmussen), 190.

12 FCA Decision Notice, 5 February 2019, Standard Chartered Bank, 4.92, https://www.fca.org.uk/publication/decision-notices/standard-chartered-bank-2019.pdf (accessed 16 April 2019).

13 Ibid (Final Notice, Standard Chartered), 4.96.

14 Julia Black, 'The emergence of risk-based regulation and the new public risk management in the United Kingdom' (Autumn 2005) *Public Law*, 512–548, 521.

15 Terje Aven, *Risk, surprises and black swans: fundamental ideas and concepts in risk assessment and risk management* (Routledge, Abingdon, England, 2014), 117–124.

16 Craig Fox and Gülden Ülkümen, 'Distinguishing two dimensions of uncertainty' in Wibecke Brun and others (eds.) *Perspectives on thinking, judging, and decision making* (Universitetsforlaget, Oslo, 2011), 8.

17 John S. Galbraith, 'The 'turbulent frontier' as a factor in British expansion' (1960) *Comparative Studies in Society and History*, 2(2), 150.

18 Michael Power, 'The nature of risk: the risk management of everything' (2004) *Balance Sheet*, 12(5), 19–28, 23.

19 SEC, Office of Compliance Inspections and Examinations (OCIE), 'The five most frequent compliance topics identified in OCIE examinations of investment advisers', OCIE National Exam Program Risk Alert, Vol VI(3), 7 February 2017, 2, https://www.sec.gov/ocie/Article/risk-alert-5-most-frequent-ia-compliance-topics.pdf (accessed 30 May 2020) and SEC, 17 CFR Parts 240 and 249 [Release No. 34–63237; File No. S7–33-10] RIN 3235-AK78 Proposed Rules for Implementing the Whistleblower Provisions of Section 21F of the Securities Exchange Act of 1934, 4, https://www.sec.gov/rules/proposed/2010/34–63237.pdf (accessed 30 May 2020).

20 The headline of 'GOTCHA – Our lads sink gunboat and hole cruiser' (4 May 1982), 'In 1982, Britain and Argentina fought a war over the Falkland Islands. In the war's deadliest moment, an Argentine ship, the General Belgrano, was sunk by the [Royal Navy], killing more than 300 people'. The Editor's Desk, Memorable headlines, 2009, https://editdesk.wordpress.com/2009/08/28/memorable-headlines-gotcha/ (accessed 25 May 2020).

21 FCA Final Notice (November 2018), Santander Bank, 4.42, https://www.fca.org.uk/publication/final-notices/santander-uk-plc-2018.pdf (accessed 10 April 2019). The bank was fine £32.8m as a result.

22 Supra note 12 (FCA Decision Notice, Standard Chartered Bank), 4.102.

23 FSA Final Notice, UBS AG, 25 November 2012, 11, http://www.fsa.gov.uk/static/pubs/final/ubs-ag.pdf (accessed 2 June 2020).

24 Ibid (Final Notice, UBS AG), 11.

25 Ibid (Final Notice, UBS AG), 11.

26 FCA Final Notice, Standard Life Assurance, 23 July 2019, 2, https://www.fca.org.uk/publication/final-notices/standard-life-assurance-limited-2019.pdf (11 December 2019).

27 Ibid (Final Notice, Standard Life), 43.

28 Ibid (Final Notice, Standard Life), 43.

29 Ibid (Final Notice, Standard Life), 43.

30 Ibid (Final Notice, Standard Life), 2.

31 FCA Final Notice Santander (November 2018), 16, https://www.fca.org.uk/publication/final-notices/santander-uk-plc-2018.pdf (accessed 10 April 2019).

32 FCA 'Dear CEO' letter, 'Firms' approval of financial promotions: the FCA expectations', 11 April 2019, https://www.fca.org.uk/publication/correspondence/dear-ceo-letter-firms-approvals-financial-promotions-fcas-expectations.pdf (accessed 22 April 2019). This follows a FCA letter of 9 January 2019 on the same topic, clarity in promotions about regulated and unregulated business: the FCA's expectations, https://www.fca.org.uk/publication/correspondence/dear-ceo-letter-promotions-regulated-unregulated-business.pdf (accessed 22 April 2019).

33 Ibid (FCA letter of 11 April 2019).

34 Ibid (FCA letter of 11 April 2019).

35 FSA Final Notice, re Standard Life Assurance, 20 January 2010, https://www.fca.org.uk/publication/final-notices/slal.pdf (accessed 11 December 2019).

36 Ibid (Final Notice, re Standard Life), 4.10.

37 Ibid (Final Notice, re Standard Life), 4.10.

38 Ibid (Final Notice, re Standard Life), 2.8.

39 Ibid (Final Notice, re Standard Life), 4.16.

40 Ibid (Final Notice, re Standard Life), 4.17.

41 Ibid (Final Notice, re Standard Life), 4.24.

42 FSA Final Notice, Barclays Bank, 14 January 2011, 1.1 and 2.10, https://www.fca.org.uk/publication/final-notices/barclays_jan11.pdf (accessed 14 December 2019).

43 Ibid (Final Notice, Barclays Bank), 4.6.

44 Ibid (Final Notice, Barclays Bank), 4.5.

45 Ibid (Final Notice, Barclays Bank), 4.5.

46 Supra note 1 ('The compliance function in wholesale banks'), 2.1.

47 Supra note 1 ('The compliance function in wholesale banks'), 2.1.

48 Martin Van Creveld, *Command In war* (Harvard University Press, Cambridge, 1985), 75.

49 Alan Brener, 'The Golden threads of compliance' (1995) *Journal of Financial Regulation and Compliance*, 3(4), 344–349, 346–347.

50 Speech by Megan Butler, FCA Executive Director of Supervision – Investment, Wholesale and Specialists, 'Cyber and technology resilience in UK financial services', 27 November 2017, https://www.fca.org.uk/news/speeches/cyber-and-technology-resilience-uk-financial-services (accessed 29 April 2019).

51 Ibid (Butler speech November 2017).

52 Parliament, House of Commons Treasury Committee, 'IT failures in the financial services sector', Second Report of Session 2019–20 (22 October 2019), 3, https://publications.parliament.uk/pa/cm201919/cmselect/cmtreasy/224/224.pdf (accessed 1 July 2020).

53 Bank of England/PRA/FCA, Discussion Paper, Building the UK financial sector's operational resilience', Bank of England DP01/18, PRA DP01/18, FCA

DP18/04, July 2018, 3, https://www.bankofengland.co.uk/-/media/boe/files/prudential-regulation/discussion-paper/2018/dp118.pdf?la=en&hash=4238F3B14D839EBE
6BEFBD6B5E5634FB95197D8A (accessed 25 May 2002).

54 Ibid ('Building the UK financial sector's operational resilience'), 32.

55 Ibid ('Building the UK financial sector's operational resilience'), 33.

56 BBC News website, 'TSB customers hit by online banking outage', 1 April 2020, 'A number of TSB customers were left unable to access online banking and mobile app services … on Wednesday. Independent website DownDetector, which tracks social-media posts on how sites are performing, showed hundreds of customers complaining of an outage', https://www.bbc.co.uk/news/technology-52121990 (accessed 28 May 2020).

57 FCA Final Notice, Linear Investments, 29 April 2019, https://www.fca.org.uk/publication/final-notices/linear-investments-ltd-final-notice-2019.pdf (accessed 1 May 2019).

58 PRA, 'Consultation Paper' (CP30/19), 'Outsourcing and third party risk management' (December 2019), 3, https://www.bankofengland.co.uk/-/media/boe/files/prudential-regulation/consultation-paper/2019/cp3019.pdf?la=en&hash=4766BFA4EA8C278BFBE77CADB37C8F34308C97D5 (accessed 28 May 2020).

59 Ibid ('Outsourcing and third party risk management'), 3.

60 Ibid ('Outsourcing and third party risk management'), 3.

61 PRA Final Notice, Raphael Bank (November 2015), 8, https://www.bankofengland.co.uk/-/media/boe/files/prudential-regulation/enforcement-notice/en271115 (accessed 7 May 2019).

62 Ibid (Final Notice, Raphael Bank), 9–11.

63 Ibid (Final Notice, Raphael Bank), 16.

64 Supra note 1 ('The compliance function in wholesale banks'), 6.4.

65 Andrew Gracie, Executive Director, Resolution, Bank of England, 'Managing cyber risk – the global banking perspective', speech at the British Bankers' Association Cyber Conference, London, 10 June 2014, https://www.bankofengland.co.uk/-/media/boe/files/speech/2014/managing-cyber-risk-the-global-banking-perspective.pdf?la=en&hash=E3DB03D027D9443D5D00C80A79BFDA24AB0EE22A (accessed 30 April 2019).

66 Bank of England, 'CBEST intelligence-led testing and implementation guide', Version 2.0 (2016) 8, https://www.bankofengland.co.uk/-/media/boe/files/financial-stability/financial-sector-continuity/cbest-implementation-guide.pdf?la=en&hash=1BFF85C8F9E6C0E8BE478BB22B422EDDA5E00DC0 (accessed 30 April 2019).

67 Supra note 65 (Gracie).

68 Supra note 66 (Bank of England, CBEST Intelligence-Led Testing and Implementation).

69 For example, the US Federal Trade Commission (FTC) data security improvement orders directed at a number of specific companies, FTC, 'New and improved FTC data security orders: better guidance for companies, better protection for consumers', 6 January 2020, https://www.ftc.gov/news-events/blogs/business-blog/2020/01/new-improved-ftc-data-security-orders-better-guidance (accessed 16 January 2020).

70 Ibid (FTC).

71 Ibid (FTC).

72 Ibid (FTC).

73 For example, FCA letter to board directors, 'Portfolio strategy letter to firms in the

Personal & Commercial Lines Insurer (PL&CL) portfolio: identifying and re-medying harms' (8 January 2020), 2, https://www.fca.org.uk/publication/correspondence/letter-firms-personal-commercial-lines-insurer-portfolio-identifying-remedying-harms.pdf (accessed 17 January 2020).

74 FCA website, Magnus Falk, 'Artificial intelligence in the boardroom', https://www.fca.org.uk/insight/author/magnus-falk (accessed 24 November 2019).

75 Ibid (Falk, FCA website).

76 Ibid (Falk, FCA website).

77 Ibid (Falk, FCA website).

78 FCA Business Plan 2019/20, 22, https://www.fca.org.uk/publication/business-plans/business-plan-2019-20.pdf (accessed 1 July 2020).

79 PSD II (EU) 2015/2366 and Payment Systems Regulator, 'Data in the payments industry: responses to our discussion paper' (DP18/1 September 2019), 97, https://www.psr.org.uk/sites/default/files/media/PDF/PSR-Responses-to-DP18-1_.pdf (accessed 24 November 2019).

80 Alan Brener, 'Payment Service Directive II and its implications' in T. Lynn (ed.) *Disrupting finance* (Springer, 2018), 104–105.

81 FCA, Christopher Woolard, 'The future of regulation: AI for consumer good', speech given on 16 July 2019, https://www.fca.org.uk/news/speeches/future-regulation-ai-consumer-good (accessed 24 November 2019).

82 Bank of England and FCA, 'Machine learning in UK financial services' (October 2019), 10, https://www.fca.org.uk/publication/research/research-note-on-machine-learning-in-uk-financial-services.pdf (accessed 7 March 2020).

83 Ibid ('Machine learning'), 19.

84 Dirk Zetzsche, Douglas Arner, Ross Buckley, and Brian Tang, 'Artificial in-telligence in finance: putting the human in the loop' (February 2020), Vol 1, Centre for Finance, Technology and Entrepreneurship Academic Paper Series, https://ssrn.com/abstract=3531711 (accessed 7 March 2020).

85 Rechtbank Den Haag (5 February 2020) Nederlands Juristen Comité voor de Mensenrechten/Staat Der Nederlanden, 1878 – Den Haag, 05-02-2020 / C-09–550982-HA ZA 18–388, https://uitspraken.rechtspraak.nl/inziendocument?id=ECLI:NL:RBDHA:2020:1878 (English translation).

86 Ibid (Den Haag).

87 Mark Paige, Audrey Amrein-Beardsley, and Kevin Close, 'Tennessee's national impact on teacher evaluation law and policy: an assessment of value-added model litigation' (Winter 2019) *Tennessee Journal of Law and Policy*, 13(2), 564–565.

88 Houston Federation of Teachers, Local 2415 v. Houston School District (2017) 251 F. Supp. 3d 1168, 1174.

89 Ibid (Houston teachers case), 1176.

90 Ibid (Houston teachers case), 1177.

91 Valérie Beaudouin and others, 'Identifying the 'right' level of explanation in a given situation' (March 2020), hal-02507316, 3, https://hal.telecom-paristech.fr/hal-02507316/document (accessed 10 April 2020).

92 Ibid (Beaudouin and others), 3.

93 James Manyika, Jake Silberg, and Brittany Presten, 'What do we do about the biases in AI?' (25 October 2019), *Harvard Business Review*, https://hbr.org/2019/10/what-do-we-do-about-the-biases-in-ai (accessed 12 April 2020).

94 Talia Gillis, 'False dreams of algorithmic fairness: the case of credit pricing' (November 2019), 85, https://scholar.harvard.edu/files/gillis/files/gillis_jmp_191101.pdf (accessed 1 July 2020).

95 Ibid (Gillis), 74.

96 Consumer Financial Protection Bureau, 'Fair Lending Report' (June 2019), Federal Register/Vol 84, No. 130/Monday, July 8, 2019/Notices, 32423, https://www.govinfo.gov/content/pkg/FR-2019-07-08/pdf/2019–14384.pdf (accessed 1 July 2020).

97 Supra note 91 (Beaudouin and others), 3.

98 Ruha Benjamin, *Race after technology: abolitionist tools for the new Jim code* (Polity, Cambridge, England, 2019), 58.

99 FCA, 'Sector views' (February 2020), 75, https://www.fca.org.uk/publication/corporate/sector-views-2020.pdf (accessed 9 March 2020).

100 HM Treasury and FCA, 'Financial advice market review – final report' (March 2016), 18, https://www.fca.org.uk/publication/corporate/famr-final-report.pdf (accessed 4 March 2020) FCA website, The retail intermediary market 2018 (June 2019), https://www.fca.org.uk/data/retail-intermediary-market-2018 (accessed 4 March 2020).

101 House of Commons, Briefing Paper No. 5528, 'Financial advice market review and the Retail Distribution Review' (14 March 2015), 19, https://researchbriefings.parliament.uk/ResearchBriefing/Summary/SN05528 (accessed 4 March 2020).

102 Supra note 100 ('Financial advice market review'), 13.

103 Supra note 100 ('Financial advice market review'), 6.

104 Financial Times, 'Putting the 'AI' into financial advice' (8 November 2019).

105 Charles Schwab, 'The rise of robo: Americans' perspectives and predictions on the use of digital advice' (November 2018), 2, https://content.schwab.com/web/retail/public/about-schwab/charles_schwab_rise_of_robo_report_findings_2018.pdf (accessed 4 March 2020), citing a report by Aite Group, 'US digital advice: consolidation, fee disruption, and the battle of the brands' (September 2017).

106 Financial Times, 'Investec shuts robo-advice service due to 'low appetite' (16 May 2019). This follows the departure of UBS from this area of the market in 2018.

107 FCA website, Automated investment services – our expectations (as at May 2018, date of most recent update), https://www.fca.org.uk/publications/multi-firm-reviews/automated-investment-services-our-expectations (accessed 28 February 2020).

108 Ibid (FCA website, Automated investment services).

109 Ibid (FCA website, Automated investment services).

110 Ibid (FCA website, Automated investment services).

111 Ibid (FCA website, Automated investment services).

112 Ibid (FCA website, Automated investment services).

113 Ibid (FCA website, Automated investment services).

114 Bank of England, 'Future of finance: review on the outlook for the UK financial system – what it means for the Bank of England' (June 2019), 80–88, https://www.bankofengland.co.uk/-/media/boe/files/report/2019/future-of-finance-report.pdf?la=en&hash=59CEFAEF01C71AA551E7182262E933A699E952FC (accessed 9 March 2020).

115 David Llewellyn, 'The economic rationale for financial regulation' (Financial Services Authority, London, April 1999), Occasional Paper No. 1, 1–57, 9–10.

116 For example, the natural resource: a field of grass, has no owner who has an economic interest in preventing overgrazing. Consequently the grass is devoured by the cattle of all the farmers thereabout with no thought or incentive by anyone farmer to protect the field's cultivation. The consequence is that all farmers are poorer as a result – that is their tragedy (William Forster Lloyd, *Two lectures on the checks to population* (Collingwood, Oxford, 1833), 30–32).

117 Mark Carney, 'Breaking the tragedy of the horizon – climate change and financial

stability', speech given at Lloyd's of London on 29 September 2015, https://www.bankofengland.co.uk/-/media/boe/files/speech/2015/breaking-the-tragedy-of-the-horizon-climate-change-and-financial-stability.pdf?la=en&hash=7C67E78565186 2457D99511147C7424FF5EA0C1A (accessed 9 March 2020).

118 Larry Fink, Chairman and Chief Executive Officer, letter to the CEOs of companies in which BlackRock is a shareholder, 'A fundamental reshaping of finance' (BlackRock website, https://www.blackrock.com/corporate/investor-relations/larry-fink-ceo-letter (accessed 10 March 2020).

119 Ibid (Fink letter).

120 FCA, Proposals to enhance climate-related disclosures by listed issuers and clarification of existing disclosure obligations, Consultation Paper, CP20/3 (March 2020), https://www.fca.org.uk/publication/consultation/cp20-3.pdf (accessed 10 March 2020).

121 Ibid (CP20/3), 46 and 48.

122 FCA website, 'FCA encourages firms to develop purposeful cultures', 5 March 2020, https://www.fca.org.uk/news/news-stories/fca-encourages-firms-develop-purposeful-cultures (accessed 10 March 2020).

123 PRA, Supervisory Statement (SS3/19), 'Enhancing banks' and insurers' approaches to managing the financial risks from climate change' (April 2019), 4–6, https://www.bankofengland.co.uk/-/media/boe/files/prudential-regulation/supervisory-statement/2019/ss319.pdf?la=en&hash=7BA9824BAC5FB313F42C00889D4E3 A6104881C44 (accessed 9 March 2020).

124 Ibid (PRA, Supervisory Statement, climate change), 4–5.

125 Ibid (PRA, Supervisory Statement, climate change), 5.

126 Ibid (PRA, Supervisory Statement, climate change), 5.

127 Ibid (PRA, Supervisory Statement, climate change), 5–6.

128 Ibid (PRA, Supervisory Statement, climate change), 5.

129 Financial Stability Board, 'Task force on climate-related financial disclosures: recommendations: final report' (June 2017), https://www.fsb-tcfd.org/wp-content/uploads/2017/06/FINAL-2017-TCFD-Report-11052018.pdf (accessed 9 March 2020).

130 David Freedman, *Statistical models: theory and practice* (Cambridge University Press, Cambridge, England, 2009), 1–2.

131 Clark Abrahams and Mingyuan Zhang, 'Regression analysis for compliance testing' in *Fair lending compliance: intelligence and implications for credit risk management* (John Wiley, Hoboken, New Jersey, 2015), 147–182.

132 Rudolf Freund, William Wilson, and Ping Sa, *Regression analysis: statistical modeling of a response variable* (Elsevier Science and Technology, San Diego, California, 2006), 1.

7

'CULTURE' WITHIN A BUSINESS

Structural and psychological issues and the role of compliance

Introduction

If the culture of the business is wrong, then regulations will be ineffective. Adapting the phrase attributed to Peter Drucker, it can be said that, 'culture eats regulatory compliance'. Viewed differently, an ethical corporate culture will produce 'ethical business practices'.[1] However, complexity exists and any business of any size will contain a number of cultures. Consequently, the compliance function has an important role in influencing the various cultures within a firm. 'Corporate culture can be viewed as a fundamental ingredient in institutionalizing ethics in organizations'.[2] Shared ethics in an organisation can help to reduce operational costs since a common ethical bond promotes coordination and cooperation without recourse to institutional structural mechanism with individuals working together through mutual trust rather because they are ordered to do so.[3]

This chapter examines the structural and psychological factors in a business culture causing firms to suffer significant failure, considering such questions as why people in an organisation act badly, and why some are incompetent and reckless. Often these behaviours are due to poor leadership and a lack of introspection coupled with self-delusion. Matters are made worse by poor communication and siloed thinking within organisations. All too often, the firms are infested by a poor culture that encourages, for example, the proliferation of products which are likely to harm customers (e.g. structured capital at risk investments) and others that are valueless, such as payment protection insurance. These products and their mis-selling are discussed in some detail with a focus on how they came about and were considered suitable by business senior management for sale to the firm's customers. At the heart of this is a lack of personal accountability resulting in dangerous business models. Earlier chapters have looked at many of these issues. This chapter develops these further, again considering them from the perspective of the compliance function.

Additionally, it is important to measure culture in the business since this may help identify areas of compliance risk. Measurement can include a range of factors such as those directly affecting customers (e.g. customer complaint levels and types of complaint); those relating to staff which may indicate significant issues (e.g. staff long- and short-terms illness, frequent use of sick days, missed staff training sessions or failure to carry out mandatory training etc.); operational failures (e.g. IT service outages) and process failings which may indicate underlying issues (e.g. dealing limit breaches etc.). These all require high levels of detailed information since significant issues may be masked by broadly satisfactory data.

Many measures may be too simplistic and too high-level and, in aggregation, may, consequently, be misleading. This is particularly true of common indicators such as customer satisfaction and net promoter scores. Often, the only useful information in customer satisfaction surveys are the data extremes: customers who are extremely satisfied and those who are very disgruntled. This results from the fact that customers who respond to surveys are normally indifferent and express no useful response. However, anger and bliss will be found at the extremes which, with sufficient detail, may be informative.

More useful are staff engagement surveys. Most medium-sized and large firms will have staff opinion surveys. Basic questions which ask if staff trust their manager or those working in other sections in the business can be very insightful but, as always, need to be analysed down to the smallest unit possible and the results followed through. These surveys also require high response levels of, at least, around 80%. Low response levels may also indicate a range of problems including poor local management and a failure to see the importance of the survey. Poor engagement results may help to identify disaffected teams and distrusted leadership and, again, risks to the firm and its customers.

Ideally, firms should all have sufficiently strong good cultures which are robust enough to ward off the pressures to act improperly. However, for a variety of reasons, considered in this chapter, it is unlikely that businesses can be left to self-regulate themselves. Nevertheless, there is much that can be done to improve and strengthen culture from within firms.

Regulation and coercion: can firms be trusted?

There are a number of ways of undertaking the task of regulation. These may include working towards a consensus which is accepted by all and implemented. At the other extreme, regulation can operate by the use of fear and coercion. For example, following the recent financial crisis the FSA, under new leadership, adopted a much more assertive tone.[4] The latter can include the fear of individuals and firms being 'named and shamed'. Nevertheless, 'it is in the nature of the many to be ruled by fear rather than by shame and to refrain from evil not because of the disgrace but because of the punishment'.[5] In parallel, the compliance function may need to employ a variety of these methods.

There is little evidence to indicate the financial firms can be trusted to act properly. The Libor and related scandals demonstrated the weak, or non-existent, oversight of these areas within banks. It also raised questions as to what level of reliance, if any, could be placed on internal controls. 'FCA enforcement notices on misconduct in foreign exchange (FX) markets showed that voluntary codes in FX and other markets had not been translated into meaningful internal guidance within firms. And trading staff in different firms attempted to collude in order to manipulate markets, against the interests both of the markets at large and, in some cases, their firms'.[6]

In parallel there is a recognition that 'it is vital to profoundly change the culture of banking. At the same time, there is a recognition that changing the culture of banking is difficult. A new culture can't just be regulated into being. Rather, culture change is something banks themselves must take responsibility for and be held accountable for'.[7] The key to change is the need to recognise the need for a more contemplative process within firms. This could be described as 'compliance by reflection'. This is considered further in this chapter.

The next sections look at a number of factors that may inhibit the development of a good culture within organisations.

Organisational structures, 'silos' and information flows

The difficulties in managing large and complex organisations results in the need for formalised rules and set procedures so that people can operate with some degree of consistency. This presents difficulties when applied to areas such as ethics and culture. Additionally, many organisations operate with structural silos and this may be exacerbated by the development of 'cultural silos'.[8] There is also a natural tendency in any organisational to hoard information and expertise and not to share it. The various units, as a consequence, lose sight of the 'purpose' of the organisation. The 'compartmentalised mind' is also subject to a range of psychological biases. All of this acts as a form of fragmentation within firms making, among other things, their consistent management difficult with an increased risk of compliance and regulatory failure.

Those working within and across the silos may act as 'tribal bankers', who amass information 'only to lavish it on others, in order to build up a capital of obligations and debts which will be repaid in the form of homage, respect, loyalty, and, when the opportunity arises, work and services', as and when needed.[9] This may produce a network of intertwined 'understandings'. These interconnected units 'trade' information and influence for their own benefit. This may not assist units which are outside these 'magic circles'. These rings of power and knowledge may not operate for the benefit of the firm nor will they work to help other stakeholders. Organisations are subject to frequent structural reorganisations but these informal networks are very resilient and the bonds will quickly re-emerge. It is a core reason why changing culture in a firm is very difficult since often only an anthropological study will identify how an organisation really functions and how these informal arrangements are the 'glue' which both holds the firm together and also act as barriers to change, cultural or otherwise. Many of the issues preventing operational compliance result from these organisational 'silos'.

These operational silos can be reinforced by management and board committee structures. For example, at some organisations risk issues are considered by risk committees while other management issues are considered separately.[10] Each has its designated committee with little apparent interchange between the two.

Similarly, reporting structural arrangements may insulate directors, company group functions and the like from disturbing news. In part this may be due to a desire to manage information flows as a control mechanism to prevent an uncontrolled reaction.[11] It may simply be a desire to suppress bad news. It was a particular issue revealed by the enquiries into the recent financial crisis. For example, Pat McFadden MP, in questioning Tracey McDermott, the then Director of Enforcement and Financial Crime at the FSA asked her why senior staff at UBS bank were not personally sanctioned by the regulator. He summarised her response saying that,'you had been asked specifically about the UBS investigation and why the trail had not gone higher. You said: 'what you do in an investigation is follow where the lines of inquiry take you … you will start working up from the bottom to get through the process, and see which direction you are pointed in, in terms of who are the people with responsibility and who are the people who are aware'.…It looks as though there is an incentive for senior people and directors in banks to be ignorant of what is going on in the company'.[12] In the United Kingdom this, and similar exchanges, resulted in new legislation creating personal accountability under the Senior Manager and Certified Persons Regime discussed elsewhere in this book. Nevertheless, the UK regulatory approach can sometimes still appear opaque. For example, Commerzbank in the United Kingdom was fined over £37m (after a 30% discount) by the FCA in June 2020 for numerous, serious anti-money laundering failures.[13] There was evidence of many policy and process failures by several units within the bank, including both 'first' and 'second' line compliance functions, spread over several years. However, it appears that the regulatory investigation was narrowly drawn. There does not appear to have been any FCA examination of the prevailing culture and governance arrangements within the business which may have been responsible for these extensive problems. No management, senior or otherwise, are mentioned in the FCA's Final Notice and no one seems to have been held personally accountable by the regulator. It is possible to draw the conclusion that there were a number fundamental issues at the bank which were not addressed in the Final Notice. It is difficult to understand why these aspects were not covered. It would appear to be a wasted regulatory opportunity.

Business models, culture and personal accountability

Regulators often complain that they ask by the management of regulated firms to do two apparently mutually exclusive things at the same time. The businesses claim that they want open textured regulations which set out the regulatory objectives (often know as 'Principles'). Managers consider that this approach allows them to meet these objectives in a flexible and proportion way. It promotes innovation and allows them to operate in a way relevant to their firm. At the same time these same managers, and more specifically, their staff who have to design systems and train other employees, want certainty. They do not want to find out later, often with the benefit of hindsight, that what they did was wrong. They prefer very clear, specific rules on what they can or cannot do. They may complain about a'box ticking' approach to regulation but most want the regulator to 'just tell us precisely what you want'.[14] Consequently, regulators will attempt to balance what may be called 'regulation by objective or outcome' or 'Auftragstaktik' and the more prescriptive rule-making styles.[15]

In recent years, this binary approach has been complicated by insights into how to use regulation to guide business model and conduct. The FCA considers that the roots of what drives misconduct are to be found in poor culture and the lack of individual accountability.[16] In parallel, a firm's business model, coupled with issues with culture and personal irresponsibility, may 'indicate high levels of risk'.[17] Risks can thrive where a business operates in a highly competitive market or on the verge of failure. These can drive the management to extremes setting targets which encourage misconduct and incentives which encourage wrong-doing.

There are also the risks arising from a 'herd' mentality. For example, other firms in the industry are launching similar products or services or buying new business assets at inflated prices. There is pressure to do the same rather than be left out. Bank customers may also ask why 'your' bank is not copying others. Sometimes following the actions of others can be the right decision. However, there is no safety in moving with the 'herd'. Deciding what to do requires calm, objective analysis. I recall an executive meeting where a senior marketing manager tried to encourage us to follow the lead of another bank and to launch a new product which might hazard the capital of customers. Before I had a chance, as the compliance officer, to intervene the business CEO questioned whether this strategy would be right for our customers and answered their own question saying that our retail customers should not be exposed the risk of loss of their capital. This was not the right product for them.

In addition, there has been an over-focus, by some banks, on short-term factors. To a large extent this is probably due to the fact that firms and their investors are impatient. A senior manager who fails in the short-term is unlikely to have a long-term future. 'Increasing short-term pressures on market valuations ... inevitably feed back to the way in which chief executives and, by inference, their boards seek to run their businesses and the pressure exerted by relative benchmarks that have sharpened fund manager attention to short-term performance'.[18] Within firms, as in all parts of society, there will be arguments and conflicts. Many organisations will mirror the fragmentations found in all communities. But most commercial firms are driven by numbers. They will have a focus which is measured in numbers. This distinguishes them from many other parts of the society within which they operate. They are bound by contracts, incomplete or otherwise, with money as their nexus. The control functions have to work within this 'numeric' culture. It is often the immediacy of the numbers that drives short-term behaviour.

However, boards and other senior executives of banks and other financial services firms need to acknowledge their accountability to other stakeholders. Accountability has been described as 'central to our understanding of justice' and combined with a requirement for responsibility results in a demand for justice 'when things go wrong'.[19] It is increasingly the direction of regulatory travel in the United Kingdom.

The board is responsible for business strategy and a failure to set the right objectives can result in spectacular failures. It is important to mention the Wells Fargo case again. It was covered at length in an earlier chapter. However, it is worth repeating that, among other things, the strategy adopted by Wells Fargo Bank did not, apparently take account of its ethical dimensions and consequences. The business model was based on cross-selling products. The then chief executive 'had initiated the 'GR-8' program to pursue cross-selling. The aim of the programme was for each customer to have at least eight bank products memorialised in the sales slogan 'eight is great'.[20]

Issues relating to the business model at Wells Fargo were never a subject for board discussion. Audit and Examination sub-committee of the board never discussed this subject nor did it consider issues relating to sales and the potential for misconduct.[21] This sub-committee was largely focused on areas which it considered would have a material effect on the bank's financial statements including the firm's internal controls of financial reporting.[22] The results constituted a very blinkered approach to the board's role which omitted many real risks.

An executive-level enterprise risk committee existed, known as the Operational Risk Management and Compliance Group. The latter focused on anti-money laundering and 'compliance with consumer credit, home mortgage disclosure and other laws'.[23] It did not see the business model and sales practices and integrity as its responsibility.[24]

Another UK example can be seen in the FCA's action against Lloyds TSB in 2013.[25] The regulator fined the bank over £28m for serious deficiencies in its employee incentive schemes. The latter included 'variable salaries, bonus thresholds which involved disproportionate rewards for marginal sales' and so on. Consequently, 'advisers who met sales targets qualified for substantial salary rises and bonus payments, while advisers who did not faced salary reductions'.[26] Additionally, the bank had a strategic focus on selling insurance products and the incentive scheme prioritised these sales. 'Advisers were able to access details of their performance against sales targets on a daily basis. There was, therefore, a significant risk that, if not adequately controlled, advisers would sell products to customers that they did not need or want in an attempt to reach salary and bonus incentive thresholds'.[27]

The bank did have various control systems to check on the quality of the sales been made but these were not risk based. It 'relied on routine business monitoring' which did consider customer and product risk profiles and the bank 'failed to supplement this with appropriately risk-based monitoring that also focused on the risk profile of advisers'.[28]

In parallel, the then CEO of the regulator, Martin Wheatley gave a speech in which he emphasised the need for managerial cultural change.[29] In his view financial institutions had come to view customers as someone to sell to rather than serve but that this view needed to change. 'Cultural change is needed, and this change can only come from the top of an organisation. CEOs are ultimately accountable for the way their staff are incentivised, so we expect them to take a real interest in fixing this'.[30] He went onto say that 'we, the regulator, intend to change this culture of viewing consumers simply as sales targets'[31].

Nevertheless, even though banks have moved aware from explicit cash incentives for rewarding sales in some instances these have been replaced by 'activity' targets and rewards, and humiliation for failures. For example, research found that at one Halifax Bank of Scotland branch 'there was a weekly 'Cash or Cabbages day'. Employees who exceeded their targets were publicly rewarded with cash. Those who missed their activity targets were given cabbages. Two tellers at branches of the bank in Glasgow and Paisley had the vegetables placed on their desks within full public view'.[32] In another example, at a different branch of the same bank, another young branch teller 'had a cauliflower placed on her desk. She was apparently told she could only pass it on when someone opened an account'.[33]

The FCA continues to move beyond process analysis towards an assessment of the underlying business. The regulator views as 'unacceptable' regulated firms 'selling products which are unsuitable or of poor value to consumers'.[34] Products must not only meet consumer needs but must also not 'deliver poor value'.[35] The FCA have also emphasised that business pricing decisions must not primarily aim to achieve business plan and financial objectives but must also consider 'consumer outcomes'.[36] The failure to consider 'outcomes' for customers was a major issue in Lloyds Bank being fined over £64m (after a 30% discount) in June 2020.[37] The issue arose from the bank's treatment of customers with mortgage arrears. Following a badly handled reorganisation in 2011 staff who were experienced in dealing with customers with mortgage arrears were largely replaced with others inexperienced in this area. The consequential problems were masked from senior management and the regulators by ineffectual compliance monitoring of these units. These reviews 'focused on compliance with policies rather than…[with] conducting an end-to-end review of the overall customer experience to determine if the outcomes were appropriate'.[38]

There are similar cultural issues where firms place obstacles in the way of customers moving to a different service provider. Business strategies which deter the market operating properly are unfair to customers and undermine consumer trust upon which the whole edifice is foundered. Consequently, 'if the sector as a whole does not attempt to raise the bar for good practice and behaviour, it will again be difficult to bring about change'.[39] Thus, it is important that boards and senior executives must not adopt strategies which 'might discourage consumers from making active decisions' such as being able to cancel or switch products with ease.[40]

The FCA sees good governance as part of a sound business culture. In the context of pricing policies this requires that firms have 'effective governance over their pricing practises'.[41] This includes only taking pricing decisions which are based on evidence of how these proposed changes may affect consumers and how the business will 'ensure fair outcomes'.[42]

The next sections consider the psychology of doing the wrong thing where strategic decisions were taken to expand the sale of Payment Protection Insurance (PPI) in the United Kingdom. These errors in judgement were the result of a number of factors, including narrow, blinkered thinking where the issues were misconceptualised in a defective cultural setting.

The example of payment protection insurance (PPI)

The UK's PPI debacle represents one of the worst examples of blinkered management thinking and poor corporate culture. The final cost of customer claims against banks for mis-selling this product could exceed £50 Bn.[43] Contrary to the popular view this is not simply a story of wicked bankers fleecing their customers. Rather it is a tale of narrow short-term thinking, and even thoughtlessness.

Through the 2000s until around 2007 banks had lots of money to lend and indeed they made many loans. This, coupled with loose monetary policy, resulted in low interest rates and reduced net interest margins (the difference between what banks pay depositors and the interest they receive for making loans) for lenders. The profitability of lending fell to zero or less. Rather than lend less, many banks looked to what they could do to make these loans profitable. They found an exceedingly profitable product in PPI – a type of insurance that had been around for a dozen or more years. The result of this strategy of selling PPI with loans was the heavy cross-subsidisation of loss-making lending. This distorted the business model and corrupted judgements. A bit late in the day it raised regulatory fears of possible market distortion, the mis-selling of complex, unclear products, and the mis-pricing of risk. This was coupled with conflicts of interest with PPI products 'manufactured' by insurance companies and provided to banks to sell to customers with profits shared between the banks and insurance firms under various arrangements in which the interests of customers seem to have been absent.[44]

Prior to its acquisition by Santander, Alliance and Leicester (A&L) bank indulged in high levels of unsecured lending. Between 2004 and 2006 its unsecured lending rose by almost 30%.[45] In 2008 the FSA took enforcement action against the bank fining it £7m. There were serious failures at all levels within Alliance and Leicester but, in particular, the compliance function appeared to have suffered a serious failure of judgement. Between 2005 and 2007 both the training workshops and the material for the 'PPI telephone sales process made references to inappropriate sales techniques that put pressure on the customer to accept the recommendation. This was described as creating a 'pressure cooker effect'[46]. The Final Notice went onto say that 'in February 2007 A&L put in place objection handling training which instructed advisers to offer life cover when faced with re-peated objections to full PPI from the customer, rather than to make a recommendation on the basis of the customer's demands and needs and the customer information obtained. All training material was submitted to, and approved by, Group Compliance prior to use'.[47] It is clear that the com-pliance function did not exercise sound judgement and failed in a number of key aspects of their role.

It is difficult to know or understand what was going through the minds of the senior executives, board members and control functions at this bank. Some possible insight was given in the oral evidence provided by Helen Weir, a senior member of the executive team at Lloyds Bank between 2004 and 2010, to the Parliamentary Commission on Banking Standards on the sale of PPI by her bank.

'throughout the whole of my tenure [at Lloyds Bank], this was not a product where we looked at the individual profitability of PPI; that was just not the way that we looked at it. PPI was never a

product that was sold in isolation; it was always sold in conjunc-
tion with a loan ... the profitability of the unsecured lending
business was highly marginal if not negative – and it was negative
for a number of years ... The dynamic of the unsecured lending
business was effectively that you had a loan product that was
marginally profitable or unprofitable, with contribution coming
through from the PPI products, so there was, effectively, a cross-
subsidy ... There was an industry structure whereby the profitability of the PPI product, which was always sold alongside the
unsecured lending', provided the necessary cross-subsidy.[48]

There may also have been an expectation that if the regulator did not ex-
plicitly comment adversely on, for example, sales practices then compliance
and the firm might conclude that these were acceptable. It appears that, in
this example, the bank was tracking the FSA's views on PPI selling but
misjudged them. The bank's chief risk officer, to whom the compliance
function reported, criticised herself 'for not having spotted quickly enough
where that was going and for thinking it was a question of mending, when
actually it was a massive step change. I do not have a clever answer, but I
have reflected on that'.[49]

What happened with PPI is important not only because of the enormous
cost but also the weak business management and serious compliance failings. PPI matched an unprofitable core banking offering with a niche highly
profitable insurance product. The regulatory response was slow to develop
and the claims management companies made handsome profits. But this
does not absolve the financial services industry. Many in the retail and
commercial banking industry promoted the products and there appears to
have been little resistance to this or reflection on the risks.

It is difficult to understand why compliance did not speak up in a number
of banks and why the issue was not properly addressed at an early stage. In
some cases the compliance function was still focused on investment business
and appeared not to have appreciate that the regulatory world had changed
when new legislation made general insurance, including PPI, subject to
regulation under the FSA in 2005. It is also possible that general insurance
products were considered much less high risk and thus subject to less
scrutiny compared with investment business. There were also, as already
mentioned, the normal business pressures and the belief which rationalised
that, 'in the round', there was no harm to customers in selling them PPI.

In addition, due, possibly, to a large element of wishful thinking, Lloyds
Bank disagreed with the findings of the research commissioned and published by the FSA. In particular, the regulator had undertaken 'mystery
shopping' of the bank using customers who pretended to be interested in
obtain credit. The FSA described the results of this review work 'as poor',
and cited a number of failings.[50] Lloyds Bank may have discounted the

FSA's work since, in Lloyds' opinion, the 'FSA did not publish its results or an analysis of the mystery shopping exercise'.[51] Lloyds Bank did not accept that the FSA's finding of extensive mis-selling of PPI was an accurate reflection of their sales process.[52] In addition, Lloyds Bank, and many other banks, did not accept that the high number of Ombudsman complaints found in favour of the customer from 2008 onwards was accurate. Instead, the view of many in the industry was that this was the result of the Ombudsman adopting a new harder line against the banks in this area.[53]

There are a number of lessons from the PPI fiasco. These include the regulatory approach and the strategic issues relating to constructing customer redress programmes.[54] However, these aspects fall outside the scope of this work. More pertinent to this book, I believe that there was a 'moral blindness' at the heart of the industry. There is no simple solution to this risk. Each individual has to keep questioning themselves and their actions on a daily basis. That which seems questionable is likely to be wrong and an attempt at justification will not make it the right course to take. It requires much greater self-reflection on the part of a bank's senior management and board. It is necessary that control functions, especially compliance, to do the same. They need to take a robust position and stand their ground.

Others have also suggested this approach. For example, the Hong Kong Monetary Authority (HKMA) has expressed a keen interest in executive self-reflection with the need for the latter to gain a clear vision by looking into their own hearts.[55] Besides the usual need to focus on corporate governance and incentive schemes, the Authority sees assessment and feedback mechanisms as a 'third pillar' using multiple data sources with the board and executive assessment process as part of the test of whether the organisation has the right culture.[56] Too many banks, according to the HKMA, rely on too few sources for this information. Moreover, the banks tend to be too insular and do not spend time considering misconduct events overseas and what lessons could be learnt.[57] As with other regulators, the HKMA advocates encouraging whistleblowing as one of these sources and goes further by specifying that the whistleblowing channels should operate day and night every day of the year and be connected to 'live operators' who, for international businesses, have multiple language translators available.[58]

The role of those that raise concerns cannot be overstated and this subject is considered in more detail in Chapter 3. Nevertheless, there are cultural and structural pressures that coerce individuals into silence. These are considered next, together with the risks of 'cultural contagion' and conflict within firms. As discussed later, the development of 'precipice bonds' illustrates aspects of these risks.

Pressure to be a 'team player, social-silence, structures, symbols and complicity'

The pressure, within a small community such as a business can be immense. There are all the trite phrases used to maintain conformity – 'be a team player', 'get on-side', 'do not to rock the boat' and so on. This is at odds with the expectations of, among others, the regulators. From the board level downwards the regulators expect there to be 'challenge' and a degree of conflict within the regulated organisation.[59] The control functions have an important role within the business to produce this desired outcome since they are a manifestation of the regulator operating continuously, 'on-site'. 'Whistleblowing' is seen as another form of 'grit' within the system. The aim is to 'encourage a culture where individuals felt comfortable raising concerns and challenging poor behaviour without fear of retaliation'.[60]

Further, the organisation is bound by a series of structural relationships and personal obligations which can operate for good or ill and can prove very resilient to change. Often these arrangements are seen as blocking the good intentions of regulators, senior managers and so on The latter come and go frequently within firms but the 'middle management' with its ethos, customs and practices goes on. Sometimes this group is, disparagingly, called the 'permafrost layer'.[61] However, this may be unfair. These are the people that get things done and, in practice, carry the organisation's ethos. They are not even a 'layer' but form part of the system of networks operating in any organisation of any size. They are, however, dependent on those who have access to resources. These can be funding, staffing, promotions, information and so on. Those with this access can 'build up a capital of obligations and debts which will be repaid in the form of homage, respect, loyalty' and so on.[62] This ties people and groups together.

Companies often specialise in the use of symbols and the power of its conventicle to inspire loyalty to the company and the 'tribe' within the firm. A corporate sales event, in full flight, with all the music, lights, imagery and audience participation and fervour can distort the field of perception of even the most objective of observers. It is designed to do so. As observed, 'no man, however highly civilized, can listen for very long to African drumming, or Indian chanting, or Welsh hymn singing, and retain intact his critical and self-conscious personality' so can the emotion of a corporate gathering with all the symbolism of a spiritual convocation.[63]

It is central to the success of compliance that they understand all of this and can use these associations, as well as challenging them, to further the regulatory purposes they are charged with. They, and the other control function teams, need to isolate themselves from 'corporate socialisation'. Additionally, they need to understand the commercial pressures faced by the business and how these influence those working within the organisation.

157

However, at the same time, they must maintain their engagement with the firm and guide it down the right path – a difficult task.

'Precipice bonds' and culture clashes and 'contagion'

Companies often host many different cultures. There is always the risk that poor cultures can seep through organisations. Honeyed words and commercial pressures and incentives may allow a 'toxic' culture to spread like a contagious disease through parts of the business.

For example, the marketing departments within investment banks and asset managers often have a portfolio of products which they would like to distribute more widely. This might involve encouraging wealth managers and private banks to sell these products to their customers. The distribution of these products could also be expanded by packaging these offerings for retail investors. Many of these sophisticated investments are based on complex financial derivatives concocted by investment bankers. Sometimes these products are described as 'toxic' which may or may not be true. It will depend on to whom they are sold and the particular circumstances. An investment fund is likely to be well equipped to understand the risk inherent in these products and to act accordingly. However, if they are targeted at retail customers and given to retail and commercial bank staff to sell the latter may not understand the product's workings and the possible risks contained within these offerings.

Sometimes these investments are manufactured by investment banks and then 'white labelled' (i.e. sold under the brand of the distributor). The former often takes no responsibility for how the product is sold leaving that to those who have the customer relationship.

It is often at this point that cultures clash. At best it arises through thoughtlessness and the absence of any introspection. However, it may be due to darker motives propelled by greed for wider sales and contempt for what they may see as 'oafish' retail banking staff and 'lumpen' retail customers. Anthony Salz in his report on culture in Barclays Bank expressed the view that, 'a culture developed within Barclays, quite possibly derived originally from the investment bank, which came across to some as being 'clever'...even arrogant and aggressive'.[64] In part, this attitude may derive from the class background of many of the senior investment bankers. Many were educated at the best public (private) schools and the most prestigious universities. They work in the rarified atmosphere of the financial districts of major cities surrounded by offices of high-quality chrome, glass and polished wood aided by banks of computer screens and with, possibly, an artistic work by, for example, Bridget Riley or Frank Auerbach on the wall. The retail bank staff probably joined the bank straight from school, often working part-time and paid a small fraction of the remuneration of the investment banker. The retail staff are usually observed and recorded on camera every day, and one day each week will take part in a team building 'huddle' and, daily, they will receive a deluge of head, area and regional office instructions. These are the employees who may be asked to sell the complex investments constructed by the remote investment bankers in their 'masters of the universe' world.

Salz saw this and said that 'Barclays should take care to ensure that complex derivatives products manufactured in the investment bank and sold to less sophisticated customers in the retail bank are properly understood by whoever oversees the sale to the Barclays customer...we consider it likely that the issues arising from the sales of derivatives to SMEs [small and medium sized enterprises] could have been reduced if the culture within the bank had placed higher priority on meeting the needs of customers'.[65]

Structured capital at risk products ('scarp') are a type of product constructed by investment banks to be marketed to retail customers. They are sometimes known as 'precipice' bonds, promising either a fixed or variable rate of return over the life of the bond. The investments are usually linked to some index. The investment value may decrease if there is a substantial fall in the index before the bond matures. The bonds come in a wide variety of forms and often include a 'buffer' or margin by which the index can fall before the capital value of the bond itself declines. Some may have additional complexities including a series of valuation periods during the bond's existence used to assess capital diminution and limits on investment returns. The underlying bond will be based on a portfolio of derivative contracts the triggering of which may cause odd effects on the primary investment vehicle. The complexity of these products are often a challenge for the investment adviser to understand never mind the retail customer.

A number of banks failed in this task. For example, Lloyds TSB (as Lloyds Bank was known then) was fined almost £2m in 2003 for mis-selling a risky investment product to its branch bank customers. The insurance company ('Scottish Widows') in the Lloyds Bank group had designed a financial product called the Extra Income and Growth Plan ('EIGP'). This was designated as 'medium to high' risk by the insurance company and was aimed at portfolio fund managers to be used as part of a balanced set of investments.

'The return of an investor's capital was dependent on the individual performance of 30 equally weighted stocks selected from the FTSE 100 Index. However, the amount of return of the initial capital invested was not guaranteed and depended on a series of put options on each of the 30 stocks'.[66] Depending on the sales tranche the value of the equities could fall between 20% and 30% before the investors capital was put at risk if the stock did not recover its value before the investment matured. This calculation applied to each of the shares one by one. There was no method for offsetting losses and gains. There were various other complications in the investment relating to when the 'trigger' was activated and the consequences.

The bank branch network sold some 51,000 of these plans taking around £720m from investors. Subsequently, as a result of market falls, customers lost between 30% and 48% of their capital.[67] The FSA calculated that over 22,000 (44% of the total sold via the branch network) of these sales were unsuitable for the customers' real needs and circumstances.

The FSA found that 'approximately 16,500 sales (84% of the investments sold) were to investors who had not, before their purchase of the EIGP, purchased an equity related investment product and who purchased the EIGP with over 20% of their financial assets; and approximately 6,000 (18%) sales to other investors who had, before their purchase of the EIGP, purchased one or more other equity related investment products and who purchased the EIGP with over 35% of their financial assets'.[68] Consequently, there was a strong risk that most customers did not understand how the investment worked and the risks to which they were exposed. In addition, a significant amount of each customers' assets were invested in these plans and subject to the risk of capital loss. This level of concentration of risk was inadvisable.

The training given to branch based investment advisers was inadequate and rushed and compliance monitoring of the sales was poor. As a result, the FSA required the bank to compensate all those who had suffered loss and to review all the sales made to check their suitability and customer understanding.

While, not covered in the Enforcement Notice, one effective method for checking customer understanding is for compliance staff to call customers a few days after they have received advice to invest in a product. Using specially trained compliance staff, working with a set of structured questions, they can check the level of understanding. The questions employed need to be open-ended. For example, the customer might be asked what would happen to the amount they would get back when the bond matured if the index fell by X amount or did they understand that at the end of the term the bond's value could be significantly lower than the amount they originally invested?

In 2011, the FSA fined Credit Suisse just under £6m for mis-selling structured capital at risk investments.[69] Over a three year period, starting in 2007, Credit Suisse sold over 1,700 of these products to some 600 of Credit Suisse customers in the United Kingdom who invested over £1.1Bn. The 2007–2008 financial crisis struck before these investments matured and customers suffered significant losses as a result. The bank had, among other failings, no adequate system for checking customer understanding of the product. The compliance checks failed to consider all aspects of the suitability of the sale of the product.[70]

Similarly, the FSA took enforcement action against Coutts & Co in 2011 and fined the bank over £6m.[71] Between 2003 and 2008 Coutts' advisers had recommended their customers invest in the AIG Life Premier Access Bond and Premier Bond Enhanced Variable Rate Fund. By the time of AIG's collapse in 2008 customers had lost some £750m. A significant proportion of the funds had been invested in floating rate notes and asset backed securities. The risks involved with these products had not been adequately explained to customers. The bonds were marketed by Coutts as a'cash' investment. For example, the marketing material said that the funds could 'be seen as an alternative to traditional bank and building society deposits'.[72] There were many other failures in the financial advice process but of particular relevance were the deficiencies in the approach taken by the compliance function.[73] These issues may have indicated, at the time, a deep-seated cultural problems with a possible lack of understanding of the role of compliance and the need to consider, fully, the customers' perspective.

For example, customer complaints in 2008 resulted in the Coutts' compliance function carrying out a review of the quality of the investment advice. However, this review failed to include customers who had exited the investments earlier. Compliance also neglected fundamental aspects of the advice process such as whether the advice was suitable for the circumstances of the customers and the adequacy of the risk disclosures by the advisers. Moreover, the review was not undertaken sufficiently quickly.[74] This was particularly an issue since these were the very problems identified by most of the customer complaints. The Coutts' compliance team undertaking the review also used a very poor quality 'checklist' which failed to prompt 'those conducting the review to consider whether the right product was recommended to the customer in view of their financial circumstances and objectives; and the questionnaire was process driven and not customer outcome focused'.[75] It is difficult to provide a rational explanation for these serious deficiencies. In a separate enforcement case the FSA also fined Coutts almost £9m for anti-money laundering process failings.[76]

The 2012 Final Notice indicates a number of cultural issues. For example, the Coutts' anti-money laundering ('AML') team was asked to approve potential customer relationships put forward by the private bankers. The team declined 5% of these but they 'failed to provide an appropriate level of challenge to the private bankers ... In particular, the AML team relied on the reputation and experience of the private banker involved to an inappropriate extent in making their assessments of customers'.[77] Further, the regulator found five cases of serious adverse information relating to these Coutts' customers. Nevertheless, 'in each case the customers were approved without proper consideration of whether further steps were necessary ... That adverse intelligence included allegations of misappropriation of state funds and close business and/or personal associations with individuals wanted by law authorities (in two such cases, there were current international arrest warrants in force)'.[78]

These two regulatory disciplinary actions covered similar time periods and may indicate serious cultural issues with both the business units and the compliance function. For whatever reason, the compliance function failed in its fundamental responsibilities.

The next sections consider, further, why people in organisations do the wrong thing.

Why people do the wrong thing

Antiphon, a Sophist, drew a distinction between 'nomos'; the formal laws and customs of a society, and 'physis'; those more internal, interior or private, guides of truth towards oneself.[79] It may be possible to view 'physis' as part of the 'ethikos' or the moral character that underpins an individual. For Aristotle the choice of action is preceded by deliberation which involves both the application of reason and thought.[80]

There are many reasons why people do the wrong thing. In many cases something changes the moment they walk through the front door of the office. They do, or omit to do, things at work that would never happen at home or in the world outside their business. There may be something wrong in the context of work. It will almost certainly be due to poor leadership and management. Often it is caused by extraordinary incompetence – which again may be a result of bad management. There are a number of other reasons which may occur alone or in combination. These include factors such as financial greed and financial desperation. For example, Harold Jaggard stole many millions over a number of years from the Grays Building Society. The amounts were so large that the Society had to be rescued in 1978.[81] Jaggard was the Society's chairman and secretary (CEO equivalent) but he ran two separate families; that of his wife and family and his mistress and her family. He was also a heavy gambler.[82] He continually juggled his finances (and the assets of the Society) in his desperation to maintain respectable living standards for all his dependents and to sustain his gambling habit.

Other reasons for wrong-doing include, for example, a desire to appear in a favourable light to one's boss; the need to meet market expectations coupled with the importance of supporting the stock's price; the firm's cultural environment ('everyone does it'), and a belief that the job requires breaking the law. Others commit bad acts because they feel omnipotent. Charles Keating probably falls into this latter category. Besides using the assets of the Lincoln Savings and Loan Association as his own personal fund he saw himself above the law. He sold bonds in the parent company of the savings and loan business and advised 'its bond salesmen to remember that 'the weak, meek and ignorant are always good targets'.[83] Keating apparently, 'walked with a swagger [and] never minced words about buying political influence. Asked once whether his payments to politicians had worked, he told reporters, 'I want to say in the most forceful way I can: I certainly hope so'.[84] There is also a desire to prove oneself. For example,

Dennis Kozlowski, former CEO of Tyco International, who was convicted in 2005 for paying himself unapproved bonuses commented that he'had a desire to prove himself as a deal maker'.[85]

The lust for power and status

I have found, in my experience, that the desire for status is a primary driver of behaviour. It provides a sense of power, personal self-worth and a reflection of one's importance in the perception of others. The measures of status vary from having a corner office (or any office), prestigious awards, a public 'name check' in a high-profile speech to selfies with important people. The importance of these feelings of recognition cannot be overstated. In many instances it motivates even more than remuneration. There is empirical evidence to support the view that staff 'ranking feedback, which is often used in organizational settings, prompts managers ... to forgo guaranteed financial gains in order to pursue a financially irrelevant higher rank'.[86] Often the lure of power and status predominates. One example, from my personal experience was Robert Kissane. 'Bob' Kissane was a UK investment adviser in the late 1960s through to the early 1990s operating with his own firm representing Royal Life, an insurance company. He was a well-known and well-respected figure in his community in Hampshire and had a 'wall of honour' behind his office desk covered with photographs of him meeting the nation's 'good and the great'. Apparently, he thought himself 'a star' at investments in the 1980s boom and encouraged his clients to borrow to invest in his schemes. As the economy turned downwards in the early 1990s the value of the investments fell; and he was charged with and convicted of theft.[87] The life insurance company had to contact almost a thousand clients and offer compensation.[88]

It is doubtful that Kissane made much, if any, money from his schemes. However, it did make him a 'big man' in his area. 'Bob' was the man to meet and know. He took great pride in his status, as evidenced and celebrated by the photos on his wall. He would meet his clients, who all lived locally, in his large expensive cars. He would remember their birthdays, anniversaries and so on. and his personal charm made those that he met feel special. He appeared to have revelled in his local, celebrity status and it is this that seemed to have motivated him.

A lack of imagination and sheer drudgery

The drudgery of work may enable unwarranted risks to be run and harm to be done. Lack of imagination is core to many financial problems and this important issue is discussed in more detail in Chapter 2. The sheer tedium and menial nature of the job may compound and reinforce this common failure of imagination. Toiling away, even at a senior level, without hope, aspiration or inspiration can dull the critical faculties. This can result in serious misjudgements. For example, George Chapman was the assistant secretary (deputy CEO equivalent) of the Grays Building Society in England from 1947 until its collapse in 1978. As mentioned above, the failure of the building society was caused by the chairman and secretary fraudulently taking large sums of money out of the institution over many years (some £5m in total – almost £30m at current calculations).[89] Chapman accepted what was going on without question since he 'like the rest of the staff, was disposed to think that if something had always been done it must be right'.[90] He was worn down by 'the sheer drudgery' of the work so that it is 'hardly surprising that he never raised his eyes above his desk' and his role 'made few intellectual demands upon him' and 'sapped his initiative'.[91]

The need for introspection and the perils of self-deception

Regulation will fail if individuals lack sufficient self-reflection. If they are unable, or unwilling, to question themselves and their actions, or lack of action, then they fail themselves and those that rely on them. To succeed the individual needs to think about the issues and their role. If they are only concerned about day-to-day concerns and have no level of deeper thinking then they 'have neutralised their introspective abilities'.[92] John Locke expected, in particular, those with positions of responsibility, to lead their lives with a level of moral introspection.[93] It is a severe moral failing if, instead, they 'satisfy themselves with lazy ignorance'.[94]

Adam Smith noted the tendency towards self-deception stating that 'we have to overcome the powerful forces of self-deceit'.[95] The senior business manager requires sufficient introspection to imagine how an 'autonomous impartial spectator' would view their actions in order to avoid the risk of self-deception.[96] The manager seeks not only praise but also desires to be seen as 'praiseworthy', as measured by this inner impartial spectator.[97]

Management 'recklessness' and incompetence

It is possible to view senior management and boards as driven by avarice. For example, one view of the savings and loan crisis in 1980s was 'pure greed on the part of too many savings and loan operators, who were contemptuous of fundamental standards of fiduciary responsibility ... spawned and fed the crisis'.[98] This may be the case with a small number of institutions. However, in many others the senior management and boards of financial institutions did not understand their business and were ignorant of the risks being run. There are a number of psychological reasons for this including overweening hubris and an excess of over-confidence.

Business leaders are particularly prone to self-deception. In part, this is due to their close identification with the firm and a tendency to view everything through a business centric lens.[99] It is assisted by a process of 'ethical fading' aided by self-deception. This 'allows the businessman to behave self-interestedly while at the same time believing that he upholds his moral principles'.[100] It is based on a process which 'routinises decisions' and employs a 'language of euphemism'.[101]

Within a complex system not given to moral introspection an 'individual never stops to deliberately ponder the punitive consequences ... and calculate the risks'.[102] This lack of introspection coupled with a certain 'arbeitsfreude' or satisfaction in achievement in the task in hand. This may be viewed a resulting in the 'mut[ing] of conscience'.[103]

This process of following the herd without any self-reflection can be seen in the debasement of language. For example, Wells Fargo Bank described its financial offering as 'solutions' to customer needs and not as 'products' to be sold and a high pressure sales campaign as 'a jump into January'.[104] In part this is due to the employment of language which 'keep thoughts at bay'.[105]

Individuals may rationalise 'wishful thinking' and to detach themselves from the emotions that would normally signify risks, creating rational logical arguments which explain their decisions and actions. The board sponsored report on the conduct failures at Wells Fargo Bank notes a culture of senior management optimism in which problems are 'minimised'.[106] The result may create a collective dynamic which reinforces perverse behaviour through the process of turning a blind eye. The extent of the self-deception is best summed up by the answer of one of the failed bank CEOs 'we thought that... we were on the side of the angels'.[107]

Failures of leadership and ownership

Ethics exist within a context. Much will depend on the situation including the immediate issues, the organisational culture, the roles and related positioning of the individuals concerned, how the issues are presented or 'framed' and the potential harm and benefits and the 'magnitude of the consequences'.[108] Many compliance issues fester when a problem is identified but no one takes ownership of the issue to progress towards a rapid resolution. Instead, there is extensive internal bickering over who should take ownership and mobilise the budget and other resources to address the matter. The consequences were seen recently in the enforcement action against Santander by the FCA. The bank delayed remedial work and customer remediation from when the probate account issues first became known in October 2013. It was not until the end of February 2015 that Santander appointed an individual to lead a team to work on scoping, organising and implementing the remediation project. It is a key part of the compliance role to take ownership and to raise concerns about delay at a very early stage and, if all else fails, quickly to take ownership itself to implement remediation projects on a timetable agreed with the regulator.

Senior management can appear to be high risk-takers. For example, there is a view that: 'sees top management at UBS as having behaved like gamblers at a casino, constantly taking greater risks as their profits and their bonuses increased, until they finally lost everything and almost landed in prison'.[109] However, the opposite was true. The 'problem at UBS was not that the bank's leadership simply ran rampant without any restraint. In fact, the contrary was the case: top management was too complacent, wrongly believing that everything was under control, given that the numerous risk reports, internal audits and external reviews almost always ended in a positive conclusion'.[110] The senior team lacked 'a sense of judgment ... which would have made it possible to recognize the essential problems independently of legal opinions, internal audits and business models. Overall, the top floor at UBS was characterized by a technocratic management style'.[111]

Feldman and Kaplan divide management 'hubris' into two distinct categories.[112] First 'self-justifying non-compliance' can be defined as 'semi-conscious' in that the individuals positive self-image 'distorts the ethical deliberation in a way that presents them in a positive light'.[113] This is particularly, evident where the individual fails to adequately understand the 'harmfulness of their actions, thereby distorting their ethical calculation'.[114] The second type of 'hubris' is described as 'self-blindness' where the perception of reality prevents 'them from recognizing a moral dilemma at all'.[115] As Locke says, self-delusion is a great temptation since 'what suits our wish is fondly believed'.[116] The wish to believe often results in a confirmatory bias where contradictory information or opinions are filtered out. Views which contradict or 'disturb' the perceived or prevailing position are excluded from thought.

This is often the case where it is difficult to identify a specific victim. The individual operating in a state of self-delusion has considerable difficulty in imagining 'the other'.[117] This requires a level of self-understanding and also an appreciation of the possible effect of one's actions on others.[118] It requires a respect for others and a degree of personal humility which some individuals find difficult.[119] It requires a form of inward mirror which 'turn'st mine eyes into my very soul'.[120]

The process of self-reflection permits both a measure of external, objective judgement and develops and reinforces the individual's own self-respect – the 'moral law within me'.[121]

Additionally, and importantly, each person casts a shadow over others around them. They can set an example of self-reflection and this influences the culture in the area within which they work. Staff are always looking at their bosses and take their lead from them. They create a 'shadow'. By employing, what has been termed, the 'management of meaning' it is possible to create important symbols which reflect the views of the senior management and strongly influence all those around them, throughout the business, and beyond.[122] However, it is possible that the 'language of accountability' ('responsibility', 'integrity', etc.) may not be wholly effective since the language is too complex in structure and content to be meaningful. The result has been described as producing 'rhetoric-as-ritual' which become 'incantations' and submerge the 'moral' meaning of words.[123]

There is a need to go beyond the black letter of the law and to think morally. That something is legal or illegal can be said to be 'morally neutral ... it does not require moral integrity but only law-abiding citizens'.[124] However, this is not sufficient. We need to think beyond the rules and regulations and consider what they are trying to do. We need to focus on these objectives and seek to achieve them even if it means going further than what is specifically required by the law. In Kantian terms a failure to exercise reason and to act on that reason threatens self-contempt. The process of reflection may end with the command 'this I ought not to do'. Part of the process of reasoning should be based on an understanding of consequences. It requires an understanding of possible causation 'if I do X it may result in Y' and this process should take account of causative responsibility and hence accountability for the end result. This chain of thinking requires the 'faculty of imagination' and 'the ability to envisage something [or someone] who is not present' or 'representations of things which are not present'.[125]

The ability to 'imagine the other' which requires understanding ourselves and the effect of our actions upon others is central to being a 'just man'.[126] The difficulty of appreciating and understanding others and their perspective 'gives rise to ethics which goes beyond any form of self-fulfilment but is based on generosity, respect and humility'.[127]

Lack of inspiration: the role of organisational purpose and narrative

Generally, financial services, as an industry, is not inspirational. It does not improve individual health or prevent or alleviate illness, nor does it, obviously, make things useful to aid peoples' lives. It does not entertain. Nor does it create works of imagination or garner looks of admiration. Acting compliantly in accord with regulations is unlikely to unleash much by way of moral commitment. 'The law does not generally seek to inspire human excellence or distinction. It is no guide for exemplary behavior – or even good practice. Those managers who define ethics as legal compliance are implicitly endorsing a code of moral mediocrity for their organizations. As Richard Breeden, former chairman of the Securities and Exchange Commission, noted, 'It is not an adequate ethical standard to aspire to get through the day without being indicted'.[128] Consequently, it falls to senior management to provide this inspiration through a number of measures including setting a clear, socially useful purpose for the organisation reinforced by a strong narrative explaining this and each and everyones' role in achieving this aim. This subject is covered at length in Chapter 3.

Many organisations shy away from 'culture' as being too vague and difficult to see and measure. This is not correct. It can be witnessed hour to hour in an organisation for those with eyes to see and it can be measured. The measurement of culture is a fundamental part of the role of the board, senior management and compliance. There are many ways of doing this which are not mutually exclusive. Based on my personal experience, the proper use of staff opinion surveys is critical to success in this area.

Staff opinion survey and the measurement of culture

As mentioned above, staff opinion surveys, if used properly, can be an important means of measuring the cultures within a firm. Further, assessing the various cultures within a business is an important part of the role of compliance. One can be certain that where a poor culture exist there will also be significant compliance and other issues, with significant deficiencies in leadership and management. Compliance does not need to carry out the surveys itself: it can make use the existing corporate reviews. However, compliance does need to make certain that the surveys are undertaken properly and that they are constructed and implemented to a high standard. A poor-quality survey, or one with a low response rate, are themselves key indicators of a firm's culture. It may also indicate how seriously the management and board take the exercise and how they see their responsibilities.

Survey attributes

At the very least a good staff option survey must have the following key attributes. It must:

- cover all the main business areas and locations,
- have a high level of granularity (probably down to a ten person unit),
- include 'engagement' type questions (e.g. 'does the firm turns a blind eye to unethical behaviour?'),
- have all the answers categorised as red, amber and green so that it is possible to compose 'dash-boards' section by section to help to identify potential troubling areas at sight,
- be carried out at least annually,
- be supported by an effective communications plan including support by local management.

Some of these areas are covered in more detail below.

Response rates

These surveys will only be of value if there is a large staff response rate. Firms should aim for a response rate of at least 80%. A low response rate may indicate a local manager who fails to take the survey seriously and sees no value in the exercise. It is possible that they have a jaundiced view of their own staff and that they see rules and regulations as optional too.

Good managers will encourage their teams to complete the surveys and provide time for them to do so. On the other hand, it needs to be made clear to managers that standing over staff as they completed the survey or in any other way intimidating or coercing staff to complete the information is wholly unacceptable and staff should understand this and report bad practices.

In addition, it would be useful if the surveys were supplemented by randomised structured staff interviews and focus groups. These would help provide additional and more impressionistic information on aspects of the firm's cultures. However, these interviews and discussion groups are highly labour intensive and costly so it would be understandable if they were not done.

Communicating the survey and its purpose

It is important that the survey's purpose and importance are clearly communicated. This needs to be done both at the time of the survey's launch and also when the data from the survey is released. The latter needs to include the positive and negative results both for their own areas and for the firm more generally and it should be presented team by team by local managers. There should be a formal process for team discussions to devise a remedial plan. Some recommendations may not be possible (e.g. allocating more staff resources), while others may be doable with little extra cost (e.g. hold joint briefing meetings with another set of teams to improve co-ordination). The results should also be compared against the best firms – outside financial services. This may help as an antidote to complacency and self-congratulation.

The information from each survey round should be considered by the senior executives and the board with a particular focus on those areas which need remedial work. These presentations should be in disaggregated version. This latter point is very important since, in most organisations, troubled teams are usually masked by the more positive attitudes of the majority of workers. Antony Salz, in his review of Barclays, including its culture, found that:

> some of the more qualitative information that could have alerted the Board to fundamental indications of cultural issues was not

169

discussed ... Most of the time, the Board was given aggregated scores which showed that employee satisfaction was increasing year-on-year across the Group. But the Board reports did not consistently include granular data indicating, for example, wide-ranging concerns about escalating ethical issues.[129]

Types of staff engagement questions

There are number of questions which can be asked to obtain a sense of staff engagement with the firm and its management and their perception of the organisation for which they work. These questions essentially test the culture of the business. The following questions are taken from the Banking Standards Board Annual Review.[130]

- I believe senior leaders in my organisation mean what they say and can be trusted,
- In my organisation I see instances where unethical behaviour is rewarded,
- My colleagues act in an honest and ethical way,
- It is difficult to make career progression in my organisation without flexing my ethical standards,
- At my work I feel that I am treated with respect,
- At my work people seek and respect different opinions when making decisions,
- In my organisation Risk and Compliance are both respected functions,
- In my organisation we are encouraged to follow the spirit of the rules (what they mean, not just the words),
- If I raised concerns about the way we work, I would be worried about the negative consequences for me,
- I see people in my organisation turn a blind eye to inappropriate behaviour,
- I feel comfortable challenging a decision made by my manager,
- I believe that my organisation responds effectively to staff feedback.

This is not a definitive list but it does provide a sense of the type of questions which should be asked.

The communication of compliance

When talking about compliance with business managers and their teams, and with senior management and boards it is important to avoid a highly theoretical approach and terminology. Talk of 'frameworks', 'toolboxes', 'matrices' and other conceptual structures becomes so much noise, lacking resonance, and is quickly filtered out by the audience. What really matters are actions which can be 'embedded in daily decision-making'.[131] This could, for example, be in the product approval process, the development of marketing material or the induction of new recruits to the business. Compliance needs to be focused on taking action and needs to use direct language to communicate these actions. For example, the compliance officer can briefly describe the issue and quickly state 'we are doing this ... we will do X by Y date. This will deliver Z. This will resolve A and I will update you by B date' and so on.

There is also the strong risk of what can be described as 'organisational fatigue'. This may occur where, for example, the objectives of change are vague and fail to engage those who have to operate the new methods.[132] For example, line management at UBS's London offices were supposed to supervise the actions of the traders including Kweku Adoboli operating in Global Synthetic Equities ('GSE') business conducted from the London Branch of UBS.

In 2011 Adoboli committed a number of fraudulent transactions which the systems failed to detect until too late causing the business substantial losses and a heavy regulatory fine.[133] The bank's management concerned by the risks posed by a rogue trader had instituted new procedures and checks. However, these all failed for organisational and operational reasons. For example, line management of Adoboli's trading desk before April 2011 rested with the Cash Equities Division in London. Supervisory reports on the trader's activities went to managers in this unit to review and check. This was aided by the fact that the managers were co-located with the traders. In April 2011, as often happens for organisational reasons, line management responsibilities were transferred, in this case to the managers in the GSE Division based in New York.

However, there was a long delay in transferring the supporting control infrastructure from London to New York. Consequently, the previous supervisor continued to receive some of the supervisory reports, despite having no ongoing supervisory responsibilities over the desk but did not review this information since Adoboli's trading desk was no longer their responsibility. Conversely, the new New York management were blissfully unaware of any issues since they received no reports of any problems.[134]

By way of background, many organisations retain cultural 'memories'. Consequently, new processes which are complex or which are not properly explained may be subverted as staff try to apply these new procedures. However, the older, previous practices re-emerge as distortions of the new ways. This can be seen when new IT arrangements are rolled-out with various sub-routines or 'work-arounds' where the full IT system is still incomplete. It is often at these points of tension in the system that failure may be found.

There was an 'historical perceptions' in the UBS/Adoboli case. The Operations Division in London formed part of the systems and controls for trading desks. However, while the controls looked sound in the process manuals, in practice their effectiveness was very weak. Under the previous systems, the Operations Division may not have seen themselves as a control function. Instead, they may have seen their purpose as increasing operational efficiency and sweeping-up trading desk errors such as mismatched trading orders.

The FSA's Final Enforcement Notice against UBS states that the Operations Division, under the old regime, had identified the trading desk 'as generating a large number of breaks [trades which did not settle which could be the result of error or, in this case, fraud]...There appears to have been an expectation from junior personnel in the Operations Division involved with the Desk that it would generate a significant number of breaks, leading them not to investigate further or escalate breaks caused by the trading activity to management'.[135] To a great extent there is a tendency by risk and compliance managers to 'focus on compliance activities and regulatory requirements, via formalised and standardised tools' while it would be better to simply talk to frontline staff about what they actually do using 'simple tools rather than sophisticated risk models'.[136]

Senior management and compliance failed to communicate the altered role of the Operations Division which continued to function as it had before and failed to look for 'trends and patterns' at the trading desk or trader level which 'may have indicated potential unauthorised trading'.[137] Consequently, compliance, and others, believed that the changes had enhanced the regulatory and fraud-prevention controls on the trading desks. Instead the new processes where very fragile and were, in practice, designed to fail. This case is also an example of control units working in closed compartments or silos, considered earlier.

Conclusion

This chapter highlights the organisational structural and psychological issues which may account for poor cultures and behaviours within firms. By way of example it examines some of the central reasons for the widespread mis-selling of structured capital at risk and payment protection insurance products in the United Kingdom. The underlying causes are complex and go beyond superficial views that these marketing strategies were simply the result of greed and misaligned incentives.

The marketing of PPI evidenced a 'moral blindness' in many firms with a complete failure to examine and to think about the details of the product and its value to customers, and the difficulties in promoting such complex products fairly. The senior management, in many cases, failed to look at what the business was doing from the customer's perspective: would both those selling the insurance and the customer understand what was being sold and bought; was it good value for the customer and how would all this look in retrospect. I call the latter the 'cold light of dawn' test – objectively, examined later, would the firm feel ashamed of what they had done – would it be a matter of regret?

The same form of analysis applies to the sale of structured capital at risk products. These types of investment are complex. The investment bankers who devised them were clever and it may have been arrogance, as well as a desire to expand the business that prompted them to push for their marketing to retail bank customers. It may also be an example of the contagious effect of an inadequate culture spreading to other areas within an organisation. Compliance needs to be aware of the business risks of siloed operations and the prevailing culture within each section.

These forms of examination do not fit neatly into a compliance programme. They are difficult to formulate in risk management frameworks. It was possible, over the years, to review sales processes and misjudge that these were fair and that the firm's policies were compliant and that staff followed them to the letter. Nevertheless, the strategy, as a whole, was misbegotten and not properly thought through. Compliance needs to be involved and to intervene at the concept and planning stage. Those devising the strategy need to be truly self-reflective, thinking of the consequences over the longer term. It also requires compliance to take a robust position and to stand its ground.

Compliance needs to be aware both of the structural and cultural risks within a business. Besides its own networks and whistleblowers, discussed in previous chapters, compliance needs to make active use of staff option surveys. The board and other senior management should be doing the same. It is armed with this detailed information that compliance can identify defective cultural 'hot-spots' and, working with others, it can direct its attention and resources accordingly.

Notes

1 Patrick Murphy, 'Creating ethical corporate structures' (1989) *Sloan Management Review*, 30(2), 81–87, 81.
2 Josep Lozano, 'Ethics and corporate culture: a critical relationship' (1998) *Ethical Perspectives*, 5, 53–70, 55.
3 Ibid (Lozano), 57.
4 Hector Sants became chief executive officer in July 2007. The change in style is clearly stated in his speech, 'Delivering intensive supervision and credible deterrence', 'There is a view that people are not frightened of the FSA. I can assure you that this is a view I am determined to correct. People should be very frightened of the FSA... The FSA has been seared by recent events but it is tougher and better as a result', at the Reuters Newsmakers event, 12 March 2009, https://webarchive.nationalarchives.gov.uk/20090320233408/http://

www.fsa.gov.uk/pages/Library/Communication/Speeches/2009/0312_hs.shtml (accessed 19 December 2019).

5 Aristotle, *Nicomachean Ethics*, 1139a22–35 (Penguin Classics edition), 145–146.

6 Bank of England, Fair and Effective Markets Review Final Report (June 2015), 59, https://www.bankofengland.co.uk/report/2015/fair-and-effective-markets-review---final-report (accessed 14 June 2020).

7 Andre Spicer, 'A report on the culture of British retail banking' commissioned by Cass Business School and New City Agenda (2014), 21, http://newcityagenda.co.uk/wp-content/uploads/2014/11/Online-version.pdf (accessed 7 December 2019).

8 Gillian Tett, *The silo effect* (Abacus, London, 2016), 104.

9 Pierre Bourdieu, *Outline of a theory of practice*, Richard Nice (tr) (Cambridge University Press, Cambridge 1977), 173.

10 Simon Ashby, Tommaso Palermo, and Michael Power, 'Risk culture in financial organisation: an interim report' (November 2012), 15, http://www.lse.ac.uk/accounting/assets/CARR/documents/Risk-Culture-in-Financial-Organisations/Risk-culture-interim-report.pdf (accessed 24 April 2019).

11 Ibid ('Risk culture in financial organisation'), 14.

12 Parliamentary Commission on Banking Standards – Minutes of Evidence HL Paper 27-III/HC 175-III, Q3013, McFadden MP, 29 January 2013, https://publications.parliament.uk/pa/jt201314/jtselect/jtpcbs/27/130129.htm (accessed 3 June 2020).

13 FCA Final Notice, Commerzbank, 17 June 2020, 1–2, https://www.fca.org.uk/publication/final-notices/commerzbank-ag-2020.pdf (accessed 2 July 2020).

14 Andrew Bailey, 'The future of financial conduct regulation', speech given on 23 April 2019, https://www.fca.org.uk/news/speeches/future-financial-conduct-regulation (accessed 24 April 2019).

15 Jochen Wittmann, 'Auftragstaktik for business organizations in volatile and uncertain environments: a competence-based view' (Autumn 2017) *IAFOR Journal of Business and Management*, 42(2), 29–49, 42, https://www.researchgate.net/publication/321756066_Auftragstaktik_for_Business_Organizations_in_Volatile_and_Uncertain_Environments_a_Competence-Based_View (accessed 24 April 2019).

16 FCA, 'Approach to supervision' (April 2019), 10–12, https://www.fca.org.uk/publication/corporate/our-approach-supervision-final-report-feedback-statement.pdf (accessed 25 November 2019).

17 Ibid ('Approach to supervision'), 10.

18 Sir David Walker, 'A review of corporate governance in UK banks and other financial industry entities: final recommendations' (November 2009), 27, http://webarchive.nationalarchives.gov.uk/+/http:/www.hm-treasury.gov.uk/d/walker_review_261109.pdf (accessed 5 June 2020).

19 Mollie Painter-Morland, 'Redefining accountability as relational responsiveness' in Mollie Painter-Morland and Patricia Werhane (eds.) *Cutting-edge issues in business ethics* (Springer, New York, 2008), 33.

20 Independent Directors of the board of Wells Fargo Sales Practices Investigation Report (April 2017), 54, https://www08.wellsfargomedia.com/assets/pdf/about/investor-relations/presentations/2017/board-report.pdf (accessed 29 October 2018).

21 Ibid (Wells Fargo Directors' report), 100.

22 Ibid (Wells Fargo Directors' report), 100.

23 Ibid (Wells Fargo Directors' report), 60.

24 Ibid (Wells Fargo Directors' report), 60.

25 FCA Final Notice, Lloyds TSB, 10 December 2013, https://www.fca.org.uk/publication/final-notices/lloyds-tsb-bank-and-bank-of-scotland.pdf (accessed 4 December 2019).
26 Ibid (Final Notice, Lloyds TSB), 2.
27 Ibid (Final Notice, Lloyds TSB), 2.
28 Ibid (Final Notice, Lloyds TSB), 2.
29 Martin Wheatley (former CEO of FSA), speech, 'FSA launches initiative to outlaw flawed sales bonuses that encourage mis-selling' (5 September 2012), https://webarchive.nationalarchives.gov.uk/20121003062553/http://www.fsa.gov.uk/library/communication/pr/2012/084.shtml (accessed 4 December 2019).
30 Ibid (Wheatley 2012 speech).
31 Ibid (Wheatley 2012 speech).
32 Supra note 7 (Spicer),15.
33 Supra note 7 (Spicer), 21.
34 FCA letter to board directors, 'Portfolio strategy letter to firms in the Personal & Commercial Lines Insurer (PL&CL) portfolio: identifying and remedying harms', 8 January 2020, 2, https://www.fca.org.uk/publication/correspondence/letter-firms-personal-commercial-lines-insurer-portfolio-identifying-remedying-harms.pdf (accessed 17 January 2020).
35 Ibid (FCA letter), 2.
36 Ibid (FCA letter), 3.
37 FCA Final Notice, Lloyds Bank, 11 June 2020, 1 and 10, https://www.fca.org.uk/publication/final-notices/lloyds-bank-plc-bank-of-scotland-plc-the-mortgage-business-plc-2020.pdf (accessed 2 July 2020).
38 Ibid (Final Notice, Lloyds Bank), 10.
39 Richard Lambert, 'Banking standards review', 19 May 2014, 6, https://www.bankingstandardsboard.org.uk/pdf/banking-standards-review.pdf (accessed 19 December 2019).
40 Supra note 34 (FCA letter), 3.
41 Supra note 34 (FCA letter), 4.
42 Supra note 34 (FCA letter), 4.
43 Financial Times, 'PPI scandal hits £50bn after claims rise at Lloyds and Barclays', 9 September 2019.
44 Supra note 16 ('Approach to supervision'), 11–12.
45 Alliance and Leicester Reports and Accounts at 31 December 2004 and 2006. Unsecured lending at the respective year ends £3,988m and £5,067m (note 19 of the Report and Accounts).
46 FSA, Final Notice, Alliance & Leicester, October 2008, 9, https://www.fca.org.uk/publication/final-notices/alliance_leicester.pdf (accessed 5 May 2019).
47 Ibid (Final Notice, Alliance & Leicester), 9.
48 Answers to Qs 511 and 512, Helen Weir, Principal Retail Distribution, 2008-10 and CFO, 2004-08, Lloyds Banking Group, on 21 January 2013, oral evidence to Sub-Committee on cross-selling and mis-selling of the Parliamentary Commission on Banking Standards, https://publications.parliament.uk/pa/jt201213/jtselect/jtpcbs/uc860-iii/uc86001.htm (accessed 5 May 2019).
49 Ibid (Oral evidence of Carol Sergeant on 21 January 2013), Answer to Q 654.
50 Parliamentary Commission on Banking Standards, written evidence from Lloyds Banking Group, 4 January 2013, https://publications.parliament.uk/pa/jt201314/jtselect/jtpcbs/27/27ix_we_j04.htm (accessed 27 November 2019).
51 Ibid (Written evidence from Lloyds Banking Group).
52 Ibid (Written evidence from Lloyds Banking Group).

53 Ibid (Written evidence from Lloyds Banking Group).
54 National Audit Office Report, 'Financial services mis-selling: regulation and redress', 24 February 2016, HC 851 Session 2015-16, 9, 'The FCA does not evaluate its chosen redress schemes formally, making it hard to assess whether schemes achieve their intended outcomes', https://www.nao.org.uk/wp-content/uploads/2016/02/Financial-services-mis-selling-regulation-and-redress.a.pdf (accessed 27 November 2019).
55 Alan Au, Executive Director (Banking Conduct), Hong Kong Monetary Authority, quoting Carl Jung, 'Our journey towards sound bank culture – reflections and beyond' (speech given on 14 January 2020), https://www.hkma.gov.hk/eng/news-and-media/speeches/2020/01/20200114-2/ (accessed 22 January 2020).
56 Ibid (Au speech).
57 Ibid (Au speech).
58 Ibid (Au speech).
59 For example, the Financial Reporting Council's comments on the special need for vigilance where companies demonstrate a 'lack of openness to challenge', 'Corporate culture and the role of boards: report of observations' (July 2016), 39, https://www.frc.org.uk/getattachment/3851b9c5-92d3-4695-aeb2-87c9052dc8c1/Corporate-Culture-and-the-Role-of-Boards-Report-of-Observations.pdf (accessed 27 November 2019).
60 FCA, 'Retail and wholesale banking: review of firms' whistleblowing arrangements', 14 November 2018, https://www.fca.org.uk/publications/multi-firm-reviews/retail-and-wholesale-banking-review-firms-whistleblowing-arrangements (accessed 27 November 2019).
61 For example, the term was used by in a speech by the FCA's Jonathan Davidson, Director of Supervision, 'Getting culture and conduct right – the role of the regulator', 13 July 2016, https://www.fca.org.uk/news/speeches/getting-culture-and-conduct-right-role-regulator (accessed 27 November 2019).
62 Supra note 9 (Bourdieu), 190.
63 Aldous Huxley, *The Devils of Loudon* (first published 1952, Harpers Colophon, New York, 1965), 268.
64 Salz review: an independent review of Barclays' business practices (April 2013), 70, https://online.wsj.com/public/resources/documents/SalzReview04032013.pdf (accessed 15 April 2019).
65 Ibid (Salz review), 59.
66 FSA Final Notice, Lloyds TSB, 24 September 2003, 6, https://www.fca.org.uk/publication/final-notices/lloyds-tsb_24sept03.pdf (accessed 29 November 2019).
67 Ibid (Final notice, Lloyds TSB), 6.
68 Ibid (Final notice, Lloyds TSB), 8.
69 FSA Final Notice, Credit Suisse UK, 25 October 2011, 1, https://www.fca.org.uk/publication/final-notices/credit-suisse25oct11.pdf (accessed 3 December 2019).
70 Ibid (Final Notice, Credit Suisse), 10.
71 FSA, Coutts & Company, Final Notice, 7 November 2011, 1, https://www.fca.org.uk/publication/final-notices/coutts.pdf (accessed 3 December 2019).
72 Ibid (Coutts Final Notice), 7.
73 Ibid (Coutts Final Notice), 11.
74 Ibid (Coutts Final Notice), 11.
75 Ibid (Coutts Final Notice), 11.
76 FSA, Coutts & Company, Final Notice, 23 March 2012, 1, https://www.fca.org.uk/publication/final-notices/coutts-mar12.pdf (accessed 3 December 2019).
77 Ibid (Coutts Final Notice), 9 and 10.
78 Ibid (Coutts Final Notice), 10.

79 Carroll Moulton, 'Antiphon the Sophist, on truth' (1972) *Transactions and Proceedings of the American Philological Association*, 103, 329–366.

80 Supra note 5 (Aristotle), 145–146.

81 Grays' rescue, by the Woolwich Equitable Building Society in 1978, was arranged by the Registry of Friendly Societies, the regulator at the time, and the Building Societies Association (a trade body). Woolwich Equitable was acquired, in turn, by Barclays Bank in 2000, Barclays archive, https://www.archive.barclays.com/items/show/5366 (accessed 4 June 2020).

82 Registry of Friendly Societies, 'Grays Building Society – investigation under section 110 of the Building Society Act 1962', May 1979, HMSO Cmnd 7557.

83 New York Times, 'Charles Keating, 90, Key Figure in '80 s Savings and Loan Crisis, Dies', 2 April 2014, https://www.nytimes.com/2014/04/02/business/charles-keating-key-figure-in-the-1980s-savings-and-loan-crisis-dies-at-90.html (accessed 3 June 2020).

84 Ibid (New York Times).

85 Financial Times, 'The executive success factors that lead directly to jail', 10 February 2020.

86 Jan Woike and Sebastian Hafenbrädl, 'Rivals without a cause? Relative performance feedback creates destructive competition despite aligned incentives' (2020) *Journal of Behavioral Decision Making*, 1–15, 2, https://www.researchgate.net/publication/339233864_Rivals_without_a_cause_Relative_performance_feedback_creates_destructive_competition_despite_aligned_incentives (accessed 2 March 2020).

87 Financial Times, 'Royal Life agent on £69,000 charge', 6/7 October 1992.

88 Hansard, written reply by Anthony Nelson MP, Economic Secretary to the Treasury (9 March 1993) Vol 220, col. 503.

89 Supra note 82 (Grays Building Society – investigation), 3–4.

90 Supra note 82 (Grays Building Society – investigation), 68.

91 Supra note 82 (Grays Building Society – investigation), 68.

92 Alan Brener, 'Developing the senior managers regime' in Costanza Russo, Rosa lastra, and William Blair (eds.) *Research handbook on law and ethics in banking and finance* (Edward Elgar, Cheltenham, 2019), 274–301, 294.

93 John Locke, *An essay concerning human understanding* (first published 1710, Thomas Tegg, London, 1846), Book IV, chapter XX, 538.

94 Ibid (Locke), 541.

95 Maria Pia Paganelli, 'Recent engagements with Adam Smith and the Scottish Enlightenment' (2015) *History of Political Economy*, 47(3), 363–394, 369.

96 Jerry Evensky, *Adam Smith's moral philosophy, a historical and contemporary perspective on markets, law, ethics and culture* (Cambridge University Press, Cambridge, 2005), 44–45.

97 Ibid (Evensky), 45.

98 Edwin Gray, 'Warnings ignored: the politics of the crisis' (1990) *Stanford Law and Policy Review*, 2, 138–146, 138.

99 Piet EenkHoorn and Johan Graafland, 'Lying in business: insights from Hannah Arendt's 'Lying in politics'' (2011) *Business Ethics: A European Review*, 20(4), 359–374, 371.

100 Ann Tenbrunsel and David Messick, 'Ethical fading: the role of self-deception in unethical behavior' (2004) *Social Justice Research*, 17(2), 223–236, 224–225.

101 Ibid (Tenbrunsel and Messick), 224–225.

102 Mollie Painter-Morland, 'Redefining accountability as relational responsiveness' in Mollie Painter-Morland and Patricia Werhane (eds.) *Cutting-edge issues in business ethics* (Springer, New York, 2008), 33–45, 38.

103 Peter Gratton, 'An Arendtian approach to business ethics' in Mollie Painter-Morland and Patricia Werhane (eds.) *Cutting-edge issues in business ethics* (Springer, New York, 2008), 202–214, 212.

104 Supra note 20 ('Independent directors of the board of Wells Fargo'), 22 and 23.

105 Harold Pinter, 'Art, truth and politics' (2005) Nobel Prize Lecture, Stockholm, https://www.nobelprize.org/prizes/literature/2005/pinter/25621-harold-pinter-nobel-lecture-2005/.

106 Supra note 20 ('Independent directors of the board of Wells Fargo'), 10.

107 Eric Daniels (former CEO of Lloyds Bank), oral evidence to the PCBS, 14 February 2013, answer to question 4247, https://publications.parliament.uk/pa/jt201213/jtselect/jtpcbs/uc606-xxxvi/uc60601.htm (accessed 4 June 2020).

108 Jeri Beggs and Kathy Dean, 'Legislated ethics or ethics education? faculty views in the post-Enron era' (2007) *Journal of Business Ethics*, 71, 15–37, 18.

109 Tobias Straumann, 'The UBS crisis in historical perspective' (2010), Expert Opinion for UBS AG, University of Zurich, Institute for Empirical Research in Economics, 1–16, 3.

110 Ibid (Straumann), 3.

111 Ibid (Straumann), 21.

112 Yuval Feldman and Yotam Kaplan, 'Behavioral ethics as compliance' in Van Rooij and Sokol (eds.) *Cambridge Handbook of Compliance* (September 2019), Bar Ilan University Faculty of Law Research Paper No. 19–18, Forthcoming: https://ssrn.com/abstract=3458582 or http://dx.doi.org/10.2139/ssrn.3458582 (accessed 16 December 2019).

113 Ibid (Feldman and Kaplan), 22.

114 Ibid (Feldman and Kaplan), 22.

115 Ibid (Feldman and Kaplan), 22.

116 Supra note 93 (Locke), 544.

117 April Capili, 'The created ego in Levinas 'totality and infinity' (2011) *Sophia*, 50(4), 677–692, 685 and 691.

118 Ibid (Capili), 685 and 691.

119 Carl Rhodes, 'Organizational justice' in Mollie Painter-Morland and René Ten Bos (eds.) *Business ethics and continental philosophy* (Cambridge University Press, Cambridge, 2011) 141–161, 150–151.

120 William Shakespeare, 'Hamlet', Gertrude, Act III, Scene 3.

121 Immanuel Kant, Critic of practical reason (first published 1788, Werner Phuhar (tr), Hackett, Indianapolis, 2002), Conclusion to Part II, line 162, page 203.

122 Dan Gowler and Karen Legge, 'The meaning of management and the management of meaning: a view from social anthropology' in *Perspectives on management: a multidisciplinary analysis* (Oxford University Press, Oxford, 1983) 197–233.

123 Ibid (Gowler and Legge), 213–214 and 229–230.

124 Hannah Arendt, *Responsibility and judgement* (first published in 1971 and reprinted by Shocken Books, New York, 2003), 68.

125 Ibid (Arendt), 139 and 189.

126 Supra note 117 (Capili), 685 and 691.

127 Supra note 119 (Rhodes), 150–151.

128 Lynn Paine, 'Managing for organizational integrity' (1994) *Harvard Business Review*, 72(2), 106–117, 111.
129 Supra note 64 (Salz review), 91,.
130 Banking Standards Board Annual Review 2018/19, Annex C, 70 and 71, https://www.bankingstandardsboard.org.uk/pdf/banking-standards-annual-review-2018–2019.pdf (accessed 15 April 2019).
131 Tommaso Palermo, Michael Power, and Simon Ashby, 'Navigating institutional complexity: the production of risk culture in the financial sector' (2017) *Journal of Management Studies*, 54(2), 165, 154–181.
132 Ibid ('Navigating institutional complexity'), 167.
133 FSA Final Notice, UBS AG (25 November 2012) – (re Kweku Adoboli), 1–2, https://www.fca.org.uk/publication/final-notices/ubs-ag.pdf (accessed 23 April 2019).
134 Ibid (Final Notice, UBS), 6.
135 Ibid (Final Notice, UBS), 8.
136 Marika Arena, Michela Arnaboldi, and Tommaso Palermo, 'The dynamics of (dis)integrated risk management: a comparative field study' (2017) *Accounting, Organizations and Society*, 62, 65–81, 67.
137 Supra note 133 (Final Notice, UBS), 14.

8

TRAINING CORPORATE ORGANISATIONS TO BE COMPLIANT

Introduction

'Believe it or not, you can become a Chief Risk Officer or a Head of Compliance or Head of Internal Audit with no formal qualifications. This is just plain wrong. These roles are now equally as important as the CFO's (Chief Financial Officer) job and we need to be totally confident in their technical competence, their skills and their integrity'.[1] All these individuals can damage both the company and its stakeholders, including customers. They can also destroy any trust in the industry as a result of their incompetence and inability to do their job. Just like all the heads of all the control functions, all board member and business employees need to be properly trained. It is critical to the success of the firm and the effectiveness of financial services regulation. Ensuring that this training is done and that it is effectively forms an important part of the role of compliance.

Except for the very smallest firms, businesses are dependent on staff to whom power and responsibility have been delegated. Clearly the actions, and inactions, of these individuals may promote or damage the firm and its stakeholders, including customers. Consequently, it is vitally important that staff understand what they should or should not do. Some of this, as discussed earlier, will come from recruiting and retaining people with the right attitude and ethos. It is also derived from the approach taken by management and, also, the whole culture of the firm itself. Ensuring a high level of continuous training and communication is important to create – and maintain – this ethos.

There are some specific roles where UK rules require training of the incumbents. For example, under the FCA's Training and Competence Rules (TC) for investment and mortgage advisers.[2] Besides these very specialised jobs it is somewhat surprising that in the United Kingdom the regulators have been largely mute in this area since the early 2000s. Additionally, the UK's financial services legislation requires that certain individuals covered by the Senior Managers and Certified Persons Regime (SM&CR) are trained and competent.[3] The regulatory requirements implementing the legislation state the need for training for the select group falling within the scope of the SM&CR, but what this should be is not specified.[4] The regulations regarding the need for competence and training for other staff is limited.[5]

The lack of specificity and the lack of regulatory emphasis on training for all those in regulated organisations forms a large gap which the compliance function must make good.

This chapter highlights the importance of training for financial services staff; training methods and how to measure their effectiveness; the misuse of training and related issues; formal compliance qualifications; and, finally, US regulatory guidance on the subject.

The importance of training

As mentioned in other chapters, much of what has gone wrong in financial services is not due to malice and, often, it is also not due to avarice. Much more frequently, it is caused by a lack of knowledge and understanding. Many board members and senior executives lacked the technical knowledge necessary to do their jobs satisfactorily and they frequently failed to appreciate this failure. In many instances they did not understand, for example, the fragility of banking and the risks being run by the business. This lack of competence and professionalism can and should be remedied by formal training.

Training is a good thing in itself. It should permeate all levels of the organisation both as a means of developing people so that they can use all their potential, and as a means of benefiting the firm directly.

Moreover, training for the board and executive team aids good corporate governance. It needs to be extended to all staff for a number of reasons, including developing staff engagement and also as part of good communications within the firm. Consequently, it should be high on the list of a firm's priorities. If done well it can engage employees; and engaging staff is part of the process of building and developing a good culture within the business.

In addition to the more usual forms of training covering, for example, professional skills, management development and the like, many firms will have a programme of mandatory training. These will address the particular risks associated with the business as well as more generic ones covering, for example, fire and accident prevention. Some of this training will be delivered face-to-face but, very frequently, it will take the form of computer-based training (CBT) which all staff are required to undertake on a regular and frequent basis. CBT is often reinforced by on-line assessments with a pass mark which must be achieved for the individual to be deemed as competent.

Although most organisations recognise the importance of training it is often delegated far down the business ranks and – shamefully – is often one of the first areas to be cut in the face of financial difficulties. For these reasons and others, it is often difficult to identify successful training schemes. These issues are considered in the next two sections, following a look at US regulatory guidance in this area.

US regulatory guidance on training

The US Department of Justice has issued guidance on what it expects to see in staff training programmes in financial service firms. Central to this is the need to ensure that training is distributed across the organisation and the extent to which the content of the training is understood and absorbed by the firm's staff.[6] Training should be risk-based with evidence of the analysis undertaken to determine who should be trained and on what subjects.

There should be an examination of past misconduct to address risks requiring specific training and the role of high-risk business areas and the appropriate training required.[7]

The effectiveness of the training needs to be tested and assessed. This process needs to address the following questions:

- has the training been offered in the form and language appropriate for the audience,
- is the training provided online or in-person (or both), and what is the company's rationale for its choice,
- has the training addressed lessons learned from prior compliance incidents,
- how has the company measured the effectiveness of the training,
- have employees been tested on what they have learned,
- how has the company addressed employees who fail all or a portion of the testing?[8]

The United Kingdom would benefit from adopting this guidance.

Indicators of an effective training programme

Much will depend on how seriously the business takes training. There are a number of measures which can be used to assess this. These include:

- ensuring that all staff undertake the training and pass the assessment. This must include all executives since they need to set an example and be held to the same standards as everyone else and must not be permitted to excuse themselves due to 'pressure of work' – there are many other staff who could claim the same,
- providing policies, procedures and training material written in clear, jargon-free language in a style which resonates with the target audience. It must at all costs be free of legal terminology,

- checking that all staff who commit to attend face-to-face training actually do attend and stay throughout the programme. Significant non-attendance, including patterns of absence, is another indicator that something is wrong; either in specific pockets or across the whole organisation,
- effective monitoring of the training to ensure that it is properly delivered and that there is no cheating or manipulation of the training assessments. This could include, for example, CBT which is completed too quickly, teams all doing the training at the same time and completing the work together, and with the same assessment marks. This might suggest an element of management 'coaching',
- ensuring that effective public action is taken against those who fail to do the training at all, or within the required time period, or who do not pass the assessments,
- updating the training material regularly to ensure it is kept relevant to the type of business,
- maintaining the training programmes, covering both content and delivery. This must be the responsibility of a senior member of staff with sufficient budget and other resources. It is not sufficient to 'bury' this responsibility within a 'training and development' team. The relevant board committee must take an active interest in training and monitor its application and effectiveness,
- Performing regular and independent assessments of the effectiveness of the training and its delivery. Essentially, this means ensuring that the training delivers its objectives.
- Reporting the results of all this work to the executive team and the relevant board committee and taking remedial action, if necessary, as a consequence.

The quality of training, and the seriousness with which it is undertaken are really tests, and a measure, of a firms' management. It assesses what the latter see as truly important and is one method by which they communicate to staff, regulators and other stakeholders what they consider important and the value they really place on compliant actions rather than mere fine words.

Measuring training effectiveness

The effectiveness of training needs to be tested. This needs to include levels of recall days, weeks and months after the training is delivered, how it is assessed (e.g. use of on-line staff tests with an acceptable pass rate requirement). The US Department of Justice will question firms as to how they assess the quality and effectiveness of their compliance training.[9] However, a global survey across a range of industries, by Deloitte, a consultancy and accounting firm, and Compliance Week, a US trade journal, found that 'organizations are still measuring their compliance program effectiveness by utilizing internal audit, monitoring compliance training completion rates'.[10]

Activity measures 'are entirely the wrong metrics to use' for assessing the effectiveness of training.[11] This provides the facade of compliance without any substance. Clearly, this fails every measure and is very unlikely to satisfy regulators, courts and the like.[12]

What are needed are assessments which measure the relevance of the training and its effectiveness (i.e. how much employees actually learn and put into practice).[13] Measuring the effectiveness of compliance training should be subject to close board scrutiny due to its importance in ensuring that companies and their staff do the right thing - anything else is likely to be a mere delusion. It is possible to use regression analysis to help understand the relationship between training as delivered and actual staff behaviour.[14] There are a number of measures which may be used to gauge not just the effectiveness of training but also the underlying culture of the organisation. As mentioned earlier, these include course attendance and last-minute candidate withdrawals from the course and a more subjective assessment of engagement on the course (e.g. use of smartphones during teaching and group work, taking phone calls etc. and levels of participation during team exercises). These types of measures are important and indicate the training culture within the firm and how seriously training is taken. However, it does not indicate the success of the training.

'The impact of training also depends on the organizational culture in which it occurs'.[15] The assessment of the effectiveness of the training needs to be divided into two elements. First, those that 'denotes the successful recall or recognition' of processes (e.g. 'know your customer' procedures as part of an anti-money laundering programme). This is known as 'skill retention' and measured over a specified 'retention interval'.[16] This is sometimes called 'procedural compliance'.[17] Second, and more importantly, is 'attitude retention' which is used to determine whether the training has enabled the employee to 'achieve desired outcomes'.[18] This important element of training is aimed at getting trainees to think about what they are doing so that they can apply what they have learnt, intelligently, to unfamiliar situations while keeping a focus on the intended outcome.

Measuring 'outcomes' is more important for assessing this aspect. It is reinforced by training that encourages a 'questioning mind' so that the trainee can 'more readily recognize when something is wrong and handle any anomaly more effectively'.[19]

There are a number of 'outcome' measures of success. These may include an increase in the number of concerns and advice requests recorded on anonymous help-lines and staff attitudinal views as evidence of individuals, for whatever reason, taking action in response to awareness and training programmes.[20] Nevertheless, there remain issues with training both in the methods used to train and in the underlying culture within the firm.

Issues with training

There remain doubts. For example, there are questions about the effectiveness of mandatory corporate training programmes. There are, for example, a number of studies of diversity training. These found that 'diversity training in the corporate arena has a checkered history and a plethora of critics who are convinced that such efforts are a waste of time and money'.[21] Afterwards, many who took part in this type of training, left feeling 'confused, angry, or with more animosity'.[22] Training in this area, and others, is fraught.[23] However, it is worth noting that much of the research work on ethics training has been focused on the reaction of participant in the training rather than an examination of behavioural effects and changes in decision making.[24]

Ethical training can also lead to a form self-justifying righteousness. For example, an organisation that goes out of its way to badge itself as ethical (e.g. the UK's Coop Bank in the lead-up to its debacle) can produce a strong feeling of identification in its staff which, in turn, increases 'employees' tendencies to feel psychologically close to the organization and to incorporate the organizational image into their own'.[25] The downside of this, in such organisations, is a view that what we do must be morally right without any objective consideration of whether this is true in fact.

Cynically, some of this training may be seen as defensive: undertaken to protect the company from enforcement action or litigation. 'For example, when training is done merely to satisfy for example certification requirements, employee performance with respect to safety is unlikely to improve'.[26]

There may also be issues with some elements of anti-bribery and corruption training in cultures where a reciprocation of gift exchanges is seen as socially acceptable and the norm. It is suggested that this issue can be best addressed by making it clear in the training 'that corrupt behavior is not justifiable and will not be tolerated, even if it is considered part of prevailing sociocultural practices'.[27]

There is evidence from research the ethics training highlights to participants the extent of unpunished corruption in their area with the result that they started to regard such behaviour as normal after the attending these courses.[28] The consequence was a reduction in the level of unethical behaviour reporting as this became the accepted norm.[29] The training could be seen as a 'consciousness-raising experience' as the scales dropped from the eyes of new entrants to the organisation.[30] The result was cynicism ('everyone is doing it'), disillusionment and a rejection of personal accountability. It has been described as a gradual process as one unreported and unpunished infraction after another produces a 'slippery-slope' of indifference and moral decay.[31] The individual with a strong moral compass will leave as soon as possible while others 'shirked the discreditable evidence which was painful, and jumped at the impressive slogans'.[32]

Training methods

This chapter does not aim to describe, in any detail, the list of possible teaching methods. It is an axiom that good, effective training is time consuming and may need to be repeated with some frequency. However, there are a number of innovative approaches. More traditional techniques such as role-playing can also be very effective but are very resource intensive.

High quality videos are a common means of CBT. Often these include a story with actors in a realistic setting, relevant to the firm, and which are immediately recognisable to those being trained. Three or four characters are developed and presented in a series of scenarios. Choices are presented to the viewer who chooses a particular course for one character and the story proceeds to show what might happen for good or ill. This leads to a further narrative and another set of choices and so on. The trainee is thus drawn in and engaged. If the trainee has not made the best decisions the video will question this and show a better set of decisions and why. There are many variants on this. The subjects covered by the interactive video can relate to raising concerns, harassment at work, various forms of corruption, data protection and so on.

I recall watching one of the first training videos as a trainee chartered accountant called the 'Auditor in court'. It took the form of an actor playing the role of an audit partner being cross-examined in court as part of a financial negligence case. It included how the audit was planned, controlled and supervised by the partner. In the cold light of the court's enquiry the work done by the partner and his explanations were unpicked one by one in cross-examination. It made a significant impression on all who viewed it and certainly changed their behaviour, with many who watched it going back to review their current work.[33]

Another innovation is the use of actor-controlled avatars in a virtual reality.[34] It allows trainees to explore difficult scenarios and permits the training to be recorded and reviewed by independent observers and trainers. This form of training may work best where there are a range of potentially acceptable approaches with no single correct answer.

A particular difficulty is, unlike other recognised professions, there is no generally accepted training or set of qualifications for compliance staff. There are some courses which help in this area but there is more to be done in raising the professional status of members of the compliance team.

Formal compliance academic training and qualifications

Without seeking to promote any one set of compliance academic training and qualifications, it is worth noting a number of developments at some of the UK and US universities in this area.

UK university post-graduate courses

In the United Kingdom a number of universities provide post-graduate Masters courses in law with a specialism in regulatory compliance (e.g. University College London and Queen Mary University London – I teach on the UCL course).[35] Others include financial services compliance as part of a more economics-focused Masters course (e.g. the Banking Regulation and Financial Stability module forms part of Bristol University's MSc on the same subject).[36] From a different perspective, some universities offer post-graduate courses which are more practitioner focused such as Reading University's MSc in capital markets, regulation and compliance, with a heavy emphasis on capital markets.[37] A number of other universities include financial services regulation as part of the post-graduate banking MSc courses (e.g. Bangor University).[38]

US university courses

The United States provides a range of specialist compliance courses including both on-line and campus based teaching (e.g. the New York City-based PACE University, Lubin School of Business) covering corporate governance, key regulatory areas and developing and leading a compliance team.[39] Others have LLM courses focused on banking and compliance (e.g. Boston University's Banking and Financial Law LLM or Boston College's LLM with modules on banking regulation).[40]

Executive training

Most firms will provide some level of training and briefings for new board directors and some updates for existing members of the executive and board. This is an area worth developing further since even experienced directors, new to the organisation, may not understand all aspects of the bank and its risks. In many instances, any formal training they had was some time ago and would merit refreshing and updating. Good directors will appreciate their own knowledge weaknesses and not view the need for more training as a personal reflection on their competence.

Training, as mentioned earlier, requires a heavy investment in time and non-executive directors may begrudge this additional call on their diaries. However, they need to reflect on their personal exposure to the risk of things going wrong and how they would respond to a subsequent enquiry or disciplinary hearing when cross-examined by a QC [Queen's Counsel] about what training they did or did not do.

There are a number of steps they could take, supported by the business. For example, the Irish Institute of Banking, a professional body for bankers, has a course designed for bank board directors – the Certified Bank Director programme.[41] It is a ten-day programme, divided into two blocks aimed at providing both non-executive and executive directors with a 'comprehensive understanding of the unique governance issues associated with banks arising from the inherent complexity of banking business models and their risk profile. It will provide a practical understanding of the duties and responsibilities of directors and the behaviours required from them and from well-functioning boards'.[42] The course includes lessons from the recent financial crisis; regulation; risk issues of all types, especially those peculiar to banking; the role of the bank board and individual directors; corporate governance; issues around strategic models and so on.

The course is assessed by each director keeping a 'learning journal' covering each module of the course. 'A learning journal is a reflective log that records a participant's learning experience of a particular topic/ module. It allows participants to reflect on how their study and learning has developed during each module, what they are learning and the relevance or application of this learning to their own experiences in a work setting. The learning journal will be evaluated and graded by the Academic Directors to assess the participant's knowledge, synthesis, analysis and development'.[43]

There will be other equivalent courses for bank board directors provided by other organisations. This may be an area where the regulators could require, or at least encourage, all bank board directors to undertake this or similar forms of training and development.

Conclusion

The importance of training as a tool of financial services regulation has not been given sufficient emphasis by the financial services regulators. It is not clear why this is the case. It is important to see it is as largely an investment by the business in its future. Many of the problems created by firms are a consequence of incompetence rather than direct malice. Other firms have suffered as a result of a lack of professionalism with a consequential failure to 'anchor' the actions and judgements of individuals on the secure ground of professional knowledge and experience. Good quality training also provides each individual with a benchmark against which to make their own judgements and for each to make their own independent assessments.

An adequate programme of training for all staff, properly delivered and reinforced, is an indicator of the firm's culture. It demonstrates a commitment both to helping to ensure the organisation's future coupled with a desire to develop the full potential of its staff.

There is a cost to all this but it is likely to be a fraction of the cost of failure due to ignorance and misjudgement. Misdirected training, used mainly as a shield to deflect regulators and litigation, will be seen as such by employees and the regulators. It will result in cynicism and distrust.

The training needs to be effective and its effectiveness measured using appropriate indicators. With the right spirit, and a high standard of execution, it should also assist in helping to build the all-important trust with the regulators. There is also a role for the regulators to support this training work at all levels in regulated firms, including those on the boards of financial institutions.

Finally, training needs to viewed as part of a bigger enterprise in developing the professionalism of the business and its employees and management. For each person to be the best they can be is beneficial not only to the individual and the firm but also to society as a whole. It helps inspire endeavour and helps sets high standards in competence and judgement.

Notes

1 Parliamentary Commission on Banking Standards, Paul Moore written evidence, 13 May 2013, 3.1, https://publications.parliament.uk/pa/jt201314/jtselect/jtpcbs/27/27v_we94.htm (accessed 24 February 2020).
2 FCA, Handbook, 'TC App 1.1 activities and products/sectors to which TC applies subject', https://www.handbook.fca.org.uk/handbook/TC/App/1/1.html (accessed 12 May 2020); TC TP 3 Regulated Mortgage Contracts: assessments of competence under the Mortgage Code Compliance Board Rules, https://www.handbook.fca.org.uk/handbook/TC/TP/3/3.html (accessed 12 May 2020).
3 'the authorised person must have regard, in particular, to whether the candidate, or any person who may perform a function on the candidate's behalf—has obtained a qualification, has undergone, or is undergoing, training, possesses a level of competence, or has the personal characteristics, required by general rules made by the regulator in relation to persons performing functions of the kind to which the application relates'. (s60A, Vetting of candidates by relevant authorised persons, Financial Services and Markets Act 2000).
4 For example, PRA and FCA, 'Consultation paper, 'FCA CP14/13 and PRA CP14/14 strengthening accountability in banking: a new regulatory framework for individuals'', April 2014, 45, https://www.fca.org.uk/publication/consultation/cp14-13.pdf (accessed 12 May 2020).
5 For example, para 24, The Money Laundering, Terrorist Financing and Transfer of Funds (Information on the Payer) Regulations 2017, 'A relevant person must take appropriate measures to ensure that its relevant employees are made aware of the law relating to money laundering and terrorist financing, and to the requirements of data protection, which are relevant to the implementation of these Regulations; and regularly given training in how to recognise and deal with transactions and other activities or situations which may be related to money laundering or terrorist financing'.

6 US Department of Justice Criminal Division, 'Evaluation of corporate compliance programs, guidance document updated', April 2019, JM 9–28.800, 5, https://www.justice.gov/criminal-fraud/page/file/937501/download (accessed 11 February 2020).

7 Ibid (DOJ guidance), 5.

8 Ibid (DOJ guidance), 5.

9 US Department of Justice Criminal Division, 'Evaluation of corporate compliance programs: guidance document', April 2019, 4–5, https://www.justice.gov/criminal-fraud/page/file/937501/download (accessed 9 April 2020).

10 'Compliance week In focus: 2016 compliance trends survey' (2016), 4, https://www2.deloitte.com/content/dam/Deloitte/us/Documents/governance-risk-compliance/us-advisory-compliance-week-survey.pdf (accessed 8 April 2020).

11 Hui Chen and Eugene Soltes, 'Why compliance programs fail—and how to fix them' (March–April 2018), *Harvard Business Review*, 116–125, 122–123, https://hbr.org/2018/03/why-compliance-programs-fail (accessed 14 May 2020).

12 Ibid (Chen and Soltes), 122–123.

13 Ibid (Chen and Soltes), 122–123.

14 Ibid (Chen and Soltes), 125.

15 Yi Lu, Karen Marais, and Shu-guang Zhang, 'Conceptual modeling of training and organizational risk dynamics' (2014) *Procedia Engineering*, 80, 313–328, 317.

16 Ibid ('Conceptual modeling'), 320.

17 James Winnefeld, Christopher Kirchhoff, and David Upton, 'Cybersecurity's human factor: lessons from the Pentagon' (September 2015) *Harvard Business Review*, 93(9), 88–96, 90–91, https://hbr.org/2015/09/cybersecuritys-human-factor-lessons-from-the-pentagon (accessed 18 May 2020).

18 Supra note 15 ('Conceptual modeling'), 320.

19 Supra note 17 ('Cybersecurity's human factor'), 90–91.

20 Linda Treviño and others, 'Legitimating the legitimate: a grounded theory study of legitimacy work among Ethics and Compliance Officers' (2014) *Organizational Behavior and Human Decision Processes*, 123, 186–205, 191.

21 Rohini Anand and Mary-Frances Winters, 'A retrospective view of corporate diversity training from 1964 to the present' (2008) *Academy of Management Learning and Education*, 7(3), 356–372, 356, http://www.wintersgroup.com/corporate-diversity-training-1964-to-present.pdf (accessed 15 November 2019).

22 Ibid (Anand and Winters), 361.

23 Frank Dobbin and Alexandra Kalev, 'Why diversity programs fail' (July/August 2016) *Harvard Business Review*, https://hbr.org/2016/07/why-diversity-programs-fail (accessed 15 November 2019).

24 Logan Steele and others, 'How do we know what works? A review and critique of current practices in ethics training evaluation' (2016) *Accountability in Research*, 23(6), 319–350, 334.

25 Sean Martin, Jennifer Kish-Gephart, and James Detert, 'Blind forces: ethical infrastructures and moral disengagement in organizations' (2014) *Organizational Psychology Review*, 4(4), 295–325, 309. The issues involving the Coop Bank are set out in a report by Sir Christopher Kelly, 'Failings in management and governance: report of the independent review into the events leading to the Co-operative Bank's capital shortfall', 30 April 2014, https://assets.ctfassets.net/5ywmq66472jr/3LpckmtCnuWiuuuEM2qAsw/9bc99b1cd941261bca5d674724873deb/kelly-review.pdf (accessed 7 July 2020).

26 Supra note 15 ('Conceptual modeling'), 325.

27 Christian Hauser, 'Fighting against corruption: does anti-corruption training make any difference?' (2019) *Journal of Business Ethics*, 159(1), 281–299, 294–295.

28 Mary Curtis and John Williams, 'The impact of culture and training on code of conduct effectiveness: reporting of observed unethical behavior' in *Research on professional responsibility and ethics in accounting* (Vol 18; Emerald Group Publishing, Bingley, England), 1–31, 23.

29 Ibid (Curtis and Williams), 23.

30 Jill Graham, 'Principled organizational dissent' (1983), Northwestern University, ProQuest Dissertations Publishing, 8.

31 Gino Francesca and Max Bazerman, 'When misconduct goes unnoticed: the acceptability of gradual erosion in others' unethical behavior' (2009) *Journal of Experimental Social Psychology*, 45, 708–719, 718.

32 The process is similar to that of 'Gleichschaltung' or 'moral and organisational coordination' employed by Nazi Germany to gain societal acceptance, 'Gleichschaltung' in Germany and Austria in CL Mowat (ed.) *The New Cambridge Modern History* (Cambridge University Press, Cambridge, 1968), 496–499, 496.

33 'Auditor in court' video, available on YouTube, https://www.youtube.com/watch?v=oEgCMZRgJLs (accessed 13 November 2019).

34 Clayton Christensen Institute website, 'Innovation worth watching: Mursion', https://www.christenseninstitute.org/blog/innovators-worth-watching-mursion/ (accessed 15 November 2019).

35 UCL website, https://www.ucl.ac.uk/laws/study/llm-master-laws/llm-modules-2020-21 (accessed 4 February 2020); Queen Mary University London website, https://www.qmul.ac.uk/law/postgraduate/courses/llm/modules/ (accessed 4 February 2020).

36 Bristol University website, https://www.bris.ac.uk/unit-programme-catalogue/RouteStructure.jsa?byCohort=N&ayrCode=20/21&programmeCode=9EFIM007T (accessed 4 February 2020).

37 Reading University website, https://www.icmacentre.ac.uk/study/masters/masters-in-capital-markets-regulation-and-compliance#%20entry-requirements (accessed 4 February 2020).

38 Bangor University website, https://www.bangor.ac.uk/courses/postgraduate/banking-and-finance-msc (accessed 4 February 2020).

39 PACE University website, https://www.pace.edu/lubin/departments-and-research-centers/center-for-global-governance-reporting-and-regulation/ccrp (accessed 4 February 2020).

40 Boston University website, https://www.bu.edu/law/academics/llm-masters-degrees/banking-financial-law/courses-of-study/ (accessed 4 February 2020); Boston College website, https://www.bc.edu/content/bc-web/schools/law/academics-faculty/fusion-search.html (accessed 4 February 2020).

41 Irish Institute of Banking website, Certified Bank Director course, https://iob.ie/programme/certified-bank-director (accessed 26 June 2020).

42 Ibid (Irish Institute of Banking website).

43 Ibid (Irish Institute of Banking website).

9

LESSONS FOR COMPLIANCE OFFICERS FROM REGULATORY ENFORCEMENT: THE UK EXPERIENCE

Introduction

This chapter looks at the regulatory risks run by UK compliance officers. It is an area of increasing personal accountability. Existing compliance officers, and those that aspire to this position, need to be aware of the dangers and the possible ways of avoiding falling foul of the regulatory supervision and enforcement teams. The risks have increased in reason years for a range of reasons including the advent of the Senior Managers and Certified Persons Regime (SM&CR) discussed in earlier chapters.

This chapter also looks at a number of regulatory enforcement actions against compliance officers. The lessons from these cases reinforce the need for compliance officers to be competent, open and honest with the regulators, and to report problems quickly and honestly. It also considers the risks relating to the regulatory use of 'attestation letters' and how these may expose the compliance officer, and others, to personal sanction.

The increasing regulatory risks run by compliance officers

There has been a move by both the UK and US regulators towards increased personal accountability. Individual board members and senior staff are now being held personally accountable. This is in addition to regulatory action against the regulated firms themselves.

Since 2011 the regulators, and the FCA in particular, have targeted compliance officers and there has been at least one example which has been made public of them rejecting an application for an appointment as a compliance office on the grounds that the individual lacked competence.[1] It is worth examining these dozen cases in detail to see what lessons may be learnt and to compare this with the approach taken by the US regulatory authorities, primarily the Securities and Exchange Commission (SEC), a subject covered in depth in the next chapter.

In the United Kingdom there are a number of examples of enforcement action against compliance officers, which, in many ways, parallel those in the United States. These include the FCA's action against Anthony Willis, the compliance officer at Bank of Beirut (UK), in 2015 for failing to be open with the regulator. He claimed in his defence that 'at times he felt under pressure from senior management to be 'careful' in his communications with the Authority and that he was not given 'licence' to explain issues fully to the Authority'.[2] This defence was sharply rebuffed by the FCA. The case is considered in more detail later in this chapter.

The most serious offence by a compliance officer is failing to be open and honest with the regulator. The latter rely almost totally on the compliance officer and, as discussed elsewhere in this book, lying breaks the bond of trust absolutely. In other cases, the regulator appears to have been vexed by the compliance officer's failure to heed earlier regulatory warnings. However, most of the cases covered in the following sections related to weak and incompetent compliance officers who failed to ensure that the processes within the regulated firms were of a sufficiently high standard. The compliance officers, generally, as far as it is possible to tell, were not highly-paid. Many had problems paying the regulatory fines levied. Some of them appear to have been bullied by senior executives and their contacts with board non-executive directors and the firm's chairman were also, apparently, limited. However, it is not possible to ascertain from the available information whether the firm, due to its poor culture, sought out weak individuals for the compliance officer role. Many of the businesses, and their business models, were clearly high risk in regulatory terms and the compliance officers in these firms may have been taking a gamble on working in such high-profile roles in such organisations. The boards and senior executives of these businesses may have sought out and got the compliance officers they wanted.

However, the central lesson from many of the major enforcement cases is the absence of any effective compliance function. The failure of compliance to intervene, and often the function's complete absence, are remarkable in all these cases. The weaknesses, in its various guises, of compliance is a theme throughout this book. In all these enforcement cases compliance had no adequate role. This book seeks to suggest how this void can be filled and compliance made more effective and engaged.

Background

There have been very few UK regulatory enforcement actions against compliance officers considering the number of enforcement cases against regulated firms each year. None have taken place in recent years in relation to issues post the introduction of the Senior Managers and Certified Persons Regime in 2016.

Every regulated business has a compliance officer and, in view of the facts, it is often difficult to see why regulatory action was not taken against the individual compliance officers in many more cases. It is not clear how they could have satisfied the regulatory expectations placed upon them. Nevertheless, it is worth considering the few, apparently, unlucky compliance officers who were taken through the regulatory disciplinary process to see what lessons can be learnt. The cases, set out below, represent every known enforcement case against a compliance officer of a firm of any substance in the United Kingdom.

Peter Johnson

Peter Johnson was the compliance officer for Keydata until the end of 2008. He was responsible for checking and approving financial product promotions by the company. He was also the man responsible for reporting the findings of his oversight work to the company's board.[3]

The regulator found that despite getting professional advice the firm's financial promotions 'contained unclear, incorrect and misleading statements', that the compliance officer's checking work was inadequate, and that the risks in the Lifemark Portfolio were not managed and were not made clear to customers and their advisors.[4] In addition, the compliance officer deliberately mislead the regulator about the product and its performance.[5] He also allowed the product to be sold, even after he was aware that it was highly illiquid and that it breached the taxation regulations.[6] Moreover, he was not proactive in notifying the regulator of the product's poor performance and the concerns expressed by professional advisors.[7] It would appear that his failure to be open and honest with the regulator and his failure to change course in the light of professional advice were central to the decision to take regulatory action against him personally.

As a consequence, following the collapse of Keydata itself, some 37,000 customers who had bought the product, investing almost £0.5Bn, were paid compensation by the Financial Services Compensation Scheme of over £300m.[8]

Sanction

But for his poor financial position Johnston would have been fined £200,000. For this reason he was not fined but he was banned from holding a regulated position in the industry.[9]

Anthony Wills

Following regulatory supervision visits to the Bank of Beirut's London-based company in 2010 and 2011 the regulator required the bank to 'develop, implement and conduct a compliance monitoring plan' to help the bank 'counter the risk of financial crime'.[10] As a result, the bank appointed

Anthony Willis as its compliance officer in July 2011. However, through 2012 he failed in his critical role and failed to tell the regulator about delays to the monitoring plan and the lack of monitoring work. Further, he actively mislead the regulator writing 'an internal email to senior management ... that he was 'fairly guarded' during a conversation with the [regulator] about the compliance monitoring plan' and stating that compliance actions had been completed when this was false.[11]

As mentioned earlier, in his defence Wills said that he had insufficient compliance resources and that 'at times he felt under pressure from senior management to be 'careful' in his communications with the [regulator] and that he was not given 'licence' to explain issues fully'.[12] The FCA was clear that this was no excuse.[13] Again, the feebleness of the compliance officer's defence, coupled with his lies to the regulator may have been behind the decision to take personal regulatory action. The FCA commented that 'we are reliant on compliance officers and internal audit to act as an important line of defence, to support effective regulation at firms and to show backbone even when challenged by their colleagues'.[14]

Sanction

After a discount for not contesting the case, Wills was fined just over £19,000 but was not banned from working in a regulated, senior post in the industry.[15] From the information available it is unclear why he was not banned.

David Watters

Watters was the compliance officer of a firm giving pensions advice between 2006 and 2009. He failed he understand his role as compliance officer and the nature of the risks relating to the advisory business.[16] Watters also failed to engage with the advisory process, nor did he seek independent expert assistance, and when consultants were engaged he failed to check that their recommendations were acted upon.[17] He also failed adequately to monitor the work of the financial advisors, nor did he identify and manage adequately the conflicts of interest arising from the incentivisation scheme.[18]

The case is usual since there was no regulatory enforcement action against the regulated firms themselves. It is possible to speculate that it is likely that the FCA considered themselves under media and political pressure to address concerns that individuals were being encouraged to take out more high-risk pension products as a result of changes in the law.[19]

Sanction

Watters was fined £75,000 but was not banned. Again, as with Wills, it is not clear from the publicly available information why he was not banned.

Stephen Bell

Between 2008 and 2013 Bell was the compliance officer of an investment advisory firm. He had a system for assessing the fit and properness and competence of new advisors but this process was inadequate.[20] He also failed to have an adequate system for assessing the competence of advisors on a continuing basis. Moreover, the process for selecting and checking the investment advise customer files was poor.[21]

This was an inadequate 'process' failing. There was no evidence presented that these failures actually resulted in incompetent or dishonest advisers dealing with clients. Nevertheless, the FCA's view was that 'a compliance director of a [financial advice] network has an important role in terms of ensuring that systems and controls across the network are focussed on minimising the risk of mis-selling and the provision of unsuitable advice to consumers'.[22] The FCA considered that Bell's failings were especially serious 'because he had been put on notice of the need for significant improvements in the firm's systems and controls and compliance'.[23]

Sanction

Bell was fined £33,800 and was banned from the working in a regulated role in the financial services industry.[24]

Steven Smith

Smith was appointed as the compliance and money laundering reporting officer in 2011 to Sonali Bank in London, a subsidiary of a Bangladeshi bank. Between 2011 and 2014 the FCA found numerous failings in Smith's anti-money laundering (AML) role. In addition, the FCA found compliance issues in a number of other areas.[25]

It may be that the key issue in the decision to take personal action against the compliance officer was an inspection visit to the bank by the regulator in 2010. This review had found serious anti-money laundering systems failures. Smith was recruited in 2011 to fix these issues but the problems persisted.[26] Some of these are described below.

Compliance monitoring plans

The monitoring plans were wholly inadequate since they were just a 'task list' and did not identify the work done, the rationale and methodology for the tests carried out. Moreover, work by the firm's internal auditors identified issues with 'assessed its conduct risk' and the lack of linkage 'between the risk register and the compliance monitoring plan'. However, Smith failed to take account of the concerns expressed by internal audit and 'the 2013 compliance monitoring plan was very similar in form and content to that of 2012'. Internal audit raised the same points in its 2013 report. But again Smith failed to improve his compliance monitoring plan for 2014 which remained 'similar in form and content to those of 2012 and 2013, providing no detail of the monitoring activity to be undertaken, no rationale for it and no link to the risks faced' by the bank.[27]

Management information

The reports by Smith to senior management and the board 'were formulaic, provided little analysis on the effectiveness of systems and controls and failed to highlight particular risks or issues for the immediate attention of management'. Moreover, when internal audit raised specific concerns with areas such as the monitoring of trade finance and the regulatory compliance processes Smith in his 2013 annual report made no reference 'to the findings of the Internal Auditors' 2012 governance and regulation assessment'. While, in the 2014 report he noted simply that 'none of these issues were considered significant and all have since been completed'.[28]

Branch staff training

The bank had five branches in the United Kingdom. The staff handbook contained the policies and procedures on anti-money laundering. However, this was stated in high level terms and the 'manual provided little practical guidance to staff to assist them with carrying out their functions effectively. Staff were provided with the AML Staff Handbook but were given limited further guidance on how to follow AML processes' and the training provided was generic and not role specific. For example, staff were instructed that prior to establishing a relationship or opening an account, they were required to obtain 'sufficient due diligence' but the guidance did not specify what would be considered as 'sufficient'.[29]

Lack of resources and overwork

Smith complained about 'suffering from being overworked personally and from a lack of resource' but he 'failed to impress upon senior management the need for further resources even when these were adversely affecting the monitoring work' and failed to recruit extra staff quickly even when 'he was given permission to recruit further resources'.[30]

Sanction

Smith was fined £17,800 and banned from working in a regulated role in the financial services industry.[31]

Tariq Carrimjee

Carrimjee was a compliance officer who demonstrated a lack of due skill, care and diligence in failing to escalate the risk that his client may have been intending to engage in market manipulation. He had had no formal compliance training during the period 2010 to 2012 and the Upper Tribunal, hearing the case on appeal, agreed with the regulator that the appellant lacked sufficient competence for the role.[32]

Sanction

Carrimjee was fined £89,000 and banned from the working in a regulated role in the financial services industry.[33]

Carl Davey

Davey was a compliance office at firm of stockbrokers which mis-sold investments to its clients during the period April 2008 to the end of 2009.[34] The failings are set out in some detail below since they give an indication of what can happen if compliance fails completely. It is worth noting that the stockbroker sold small capitalised unlisted securities to the public and that the CEO Sam Kenny was himself fined almost £0.5m.[35]

It is possible to surmise that the CEO sought out a compliance officer that would not get in the way of his operations and who would not trouble the senior management.

Withholding of call recording

Davey was complicit with senior management in the decision to withhold the recording of a call between an investment advisor and a client claiming, falsely, that the relevant call recording could not be found. Davey claimed that he was under pressure to do this. The FSA considered that this demonstrated a serious lack of integrity and went directly to his fitness and properness for the role.[36]

Advisers pressurise clients to invest

The FSA listened to recording of a number of client calls by advisers and found evidence of persistent pressure sales practices including persistent calling, ignoring client objections to the sales techniques and out-right lying, including mis-representing the nature and risks of the investments.[37]

Davey's training of his call monitoring staff was poor. Nevertheless, he had still discovered these issues as a result of his own, albeit inadequate, call monitoring.[38]

Client survey prevented

The FSA in 2008 had published guidance recommending that investment firms send out client questionnaires to ascertain if they had been treated fairly in accordance with the regulations. Davey proposed this to the firm's CEO. However, the latter vetoed this because it might prompt client complaints.[39]

Allowing an unauthorised person to work in a senior role

An individual applied for FSA authorising as a senior manager at the firm but Davey withdrew the application since the applicant was under FSA investigation at his previous company. However, the individual was allowed by Davey to work in an unauthorised capacity within his firm without telling the FSA.

Contrary to the statutory requirements the relevant individual nevertheless continued to work at the firm for at least another 8 months after the approval application was withdrawn. Davey told the CEO of his concerns and that the individual was mis-training sales staff and encouraging them to mis-sell investment products. The CEO took no action.[40]

Investment risk warnings

The investment advisers gave generic risk warnings to clients at the end of the sales process after the client had agree to buy the investment. Specific warnings should have been provided early on in the conversation. Davey permitted this practice and also allowed advisers to commit clients to invest above individual client investment risk limits. There was no adequate compliance monitoring of these practices.[41]

Mis-describing client attitudes to risk

Davey set the guidance for client risk profiles. These were seriously misaligned. For example, so that they 'specified that a client choosing a conservative growth investment strategy had ... a willingness to take 'high' overall risk such that 'capital returns may be negative over short to medium time horizons". Consequently, clients were invested in higher products when this is not what they had wanted.[42]

Monitoring telephone calls between advisors and clients

The regulator found that only a very small portion of advisor/client telephone calls were monitored by compliance. The process for monitoring calls was itself flawed with undertrained and inexperienced staff undertaking the work. Consequently, they failed to detect many of the issues. Moreover, there was no ranking by significance of any problems found. Even when calls were checked, Davey failed to ensure that adequate remedial work was undertaken where issues were found.[43]

Adviser remuneration

Davey provided advice on the design of the investment advisor remuneration scheme. Advisors were paid a small base salary but were, in addition, paid commission based entirely on the financial value of sales made by each advisor.

Poor quality advice only had a limited effect on reducing the level of these commission payments. For example, flawed advice calls could be off-set by unchallenged telephone advice conversations with the result that commission payments were not reduced. In an echo of Glengarry Glen Ross adviser promotion depended on making sales and promotion brought better quality leads and clients.[44]

Representations to the regulator by Davey that he did his best

Davey made representations to the FSA in 2009 that he had tried to do his best and had acted in good faith. The FSA accepted that Davey believed that had he tried to raise the problem issues that, 'he would be ignored or frustrated and might be victimised'.[45] However, the FSA was clear that they expected the compliance officer to take reasonable steps and to 'raise the alarm' on all the issues disclosed in the Enforcement Notice. Davey's 'failure to raise the alarm and/or challenge his colleagues indicates that [he] failed to understand the importance of his [compliance] role and the regulatory obligations it brings. He failed to properly discharge his responsibilities as the Firm's compliance officer'.[46]

Sanction

Davey would have been fined £175,000 but the FSA did not exact this fine since it accepted that he would suffer 'serious financial hardship'. Davey was, however, banned from the working in a regulated role in the financial services industry.[47]

Alexander Ten-Holter

Ten-Holter was a compliance officer at an investment firm in 2009. He executed a securities sale order with knowledge of information which might amount to market abuse.[48] The regulator considered that he should have been alert to the warning signs of market abuse and should have made enquiries first before executing the sale order. As a consequence, he failed to demonstrate due skill, care and diligence as required by the regulations.[49]

In his defence Ten-Holter claimed that he did not make these enquiries since in his opinion the investment firm 'had high standards of compliance and a strict market abuse policy'. However, the FSA took the view that no matter how high the standards are at a firm it does not preclude the business from making mistakes and breaking rules. The FSA went on to say that it is the role of compliance 'to ensure, so far as possible, that no mistakes, mis-judgements or deliberate breaches occur and that policies, procedures and regulatory requirements are adhered to'.[50] Compliance fails if closes its mind to warning signs that might reasonably alert it to market abuse on the grounds that it has assessed the risk of market abuse as low, based on the fact that the firm has appropriate policies and procedures.[51]

Sanction

Ten-Holter was fined £130,000 and banned from working in a regulated role in the financial services industry.[52]

Robert Addison

Addison was compliance officer between 2007 and 2009 at a group of in-vestment companies. These had two main businesses: corporate finance ad-visory which involved advising on corporate transactions and investment management. This had the potential to produce significant conflicts of in-terest. The corporate advisory work depended on obtaining the highest price for a transaction for a client. The Upper Tribunal, hearing the case on appeal, described the conflicts 'as serious as could be imagined, involving the payment of a substantial fee to [corporate advisory business] where that fee would only be payable if the transaction completed'.[53] The corporate advisory firm procured the investment business to 'make the necessary investment to enable the transaction to proceed … and there being no serious attempt to manage the conflict'.[54] The Tribunal expressed the view that 'the only right course of action to take in the absence of any other meaningful steps to manage the conflict would be to decline to enter into the transaction'.[55]

Addison understood the conflict of interests problem and in August 2007 met a compliance consultant for advice on addressing the issue. The latter, among other steps, advised documenting the fair treatment of investors and the appointment of a different investment fund manager.[56] In October 2007 the corporate advisory firm produced its first conflicts of interest policy. This set out high level standards but lacked information relating these to the business and how the issues should be addressed. A new compliance manual was issued in February 2008. It described the relevant rules on conflicts of interest and referred to a detail appendix covering the firm's conflicts of interest policy. There was no appendix and none was ever produced.[57]

The Tribunal found that Addison had failed to take reasonable steps to ensure that such systems were in place to manage a conflict of interest and that this breached the regulations.[58] There were also other failings regarding at the lack of adequate compliance monitoring and the protection of non-public confidential information.[59]

Sanction

Addison was fined £200,000 and banned from the working in a regulated role in the financial services industry.[60]

Oluwole Fagbulu

Fagbulu was the compliance officer at a hedge fund and between 2006 and 2008 he was involved in market manipulation, recording fictitious transactions, disregarding restrictions on the investments and issuing 'misleading investor communications, and deliberately failing to inform investors of important developments with the intention of misleading them as to the performance' of the investment fund.[61]

He claimed in his defence that the CEO was a dominant and forceful personality and that he directed the compliance officer who was 'out of his depth, having taken on duties for which he had little or no training and of which he had little experience, and for which he was ill-equipped'.[62] It is possible that Fagbulu may not have known or understood what he was doing. However, the Upper Tribunal concluded that he must have known that what he 'was doing was designed to deceive and was wrong'. However, 'lack of understanding does not afford him a defence, or even an excuse'.[63]

Sanction

Fagbulu would have been fine £350,000 but due to financial hardship the Upper Tribunal reduced this to £100,000 and banned him from working in a regulated role in the financial services industry.[64]

Other issues

The next two sections consider two potential problem issues for compliance officers. Failures in these areas may expose both the compliance officer and the business to regulatory sanction. The first considers the long delay in notifying the regulator and misleading policyholders and the second highlights the risks arising from the use of 'attestation letters' by the regulators and the implications for compliance officers.

Possible delays in notifying the regulator: Royal Scottish Assurance

In 1989 the Royal Bank of Scotland (RBS) and Scottish Equitable Life created a joint venture under which Royal Scottish Assurance, a RBS subsidiary, would market investment and insurance products created and serviced by Scottish Equitable Life. An important joint venture product was the 'mortgage endowment'. In summary, a customer of RBS would take out a mortgage to buy a property paying just the monthly interest on the loan. At the same time they would buy a Royal Scottish Assurance endowment policy, paying monthly premiums, with the same term as the mortgage. It was hoped, and expected, that the value of this policy, at maturity, would be sufficient to pay off the outstanding mortgage. The level of monthly premium was tied to projected growth rate of the policy's underlying investments. It was easier to sell policies which had a low premium. For reasons that are difficult to fathom, the premiums quoted by joint venture salesmen were significantly lower than would be necessary to pay off the mortgage. The mis-pricing error was spotted by the joint venture company in 1996. Early in 1999 it became clear that policyholder premiums would have to double to have a chance of meeting the objectives of the investment (i.e. to pay off the mortgage).[65] However, there were two issues which really concerned the regulator:

- in 1996 Royal Scottish Assurance had written to some 300 policyholders suggesting that they increase their monthly premiums. 'The letter misleadingly explained that the increase was necessary because of reductions in projected rates of return. In reality, the main reason was to address the shortfall that would arise as a result of the firm's undisclosed policy pricing errors',[66]
- Royal Scottish Assurance, having identified the issue early in 1996, waited until June 1997 to notify the regulator.[67] It is not clear why it took so long to tell the regulator. Whatever, the reason this was clearly unsatisfactory and there are no circumstances which would condone any delay in making the necessary full and frank disclosure to the regulators.

The regulator described all of this as evidence of a 'lack of high standards, integrity and fair dealing'.[68] The result was a fine of £2m.[69] The joint venture company also had to pay some £50m in compensation to around 30,000 customers.[70] In all of this it is not clear what the compliance officer was doing and why they did not ensure that the firm acted properly.

Attestation letters: Deutsche Bank AG

In 2015 Deutsche Bank AG ('Deutsche') was fined almost £227m (reduced from £324m since the bank did not contest the enforcement action) for breaching FCA's Principles for Businesses. Specifically, the breaches were of Principles 3 (the requirement that the firm have proper systems and controls), 5 (the need for proper market conduct) and 11 (that regulated firms are open and honest with the regulator and cooperative). The issues related to an attempted to manipulate of the Libor rates by certain of the bank's traders.[71] In 2011, 'the FSA requested that a number of banks, including Deutsche, provide an attestation that the systems and controls that they operated to oversee the integrity of their [libor] submissions were adequate'.[72]

Attestation letters are used by the FCA to make one or more senior managers confirm direct to the regulator that particular review work has been undertaken and that all the systems of control in that area are working properly and that there are no issues that the regulator should be aware of. The letters are short and are not permitted to contain any caveats or disclaimers. The use of attestation letters makes it easy for the FCA to take action against individuals if it subsequently transpires that the facts attested to were incorrect. Besides the substantive issues underlying the firm's failures, the regulator can take action on the basis that the individual mis-lead the regulator by signing a false attestation letter. This would be a breach of Principle 11 (not being open and honest with the regulator).[73]

At Deutsche Bank the senior manager delegated the work of preparing the attestation letter to the compliance officer. The latter 'undertook some investigations around systems and controls relating' to Libor at the bank and found 'that there were no Libor-specific systems and controls designed to ensure the integrity of Deutsche Bank's' submissions.[74] 'The attestation was approved by senior managers at Deutsche and signed by one such manager before being' sent to the regulator.[75] However, 'in light of the earlier investigations, the compliance officer was aware that the attestation was false'.[76]

Conclusion

Being a compliance officer is a high-risk occupation because of the raised expectations of regulators and the boards and other senior management of regulated firms. As can be seen from the enforcement cases noted above the compliance officer needs to competent and professional in all that they do. They need to select carefully the people to help them. However, it is only by good judgement and the exercise of their authority that they can hope to ensure that matters are done to their satisfaction, as they ought to be, and that they are not overborne by other senior managers who mistake their obligations and who may not share the necessary ethical perspective.

Notes

1 FCA Final Notice, Gregory Nathan re his proposed appointment to be the compliance officer and money laundering reporting officer at Goldenway Global

Investments, 21 August 2017, https://www.fca.org.uk/publication/final-notices/goldenway-global-investments-uk-limited.pdf (accessed 14 May 2019).

2 FCA Final Notice, Anthony Wills, March 2015, 3, 10, https://www.fca.org.uk/publication/final-notices/anthony-rendell-boyd-wills.pdf (accessed 15 May 2019).

3 FCA Final Notice, Peter Johnson, May 2016, 3–5, https://www.fca.org.uk/publication/final-notices/peter-francis-johnson.pdf (accessed 15 May 2019).

4 Ibid, Final Notice (Johnson), 3–5

5 Ibid, Final Notice (Johnson), 3–5

6 Ibid, Final Notice (Johnson), 3–5

7 Ibid, Final Notice (Johnson), 3–5

8 Ibid, Final Notice (Johnson), 5

9 Ibid, Final Notice (Johnson), 34

10 FCA Final Notice, Anthony Wills, March 2015, 2, https://www.fca.org.uk/publication/final-notices/anthony-rendell-boyd-wills.pdf (accessed 15 May 2019)

11 Ibid, Final Notice (Wills), 2–3

12 Ibid, Final Notice (Wills), 2–3

13 Ibid, Final Notice (Wills), 2–3

14 FCA, Georgina Philippou, acting director of enforcement, FCA press release, 5 March 2015, https://www.fca.org.uk/news/press-releases/financial-conduct-authority-imposes-£21m-fine-and-places-restriction-bank-beirut (accessed 16 May 2020)

15 Supra note 10, Final Notice (Wills), 4

16 FCA, Final Notice, David Watters, July 2017, 3, https://www.fca.org.uk/publication/final-notices/david-samuel-watters.pdf (accessed 16 May 2019)

17 Ibid, Final Notice (Watters), 3–4

18 Ibid, Final Notice (Watters), 4–5

19 Financial Times, 'Pension firms report increased demand for DB transfer quotes: members of 'gold plated' final salary schemes are increasingly tempted to cash them in', 1 May 2015, https://www.ft.com/content/eb9b0de2-f011-11e4-ab73-00144feab7de (accessed 16 May 2020)

20 FCA, Final Notice, Stephen Bell, March 2015, 19, https://www.fca.org.uk/publication/final-notices/stephen-edward-bell.pdf (accessed 16 March 2019)

21 Ibid, Final Notice (Bell), 19–20

22 FCA, Georgina Philippou, acting director of enforcement, FCA press release, 13 March 2015, https://www.fca.org.uk/news/press-releases/fca-fines-and-prohibits-mr-stephen-bell-former-director-network-financial-group (accessed 17 May 2020)

23 Ibid, FCA press release (re Bell)

24 Supra note 20, Final Notice (Bell), 20–22

25 FCA, Final Notice, Steven Smith, October 2016, 2, https://www.fca.org.uk/publication/final-notices/steven-smith-2016.pdf (accessed 17 May 2019)

26 Ibid, Final Notice (Smith), 2

27 Ibid, Final Notice (Smith), 11–15

28 Ibid, Final Notice (Smith), 11–15

29 Ibid, Final Notice (Smith), 14–15

30 Ibid, Final Notice (Smith), 2

31 Ibid, Final Notice (Smith), 1

32 Upper Tribunal case Tariq Carrimjee v FCA [2016] UKUT 0447 (TCC), 3, http://taxandchancery_ut.decisions.tribunals.gov.uk/Documents/decisions/Carrimjee%20v%20FCA%20for%20website.pdf (accessed 17 May 2019)

33 Revised FCA Final Notice re Carrimjee, 2, https://www.fca.org.uk/publication/final-notices/tariq-carrimjee-2016.pdf (accessed 17 May 2019)

34 FSA, Final Notice, Carl Davey, December 2012, https://www.fca.org.uk/publication/final-notices/carl-davey.pdf (accessed 19 May 2019)
35 FCA press release re Sam Kenny, 13 March 2015, https://www.fca.org.uk/news/press-releases/former-chief-executive-stockbroker-firm-fined-£450000-and-banned, https://www.fca.org.uk/news/press-releases/former-chief-executive-stockbroker-firm-fined-£450000-and-banned (accessed 17 May 2020)
36 Supra note 34, Final Notice (Davey), 7
37 Supra note 34, Final Notice (Davey), 5–7
38 Supra note 34, Final Notice (Davey), 10
39 Supra note 34, Final Notice (Davey), 7
40 Supra note 34, Final Notice (Davey), 7–8
41 Supra note 34, Final Notice (Davey), 8
42 Supra note 34, Final Notice (Davey), 9
43 Supra note 34, Final Notice (Davey), 9–10
44 Supra note 34, Final Notice (Davey), 10–11. See David Mamet, *Glengarry Glen Ross* (Methuen, London, 1984), Author Note
45 Supra note 34, Final Notice (Davey), 16
46 Supra note 34, Final Notice (Davey), 16
47 Supra note 34, Final Notice (Davey), 18
48 FSA, Final Notice, Alexander Ten-Holter, January 2012, https://www.fca.org.uk/publication/final-notices/ten-holter-greenlight.pdf (accessed 21 May 2019), 2–3
49 Ibid, Final Notice (Ten-Holter), 7
50 Ibid, Final Notice (Ten-Holter), 7
51 Ibid, Final Notice (Ten-Holter), 7
52 Ibid, Final Notice (Ten-Holter), 9
53 Upper Tribunal, Robert Addison v FCA [2015] UKUT 0013 (TCC), para 336, http://taxandchancery_ut.decisions.tribunals.gov.uk/Documents/decisions/Arch-v-FCA.pdf (accessed 21 May 2019)
54 Ibid, Upper Tribunal (Addison), 336–338
55 Ibid, Upper Tribunal (Addison), 336–338
56 Ibid, Upper Tribunal (Addison), 147
57 Ibid, Upper Tribunal (Addison), 153–157
58 Ibid, Upper Tribunal (Addison), 369–374
59 FCA Final Notice, Robert Addison, March 2015, 4–5, https://www.fca.org.uk/publication/final-notices/robert-addison.pdf (accessed 21 May 2019)
60 Ibid, Final Notice (Addison), 1
61 FSA Final Notice, Oluwole Fagbulu, September 2011, 5, https://www.fca.org.uk/publication/final-notices/oluwole_fagbulu.pdf (accessed 22 May 2019)
62 Oluwole Modupe Fagbulu v FSA [2011] FS/2010/0001 FS/2010/0006, para 123, http://taxandchancery_ut.decisions.tribunals.gov.uk/Documents/decisions/VisserandFagbulu_v_FSA.pdf (accessed 22 May 2019)
63 Supra note 61, Upper Tribunal (Fagbulu), 106
64 Supra note 61, Upper Tribunal (Fagbulu), 124–126
65 Scottish Courts and Tribunals, Royal Scottish Assurance PLC v Scottish Equitable Life PLC [2006] CSIH 47, para 10, https://www.scotcourts.gov.uk/search-judgments/judgment?id=ef4886a6–8980-69d2-b500-ff0000d74aa7 (accessed 14 April 2020)
66 The Herald, Scotland, 'Royal Bank subsidiary fined record amount for mis-selling endowments', 1 December 2000, https://www.heraldscotland.com/news/12165500.royal-bank-subsidiary-fined-record-amount-for-mis-selling-endowments/ (accessed 14 April 2020)

67 Ibid (The Herald)
68 Ibid (The Herald)
69 The Daily Telegraph, 'Another fine insurance mess', 3 December 2000
70 Ibid (The Telegraph)
71 FCA Final Notice, Deutsche Bank AG, April 2015, 1, https://www.fca.org.uk/publication/final-notices/deutsche-bank-ag-2015.pdf (accessed 8 May 2019)
72 Ibid, Final Notice (Deutsche Bank), 29
73 FCA website, Use of attestation letters, Exchange of letters between Clive Adamson, FCA director of supervision and Graham Beale, Chairman of the FCA Practitioner Panel clarifying the FCA's use of Attestations, 28 August 2014, https://www.fca.org.uk/news/news-stories/fca-use-attestations (accessed 18 May 2020)
74 Supra note 71, Final Notice (Deutsche Bank), 29
75 Supra note 71, Final Notice (Deutsche Bank), 30
76 Supra note 71, Final Notice (Deutsche Bank), 38

10

LESSONS FOR COMPLIANCE OFFICERS FROM REGULATORY ENFORCEMENT ACTIONS AND GUIDANCE

The US experience

Introduction

The role of the chief compliance officer (CCO) is growing in importance in the United States. This can be seen, for example, in the area of investment firms where each regulated firm is required to have a chief compliance officer.[1] This individual 'should be competent and knowledgeable [regarding the regulations] and should be empowered with full responsibility and authority to develop and enforce appropriate policies and procedures for the firm. Thus, the compliance officer should have a position of sufficient seniority and authority within the organization to compel others to adhere to the compliance policies and procedures'.[2] The increased importance of the role also comes with greater personal risk from legal and regulatory action.

There are many examples, drawn from regulatory enforcement cases, which help to illustrate many of the points made in this book. For example, in 2017, Thomas Haider, the former compliance officer of MoneyGram International, agreed to pay a regulatory penalty and accepted restrictions placed on him working as a compliance officer. He had made recommendations to management to terminate fraudulent money transmission outlets but was overruled. However, the compliance officer failed to take adequate follow-up action.

Other examples include the action by the Securities Exchange Commission (SEC) against Eugene Mason, former compliance officer of SFX Financial Advisory Management Enterprises in 2015. He was found to be negligent for failing to implement compliance policies. Other cases consider compliance outsourcing. The issues with this are evident in the SEC's 2017 action against David Osunkwo who was the principal of SC Consulting and acted as the outsourced compliance officer to both Aegis Capital and Circle One.

These and others cases are considered in more detail later in this chapter.

This chapter examines the developing US regulatory expectations of compliance officers. The regulators continue to place increasing levels of reliance on the latter's work. This is doubled edged. It indicates the importance of the role and, at the same time, the increased personal risks faced by these individuals.

The SEC's new approach

Both the US's SEC and the Financial Industry Regulatory Authority (FINRA) have started to target compliance officers. This increased focus on the role of the chief compliance officers can probably be dated back to 2014 when Andrew Ceresney, the then new SEC director of enforcement, enunciated this new policy in a speech in Washington, DC.[3] He stated that SEC enforcement action would be brought against chief compliance officers where:

- the chief compliance officers had engaged in efforts to obstruct or mislead SEC staff,
- the chief compliance officers had exhibited a wholesale failure to carry out their responsibilities.[4]

Ceresney identified a number of 'predictor' questions which might indicate the likelihood of regulatory enforcement action. The wrong answers to these questions could predict a strong risk of a compliance lapse leading to regulatory action.[5] The questions included:

- are legal and compliance personnel included in critical meetings,
- are their views typically sought and followed,
- do legal and compliance officers report to the CEO and have significant visibility with the board,
- are the legal and compliance departments viewed as important partners in the business and not simply as support functions or a cost center?[6]

The SEC's Enforcement Division continues to see its focus on individual accountability as one of its five key areas.[7] There is more on the SEC's approach later in this chapter.

Examples of the growing trend to hold individual compliance officers personally responsible

As mentioned earlier, there are a number of examples of regulatory action against individual compliance officers working in financial firms. These largely originate from the SEC but more recently the US Treasury Department's Financial Crimes Enforcement Network ('FinCEN') has brought some cases of its own. For example, against the chief operational risk officer, Michael LaFontaine, who also oversaw US Bank's anti-money laundering compliance department and the earlier case involving Wachovia Bank. This, and other cases are considered in the next section. They provide example of key themes underpinning regulatory actions against individual compliance officers.

Regulatory action examples

David Osunkwo

Between 2010 and 2011 Osunkwo provided outsourced compliance service to a number of investment management firms. He was found to have made untrue statements in relation to the registration applications and reports filed with the SEC.[8] For example, he overstated the assets under management by almost 200% and the number of clients by over 300%.[9] He was fined $30,000 and permanently banned from working in the securities industry.[10]

Thaddeus North

The regulatory action against North is particularly interesting since it includes some pertinent thinking by the SEC on the subject of enforcement action against compliance officers.[11] These are considered in detail in sections 7.2–7.5, below. In North's case the compliance officer, employed by a broker-dealer between 2009 and 2011, was responsible for checking electronic correspondence. However, he did not to this properly since 'it was boring' and he also failed to notify the regulator about the firm's business relationship with a statutorily disqualified person.[12] This the SEC viewed as 'egregious' behaviour.[13] As a consequence he was suspended from his role for three months and fined $40,000.

Treasury Department's Financial Crimes Enforcement Network ('FinCEN') action against Michael LaFontaine, the chief operational risk officer at US Bank National Association

In March 2020, the Financial Crimes Enforcement Network ('FinCEN') using a consent order required the chief operational risk officer, Michael LaFontaine, at US Bank National Association (US Bank) to pay $450,000 as a civil penalty. The central issue was LaFontaine's alleged failure to prevent data security and money laundering breaches.[14]

As chief operational risk officer, LaFontaine oversaw US Bank's anti-money laundering compliance department, and reported direct to the bank's CEO and regularly reported to the firm's board of directors.

Between 2004 and 2014, in common with many banks, US Bank used an automated IT system to identify suspicious transaction activity. These computer-generated reports would need to be investigated by anti-money laundering staff. Since he lacked sufficient staff to carry out all these investigations LaFontaine artificially capped the number of potential money laundering alerts to match the number of investigators available. Further, the bank's compliance function did not have sufficient people to review even the capped level of alerts.

There are a number of factors which told against LaFontaine. These included:

- LaFontaine's own staff and the regulators had warned him against limiting the number of alerts and had pointed out the risks involved in doing so. LaFontaine suppressed concerns from his senior staff and failed to notify the bank's CEO or the regulators of these issues,[15]
- LaFontaine's actions limited the number of suspicious activity reports to investigate, a matter of particular concern to the regulators,
- LaFontaine limited the workings of the IT systems – central to the fight against money laundering – and in so doing effectively neutered them,
- there had been a recent previous anti-money laundering failure by the bank. 'In February 2018, FinCEN, in coordination with the Office of the Comptroller of the Currency (OCC) and the US Department of Justice, issued a $185m civil money penalty against US Bank for, among other things, wilfully violating' the requirements to implement and maintain an effective anti-money laundering program and to file Suspicious Activity Reports (SAR) in a timely manner,[16]
- the OCC 'had warned US Bank on several occasions that using numerical caps to limit the bank's monitoring programs based on the size of its staff and available resources could result in a potential enforcement action, and FinCEN had taken previous public actions against banks' for similar failures,[17]
- FinCEN and the OCC had taken action, in 2010, against Wachovia Bank for setting an artificial limit on the alerts generated by its automated transaction monitoring system. LaFontaine should have been aware of this and assessed his, and US Bank's, arrangements in the light of this,[18]
- this was compounded by the fact that 'LaFontaine received internal memos from staff claiming that significant increases in SAR volumes, law enforcement inquiries, and closure recommendations, created a situation where the [anti-money laundering] staff 'is stretched dangerously thin',[19]
- all these failures had persisted for some 5 years. The issues only came to

the attention of the regulators when the anti-money laundering officer by-passed LaFontaine and went straight to the bank's chief risk officer.

The bank itself was fined $613m by a variety of regulators. While LaFontaine was not subject to an industry-wide ban he was, under the consent order, required to represent that he had not served in a compliance management function for any financial institution since he left US Bank in June 2014.

FinCEN's assessment of a civil money penalty against Wachovia Bank (4 March 2010)

As mentioned earlier, FinCEN fined Wachovia Bank for a range of failings. Of particular relevance to this work are the specific findings against Wachovia relating to its compliance organisation. These included:

- a failure to allocate adequate compliance resources,[20]
- 'where employees of the Wachovia identified anomalies in the volume or mix of bulk cash deposits that should have warranted further review, these anomalies were not brought to the attention of the bank's compliance' operation,[21]
- 'Wachovia failed to adequately staff the ... compliance function ... with individuals responsible for coordinating and monitoring day-to-day compliance' and the unit 'was understaffed, and personnel lacked the requisite knowledge and expertise to adequately perform their duties'.[22]
- Wachovia 'also suffered from an apparent lack of effective communication between audit, compliance, and management'.[23]

There are number of key messages from these cases which reinforce the themes in this book. They include the need to ensure adequate compliance resources; the need to ensure that compliance monitoring is not undertaken in a mindless, mechanical fashion but that it is designed to focus on the key risks; and the need of the compliance officer to ensure the rapid and timely escalation of significant concerns and any major issues promptly corrected. Underpinning all this is the need to ensure that the compliance officer has sufficient 'authority' within the organisation and that they operate with a high-level of competence and professionalism.

FinCEN action against Thomas Haider (4 May 2017)

As mentioned above, Haider allowed his judgement to be over-ruled regarding 'terminating [MoneyGram] outlets that posed a high risk of fraud' and he also arranged to suppress suspicious activity reports of fraud to

FinCEN.[24] In his unsuccessful plea in mitigation 'Haider said that proposals made by MoneyGram's fraud department to terminate and discipline agents at its outlets had been shot down by the sales division'.[25]

It is worth noting the clarity of Acting FinCEN Director Jamal El-Hindi's statement,

> FinCEN relies on compliance professionals from every corner of the financial industry ... Compliance professionals occupy unique positions of trust in our financial system. When that trust is broken, it is important that we take action ... Holding him [Haider] personally accountable strengthens the compliance profession by demonstrating that behavior like this is not tolerated within the ranks of compliance professionals.[26]

SEC action against Eugene Mason (15 June 2015)

In a more straightforward example, the SEC took action against Mason, the compliance officer at SFX Financial Advisory. A financial adviser, working for SFX, stole money from the account of one of the firm's clients. The SEC found that Mason's compliance arrangements to prevent such occurrences were wholly inadequate. He was required to pay a personal civil penalty of $25,000.[27] SFX was also fined.

The role of the chief compliance officer in the United States in financial service firms

The expectations placed on chief compliance officers in the United States are similar to that in other countries.[28] There is a heavy focus on training new staff, developing and promulgating procedures and policies, monitoring and reporting, regulatory risk assessments, advising on and monitoring remediation work, interacting with the regulators and addressing regulatory queries.

A decision by the chief compliance officers on what type of relationship to have with the regulators is central to the role. In contrast to the United Kingdom, in the United States there appears to be a greater emphasis on having a more legalistic and confrontational attitude to the regulators. This is based on anecdotal evidence rather than empirical research. Norm Champ was, at different times, Director of the Division of Investment Management at the SEC and a chief compliance officer, has recommended that chief compliance officers exercise a process of 'constructive engagement' with the SEC.[29] This includes briefing the regulators on what is happening generally in the industry and, more specifically, within the business. This helps the regulator gain some insights, and they are likely to appreciate the compliance officer's cooperation.[30] As discussed elsewhere in this work, it helps in building up trust with the regulator and this may be decisive in the latter determining whether to take enforcement action against the firm.

Department of Justice (DoJ) Guidance on the work of compliance and its relevance to enforcement action

In 2019, the DoJ issued updated guidance on how it will evaluate corporate compliance programmes.[31] It is almost twice the length of the earlier 2017 document with, among other areas, an increased emphasis on training.[32] The detailed points on training are covered in Chapter 8 of this book.

While the extent of a firm's compliance with the guidance forms part of the input into DoJ's decision making process on the need to conduct an investigation and whether to bring charges and so on., it has a much wider application. It sets the standard for how a competent compliance operation should be undertaken. It requires compliance (or whoever is carrying out the programme) to understand the business and its risks and to design a programme that will 'detect the particular types of misconduct most likely to occur ... in a [firm's] line of business and complex regulatory environment'.[33]

Of particular relevance is the need for the programme designers to consult with business units about the design; ensure that there is adequate communication with all employees and third parties; and that 'linguistic or other barriers to foreign employees' access' to the programme have been addressed.[34]

The Guidance also makes clear that a 'hallmark of a well-designed compliance program is appropriately tailored training and communications' and the Guidance places a considerable emphasis on this area.[35] The Guidance also covers a range of areas, including whistleblowing, the effectiveness of the compliance function, the effectiveness of the compliance programme in practice and its oversight and testing and evaluation.[36] These aspects are considered in greater detail elsewhere in this book.

The Guidance also highlights the compliance risks posed by mergers and acquisitions.[37] The Guidance makes clear that the acquiring firm's compliance function needs to identify any mis-conduct in the target company and to take steps to address this, including remediating wrongs.[38] Work on integrating the two compliance areas should also be a high priority. It is important to ensure that cost reductions, promised as part of the acquisition, do not damage compliance in the larger and, probably, more complex operations of the merged entities.

Finally, in this area, the DoJ Guidance highlights the importance of compliance under the US Foreign Corrupt Practices Act (FCPA).[39] This aspect was covered in the DoJ and SEC Resource Guide issued in 2012.[40] The lack of adequate compliance programmes in this area has been noted by the SEC in its enforcement actions.[41]

SEC expectation for compliance

The SEC has issued detailed rules on what they expect of compliance as a function and how it should integrated into the regulated firm's business and operations.[42] In summary, the rules emphasise the key relationship between the firm's board and the compliance officer:

- the compliance officer must report directly to the board and the rules specify what must be covered in these reports. 'A chief compliance officer who fails to fully inform the board of a material compliance failure, or who fails to aggressively pursue non-compliance within the service provider, would risk her position. She would also risk her career, because it would be unlikely for another board of directors to approve such a person as chief compliance officer',[43]
- the compliance officer serves at the pleasure of the board and only the latter (including a majority of the independent directors) can appoint or remove a compliance officer. The board also sets the compliance officer's remuneration,
- the compliance officer and the independent directors should meet at least once each year in 'executive session'. The aim is to create 'an opportunity for the chief compliance officer and the independent directors to speak freely about any sensitive compliance issues of concern to any of them',[44]
- the compliance officer must observe the rules prohibiting 'the fund's officers, directors, employees or its adviser, principal underwriter, or any person acting under the direction of these persons, from directly or indirectly taking any action to coerce, manipulate, mislead or fraudulently influence the fund's chief compliance officer in the performance of her responsibilities'.[45]

These issues have been noted by compliance officers. The US International Association of Risk and Compliance Professionals (IARCP), an organisation for compliance officers and others, has highlighted the following 'challenges' for chief compliance officers:

- the role is not clearly or properly defined,
- there are conflicts of interest,
- there is a lack of independence,
- chief compliance officers do not report directly to the board,
- the role, and who does it, is determined by others, beyond the board,
- there is a lack of financial and staff resources to undertake the role adequately,
- there is a lack of ability to implement effective monitoring and reporting policies and procedures.[46]

These are all fundamental issues and any compliance officer faced with any of these 'challenges' needs to consider their position at the firm. In the worst case, if changes are not made quickly, to their satisfaction, they may need to take their own legal advice on their next steps.

The next section considers in detail, other compliance 'warning indicators' identified by the SEC.

Other important warning indicators

Need to report to CEO and be visible to the board

Other warning indicators include a chain of command where the chief compliance officer does not report to the CEO and is not sufficiently visible to the board.[47] Compliance staff should provide advice to the business and get engaged and remediate problems.[48] This latter aspects can be seen as 'litmus-test' indicators of the firm's attitude to compliance and its responsibilities.

Trying to do the right thing and acting in good faith

Although not really a warning indicator, a key factor in determining a SEC decision on whether to take action is the extent to which the chief compliance officer had tried to do the right thing and that they had acted in good faith. This was clearly described in a SEC disquisition on the role of compliance and the decision by the regulators to take personal action against the chief compliance officer.[49] Consequently, a decision not to take action reflects 'the principle that, in general, good faith judgments of CCOs made after reasonable inquiry and analysis should not be second guessed. In addition, indicia of good faith or lack of good faith are important factors in assessing reasonableness, fairness and equity in the application of chief compliance officer liability'.[50] The SEC is clear that 'disciplinary action against individuals generally should not be based on an isolated circumstance where a chief compliance officer, using good faith judgment makes a decision, after reasonable inquiry, that with hindsight, proves to be problematic'.[51]

More broadly, the SEC has expressed reluctance to take action against compliance officers since enforcement may have a 'chilling effect' across the industry and the SEC are 'troubled by the prospect of running [compliance officers] out of the industry'.[52] In the recent past, between 2009 and 2014, on average the SEC took enforcement action against compliance officers in around 10% of all cases against investment advisers.[53] It appears that for the SEC to take individual action there needs to have been not only a breach of the regulations but also some other aggravating element. A regulatory failure on its own seems not to be sufficient. There also needs to be some other serious problem indicating some individual ethical defect. This could include factors such being involved directly in the misconduct, lying to the regulator, operating with a significant conflict of interest and the like.

Issues with delegation

The Commission's views on personal liability as a result of delegating some function is still in doubt. For example, in 2018 in the action against Thaddeus North reinforced the SEC's stated position: that 'the 'chief executive officer of a brokerage firm is responsible for compliance' with all of the requirements imposed on his firm 'unless and until he reasonably delegates particular functions to another person in the firm and neither knows nor has reason to know' that a problem has arisen'.[54] This 'know-nothing' approach applies to others in the firm, including the chief compliance officer.[55]

However, this statement needs to be treated with considerable caution since the SEC in its disciplinary hearing against Castle Securities in 1998 had stated that it is insufficient 'for the person with overarching supervisory responsibilities to delegate supervisory responsibility to a subordinate, even a capable one, and then simply wash his hands of the matter until a problem is brought to his attention...implicit is the additional duty to follow-up and review that delegated authority to ensure that it is being properly exercised'.[56]

Good record keeping

The SEC carries out a number of routine inspection visits each year of regulated firms. As part of these reviews SEC staff will examine the firm's record keeping, less because they are concerned about record keeping infringements, but rather poor record keeping may be an indication of more serious problems. A business that fails to maintain proper records is likely to have difficulty maintaining compliance more generally.[57]

Knowledge of the business, adequate resources and good leadership, good communication skills underpinned by 'rock-solid integrity'

The SEC also expects compliance officers to not only know the business and have financial and legal knowledge but also to demonstrate leadership, good communication skills underpinned by 'rock-solid integrity'.[58] The SEC has also been clear about the responsibility of regulated firms to ensure that there is 'effective staffing, sufficient resources and a system of follow-up and review'.[59] The SEC has stated that there are two principles which need to be balanced when determining whether the regulator will hold a compliance officer personally responsible. These are the need to protect 'investors and the public interests' and the 'principles of fairness and equity' towards chief compliance officers.[60]

It is interesting that in North's case mention is made of the National Association of Securities Dealers action against Richard Rouse in 1993 and the North case appears to demonstrate a softening of the regulatory stance where the chief compliance officer may have been over-whelmed by regulatory requests for information. In the Rouse case the SEC set aside the fine and re-qualification requirement imposed on the compliance officer 'acknowledging the extraordinary demands placed on Rouse at the time of the violations because of the numerous federal and state investigations' relating to the firm for which they worked. The SEC also noted the good work Rouse had previously done in improving 'compliance procedures and had maintained good relations with regulators' but went on to emphasise that its decision to set aside certain sanctions 'should in no way be read to diminish the importance of timely compliance'.[61]

The next sections consider the US regulatory position on compliance officers raising concerns and also issues relating to their 'authority' and competence. These are general themes of this book.

What a chief compliance officers should do if they find a serious breach of the regulations

The chief compliance officer should request permission to obtain advice from an independent outside legal firm if there is a disagreement with senior management. The chief compliance officers needs to keep the possibility of resigning at the forefront of their mind as well as the need to make full disclosure to the regulators.

A chief compliance officer may need to resign to protect themselve from regulatory action and third-party litigation and for reasons of their own personal integrity. This position may come about because they have exhausted all possible avenues within the firm to express their views and for these to be accepted and acted upon. It may relate to a range of issues, including specific points of policy; the operations of the business or concerns about a lack of adequate resources. It may be because the chief compliance officer senses that the firm's business ethics diverge from their own. This could occur where the chief compliance officers loses trust in the honesty and integrity of the senior management. The threat of resigning should have a salutary effect on the board and senior management of the firm since it is likely that the regulators will track chief compliance officers' departures at a firm and may investigate.

The chief compliance officers will need to ensure that their concerns have been escalated within the firm and have been reported and considered by the board. They should also be formally recorded in the most recent compliance report. The chief compliance officers will want to ensure that they take with them copies of key documents which support and explain the reasons for their resignation. However, there may there may be issues in taking away papers and other records which could be deemed to belong to the company. There may be some protection if the chief compliance officer's chief sends this information to the SEC under the umbrella of a whistle-blowing process. Again, this is an area where the chief compliance officers may need to take independent legal advice before acting.

The competence, status, and authority expected of a chief compliance officer

The SEC expects that a 'chief compliance officer should be competent and knowledgeable regarding the [Investment] Advisers Act and should be empowered with full responsibility and authority to develop and enforce appropriate policies and procedures for the firm. Thus, the compliance officer should have a position of sufficient seniority and authority within the organization to compel others to adhere to the compliance policies and procedures'.[62]

Part of the assessment of a chief compliance officer's 'authority' rests on the resources they command to do the job. As already mentioned, this will be one of the factors considered by the SEC. An estimate is that, 'firms should spend no less than 5% of revenue or 7% of operating budget on compliance, with most SEC-regulated entities spending between 7% and 20% of total operating costs'.[63] Since almost all the costs are going to be based on staff salaries (or the equivalent in outsourced costs) these percentages readily translate into compliance headcount.

There is no requirement for a chief compliance officer to have any specific qualifications or any particular industry experience. However, the regulators, when they carry out inspections, will be assessing their authority within the firm. This will include whether they have sufficient power to require remedial action such as disciplinary steps against staff at the business, including those in senior positions. The examiners will also consider the individuals' ability and knowledge and the amount of time they spent performing the role of chief compliance officer.[64] If, in their view, it is inadequate they will re-commend additional training for the individual.[65] There are also doubts as to whether the company's general counsel should also undertake the com-pliance officer roles since the general counsel are seen too often as advocates for their business and lacking in sufficient independence.

Conclusion

The UK and US systems of financial services regulation are very different. However, the regulatory expectations of the compliance functions are similar. Both expect to see high quality, well documented processes and procedures supervised by a risk-based compliance monitoring programme. It is the responsibility of the compliance officer to ensure the rapid and timely escalation of significant concerns and ensure that any major issues are promptly remediated. The compliance function must be independent with access to the CEO and board. It must be properly resourced. The whole edifice is based on the compliance officer having sufficient 'authority' within the organisation and that they operate with a high-level of competence. Compliance professionalism is key.

The US regulators have, in recent years, taken action against deficient chief compliance officers. The SEC's decision to take this action appears to be based on there being a combination of a regulatory failure with some serious, aggravating, factor such as compliance misconduct, lying to the regulator, a significant conflict of interest, and so on. The regulator is unlikely to take personal action against the compliance officer if they evidently acted in good faith and their judgement was not completely unreasonable.

Notes

1 Rule 206(4)-7 for investment advisers and Rule 38a-1 for investment companies, SEC Final Rule: 17 CFR parts 270 and 275 [Release Nos. IA-2204; IC-26299; File No. S7-03-03], RIN 3235-AI77 Compliance Programs of Investment Companies and Investment Advisers, SEC website, https://www.sec.gov/rules/final/ia-2204.htm (accessed 24 May 2019).
2 Ibid (SEC Final Rules).
3 Andrew Ceresney, SEC Director of the Division of Enforcement, Keynote Address at Compliance Week 2014, Washington DC, 20 May 2014, https://www.sec.gov/news/speech/2014-spch052014ajc (accessed 23 May 2019).
4 Ibid (Ceresney speech).
5 Ibid (Ceresney speech).
6 Ibid (Ceresney speech).
7 'Our decision making is guided by five core principles: (1) focus on the interests of Main Street investors; (2) focus on individual accountability; (3) keep pace with technological change; (4) impose sanctions that most effectively further enforcement goals; and (5) constantly assess the allocation of our resources', evidence given by Stephanie Avakian and Steven Peikin SEC Co-Directors, Division of Enforcement, 16 May 2018, before the House Committee on Financial Services, Subcommittee on Capital Markets, Securities, and Investment, https://www.sec.gov/news/testimony/testimony-oversight-secs-division-enforcement (accessed 24 May 2019).
8 SEC File No. 3-18280, Release No. 82070, 14 November 2017, 2, https://www.sec.gov/litigation/admin/2017/34–82070.pdf (accessed 22 May 2019).
9 SEC Order making findings and imposing remedial sanctions, 15 August 2017, 3–5, https://www.sec.gov/litigation/admin/2017/34–81405.pdf (accessed 22 May 2019).
10 Supra note 8 (SEC 18280), 3.
11 SEC, Thaddeus North, Review of Disciplinary Action taken by FINRA, Release No. 84500, 29 October 2018, 11–13, https://www.sec.gov/litigation/opinions/2018/34–84500.pdf (accessed 23 May 2019).
12 Ibid (North), 17.
13 Ibid (North), 12.

14 Financial Crimes Enforcement Network website, 4 March 2020, 'FinCEN Penalizes US Bank official for corporate anti-money laundering failures', https://www.fincen.gov/news/news-releases/fincen-penalizes-us-bank-official-corporate-anti-money-laundering-failures (accessed 19 March 2020).

15 FinCEN assessment of a civil money penalty against Michael LaFontaine, 4 March 2020, 10–11, https://www.fincen.gov/sites/default/files/enforcement_action/2020-03-04/Michael%20LaFontaine-Assessment-02.26.20_508.pdf (accessed 24 March 2020).

16 Ibid (FinCEN assessment of a civil money penalty against Michael LaFontaine), 3.

17 Ibid (FinCEN assessment of a civil money penalty against Michael LaFontaine), 7 and 8.

18 FinCEN's assessment of a civil money penalty against Wachovia Bank, 4 March 2010, 4, 'The number of alerts or events generated by the Bank's automated transaction systems was capped to accommodate the number of available compliance personnel', https://www.fincen.gov/sites/default/files/enforcement_action/100316095447.pdf (accessed 24 March 2020).

19 Supra note 15 (FinCEN website).

20 Supra note 18 (FinCEN's assessment of a civil money penalty against Wachovia Bank, 4 March 2010), 6.

21 Ibid (Wachovia Bank), 7.

22 Ibid (Wachovia Bank), 10.

23 Ibid (Wachovia Bank), 11.

24 Haider has agreed to a three-year injunction barring him from performing a compliance function for any money transmitter and has agreed to pay a $250,000 penalty, 'FinCEN and Manhattan U.S. Attorney Announce Settlement with Former Money Gram Executive Thomas E. Haider', FinCen website, 4 May 2017, https://www.fincen.gov/news/news-releases/fincen-and-manhattan-us-attorney-announce-settlement-former-moneygram-executive (accessed 21 July 2020).

25 Reuters website, 'Former MoneyGram executive settles closely watched U.S. money laundering case', 4 May 2017, https://www.reuters.com/article/us-moneygram-intl-moneylaundering-idUSKBN1802P3 (accessed 21 July 2020).

26 FinCEN press release, 'Haider Settlement', 4 May 2020, https://www.fincen.gov/sites/default/files/2017-05/HaiderSettlement_050417.pdf (accessed 21 July 2020).

27 SEC, SFX Financial Advisory Management Enterprises, Inc. and Eugene S. Mason, 15 June 2015, Administrative proceedings, File No. 3-16591, https://www.sec.gov/litigation/admin/2015/ia-4116.pdf (accessed 21 July 2020).

28 International Association of Risk and Compliance Professionals (IARCP) website, The Chief Compliance Officer, https://www.chief-compliance-officer.org (accessed 24 May 2019).

29 Norm Champ, 'Building effective relationships with regulators', 22 October 2015, https://corpgov.law.harvard.edu/2015/10/22/building-effective-relationships-with-regulators/ (accessed 24 May 2019).

30 Ibid (Champ).

31 US Department of Justice (DoJ) Criminal Division, 'Evaluation of corporate compliance programs, guidance document updated', April 2019, https://www.justice.gov/criminal-fraud/page/file/937501/download (accessed 11 February 2020). The guidance was further updated in 2020. These changes are mainly with regard to degrees of emphasis on, for example, continuous risk assessments and also the need for the firm to monitor third-parties throughout the relationship, US DoJ, Criminal Division, Evaluation of corporate compliance programs (updated June 2020), https://www.justice.gov/criminal-fraud/page/file/937501/download (accessed 28 June 2020).

32 Ibid (DoJ guidance 2019), 5.
33 Ibid (DoJ guidance 2019), 2.
34 Ibid (DoJ guidance 2019), 4.
35 Ibid (DoJ guidance 2019), 4.
36 Ibid (DoJ guidance 2019), 6–18.
37 Ibid (DoJ guidance 2019), 8.
38 Ibid (DoJ guidance 2019), 8.
39 Ibid (DoJ guidance 2019), 18.
40 DoJ and SEC, A resource guide to the US Foreign Corrupt Practices Act, November 2012, 79, https://www.justice.gov/sites/default/files/criminal-fraud/legacy/2015/01/16/guide.pdf (accessed 21 May 2020).
41 SEC website, Enforcement actions: FCPA cases, https://www.sec.gov/spotlight/fcpa/fcpa-cases.shtml (accessed 21 May 2020).
42 SEC, Final Rule: compliance programs of investment companies and investment advisers, 17 CFR Parts 270 and 275 [Release Nos. IA-2204; IC-26299; File No. S7-03-03], RIN 3235-AI77 (2004), https://www.sec.gov/rules/final/ia-2204.htm (accessed 20 May 2020).
43 Ibid, Part 270 - Rules and Regulations, Investment Company Act of 1940, §270.38a-1 Compliance procedures and practices of certain investment companies, (a) 1–4.
44 Ibid (Part 270).
45 Ibid (Part 270).
46 International Association of Risk and Compliance Professionals (IARCP) website, https://www.chief-compliance-officer.org (accessed 21 May 2020).
47 Supra note 3 (Ceresney speech).
48 Supra note 3 (Ceresney speech).
49 Supra note 11 (North), 11–12.
50 Supra note 11 (North), 12.
51 Supra note 11 (North), 12.
52 SEC Commissioner Hester Peirce, Remarks at the National Membership Conference of the National Society of Compliance Professionals, 30 October 2018, https://www.sec.gov/news/speech/speech-peirce-103018 (accessed 23 May 2019).
53 SEC website, Luis Aguilar, Public Statement, 'The role of chief compliance officers must be supported', 29 June 2015, https://www.sec.gov/news/statement/supporting-role-of-chief-compliance-officers.html (accessed 21 May 2020).
54 Supra note 11 (North), 12.
55 See Thomas White, Release No. 34398, 1994 WL 389903, https://www.sec.gov/news/digest/1994/dig072694.pdf (accessed 23 May 2019). This position was reaffirmed in Michael Markowski, Release No. 43259, 2000 WL 1264292, IV, https://www.sec.gov/litigation/opinions/34–43259.htm (accessed 23 May 2019).
56 SEC, Castle Sec Corporation, Corp., Exchange Act Release No. 39523, 1998 WL 3456, 7, https://www.sec.gov/litigation/opinions/34–39523.txt (accessed 23 May 2019).
57 Supra note 52 (Peirce remarks).
58 Supra note 52 (Peirce remarks).
59 Supra note 11 (North), 13.
60 Supra note 11 (North), 11.
61 Richard Rouse, Release No. 32658, 1993, WL 276149, 2, https://www.sec.gov/news/digest/1993/dig072693.pdf (accessed 23 May 2019).
62 Supra note 42 (Final Rule: Compliance Programs of Investment Companies and Investment Advisers), Rule 206(4)-7 (Investment advisers) and Rule 38a-1 (Investment companies).

63 Financial Planning website, Todd Cipperman, 'Voices: my predictions for 2019s regulatory agenda', 7 January 2019, https://www.financial-planning.com/opinion/sec-intensifies-scrutiny-on-doubled-up-compliance-officers (accessed 21 May 2020).
64 Supra note 53 (Luis Aguilar, Public Statement).
65 SEC Report, Examination priorities 2020, 4, https://www.sec.gov/about/offices/ocie/national-examination-program-priorities-2020.pdf (accessed 21 May 2020).

11

CONCLUSION

Compliance in financial services can be summed up in a number of words: being trustworthy; possessing 'authority', competence and professionalism; being a good interlocutor and communicator; having imagination; taking a customer-centric perspective and always being persistent.

Compliance has failed in some, or all, of these areas in many regulated firms. This is evident from the examples given in this book including the mis-design and wide spread mis-selling of **PPI and structured capital at risk products in the United Kingdom and the many issues with Wells Fargo bank in the United States.**

There are **many reasons for these compliance failures.** Some firms have employed weak and incompetent compliance staff. Compliance officers, for a range of reasons, may not have spoken up or taken the necessary action. This could have been due to fear, a culture of subservience and bullying, narrow 'siloed' thinking, a lack of perspective or a failure of imagination as the consequences were not thought through. Often compliance functions are affected by complacency. They fall into a form of torpor and do not sense the changes going on around them. As a consequence, they provide misleading but comforting reports to boards and regulators. Frequently, those that could have helped, such as whistleblowers, were ignored, persecuted and hounded out of the organisation. To counter this compliance needs to constantly challenge itself. The starting point should be that there *are* significant issues – they have just not yet been identified.

It should be possible to learn from the regulatory failures. This includes understanding better the drivers of corporate ineptitude and bad behaviour. All too often there are **structural and psychological reasons why doing the wrong thing prevails.** These reasons include hubris, greed, moral blindness and a lack of imagination. This latter error frequently occurs due to a failure to think through issues from other perspectives and an inability to imagine possible consequences. These failings may arise from a number of sources including individuals concentrating on the task in hand, day-to-day work pressures, the simple, mind-numbing drudgery of many jobs, the stress of meeting business targets and the like. The task of compliance is to give voice to the full imagination of thought. This may be a difficult role since it may mean standing up to confront all the pressures which act against doing the right thing. It is too tempting to go along with the herd and just to keep quiet. Consequently, compliance has to ensure that the business retains its 'moral compass' and compliance needs to be authoritative and to provide leadership. Offering advice and then doing nothing if that advice is ignored is a grave failing.

Although this book concentrates on financial services in the United States and the United Kingdom, the issues considered have broader application. They should resonate with those working in other highly-regulated industries such as pharmaceuticals, aerospace, extractive industries and so on. In many ways, although legislation and the actions of regulators are the catalysts for the approach taken in the financial services industry, they should not be the factors that drive good practice. As explained throughout this book, firms need to comply with the spirit, and not simply the letter, of the law. All organisations should consider the interests of all stakeholders and set and publicise the outcomes they seek to achieve to meet these expectations as best as possible. The mechanisms to gain these goals and their measurement and reporting follow on from this and forms part of good corporate governance.

In part, many problems arise because many compliance departments see their scope too narrowly. They are not alone in this since some of those in business line and in senior management roles also view the role of compliance in limited terms. Many individuals in firms see their objective as simply complying with the black-letter law set out in the various regulations. However, as we have seen this is a necessary but not sufficient goal. The board, senior management and compliance need to understand what the regulations are seeking to achieve and the target should be to deliver these outcomes. Those working in the business need to follow the 'spirit' as well as the 'letter' of the regulations. The various stakeholders such as the regulators, customers and so on are increasingly focused on regulatory outcomes as opposed to compliance 'activities' and this too must be the focus of the compliance function within firms, as well as the board and other senior management.

Compliance has been hampered in the past by a number of failings within its own arrangements and thinking. There is a strong risk that compliance staff may over-concentrate on the technical aspects of the regulations without understanding the full purpose of the requirements. These include an over-focus on operational procedures. Setting and complying with business procedures is important and the regulators have somewhat set the agenda in this area with much of regulatory inspections concerned with process. This is reflected in many of the regulatory enforcement actions. However, in addition to process, outcomes for stakeholders are even more important. Process is a means to an end and compliance must question not only whether processes are followed but whether they deliver the desired outcomes.

As discussed earlier in this book the 'tools' of compliance such as risk maps, monitoring and the like are all important but much more is required. Compliance needs to provide an **authoritative voice** for the key stakeholders and the long-term interests of the business. The board and other senior executives should already being doing this and the role of compliance should be to reinforce this view. However, from time to time some stakeholder interests may be overlooked and it is for compliance to act as a 'powerful, vocal conscience' in these circumstances. Stakeholders rely on compliance to act with authority and speak up clearly, and to do so firmly. Ultimately, if the compliance officer considers that they are not being listened to then they must, quickly take effective action to remedy this. This could include first speaking to the CEO and, if this fails, to the non-executive director chairing the board risk or compliance committee. In the worst case scenario, the compliance office may need to take their own legal advice and they may need to speak directly to the regulator. Knowledge that the compliance office possesses this level of implacable resolution should be sufficient to compel firms to act properly well before any of these steps are necessary. Additionally, compliance officers have an added incentive to act conscientiously since it is evident that regulators are **holding more compliance officers personally accountable with enforcement fines and industry bans.**

Whistleblowers have an important role in ensuring compliance within any organised body. In every organisation one or more people know what is going on and may suspect wrong-doing. They need to be given a 'voice' and be encouraged to speak-up without fear of retribution. Compliance has a central role in this. The importance of those who raise concerns cannot be over-stated. Their contribution should be welcomed by boards, senior executives and the various control functions. Some managers in the organisation will try to suppress them with a mixture of threats and psychological denigration or will just ignore them. Compliance, and others, should combat those attempting to silence those trying to speak up. This includes using a combination of staff training, publicly welcoming and celebrating those that whistleblow, ensuring that action is taken on their information and that those that attempt to render them silent are punished.

Compliance also has an important role as an **interlocutor** between the business and the regulators. Compliance fails if it simply cuts and pastes the regulations into policy documents. The regulatory requirements need to be brought to life for the business and operationalised in terms and methods applicable and comprehensible to those who need to implement them. This requires compliance staff to have a **good understanding of the business and its procedures and to be exceptional communicators.**

All this means that the compliance officer must have a sound **conceptual framework for compliance.** All compliance staff needs to have a strategic understanding of both the business and the role and purpose of

226

compliance. Compliance's conceptual framework and its role and purpose needs to be communicated clearly to all compliance staff, the board and other senior management and across the organisation. As part of this process of **communication**, compliance needs to make clear that it will not tolerate any failure to achieve the outcomes expected by the regulators. This level of clarity is likely to have the effect of preventing any future misunderstandings.

The risks are changing and 'blinkered' views need to change too. Traditional compliance perspectives need to change. Compliance needs to think more broadly about its role. Working with elements in the business, compliance needs to ensure that the products and services offered by the business are socially responsible; that the firm is publicly accountable; that no significant disadvantaged groups or individuals are neglected; and that insidious harms such as environmental damage and corruption are avoided.

As part of this new conceptual framework for compliance the latter needs to work with the board and the other senior executives to ensure that firms operate in the interests of all stakeholders, including – in particular – the **wider community**. This involves helping the business to prosper, sustainably, for the benefit of the whole community. The extent of the community ranges from the immediate localities where employees work and live through local regions to communities in the wider world.

To achieve all these objectives it is vitally important that compliance seeks **to attract and recruit the right staff**. These individuals need to come from a diversity of backgrounds bringing new ways of thinking, all buttressed by high-quality training and professionalism. The need for training extends across the business, both as a means of preventing problems which may arise from incompetence and also as a means of developing each individual so that they can use their abilities to the fullest extent. The effectiveness of staff training needs to be measured and improved, as necessary. **Training** should also extend to include board directors and other senior executives. It sends a message to other staff and managers that the organisation takes training seriously. It will also help ensure that senior management and boards all understand their roles and the risks run by the business. It will widen horizons and increase self-introspection. It will identify knowledge and skills gaps which can be addressed.

The authority of the compliance officer and the conviction of the compliance function needs to be reinforced by various **'signals'** such as ensuring that the compliance officer is a member of the executive committee of the business and has regular and frequent meetings with the firm's board and bilateral meetings with the non-executive directors and chairman.

Compliance need to consider where best to locate the compliance function within the organisation and how best to structure the unit. The standard 'three lines of defence' model needs to be challenged. It has often been found to be confusing and defective. As already mentioned, compliance needs to be proactive and intrusive to prevent problems and to take ownership of an issue and fix it quickly if no one else will act. In the United Kingdom the Senior Managers and Certified Persons Regime should also aid in encouraging the remediation of concerns. Much of the work of compliance should be aimed at preventing problems. This will include assessing the attraction strategies and recruitment of key business staff, including traders and financial advisers and their managers. It covers the design of products and services and their marketing. This may annoy senior managers but there may be among them many who regret that some of their actions were not prevented by compliance at the time.

Finally, compliance needs to look to the future and the developing areas with compliance implications. These include the uses and implications of artificial intelligence and automated advice systems. In addition, compliance needs to take account of the increasing expectations being placed on businesses covering areas such as climate change and the need both to improve corporate governance and to address societal expectations. All this means that the compliance staff must speak and operate with authority. Many compliance functions already do all of this but some do not – and this needs to change. The lessons from Wells Fargo and others demonstrate the need for fundamental change throughout many organisations.

BIBLIOGRAPHY

Books and articles

Abrahams, Clark and Mingyuan Zhang, 'Regression analysis for compliance testing' in *Fair lending compliance: intelligence and implications for credit risk management* (John Wiley, Hoboken, New Jersey, 2015), 147–182.

Alford, Charles Frederick, 'What makes whistleblowers so threatening? Comment on 'Cultures of silence and cultures of voice: the role of whistleblowing in healthcare organisations'' (2015) *International Journal of Health Policy and Management*, 5(1), 71–73, https://www.ncbi.nlm.nih.gov/pmc/articles/PMC4676977/pdf/IJHPM-5-71. pdf (accessed 8 January 2020).

Alliance and Leicester Reports and Accounts at 31 December 2004 and 2006, https://www.investegate.co.uk/article.aspx?id=200502250700040142J (accessed 15 June 2020).

Anand, Rohini and Mary-Frances Winters, 'A retrospective view of corporate diversity training from 1964 to the present' (2008) *Academy of Management Learning and Education*, 7(3), 356–372, http://www.wintersgroup.com/corporate-diversity-training-1964-to-present.pdf (accessed 15 November 2019).

Anglin, Stephanie, 'Do beliefs yield to evidence? Examining belief perseverance vs. change in response to congruent empirical findings' (2019) *Journal of Experimental Social Psychology*, 82, 176–199.

Arena, Marika, Michela Arnaboldi, and Tommaso Palermo, 'The dynamics of (dis) integrated risk management: a comparative field study' (2017) *Accounting, Organizations and Society*, 62, 65–81.

Arendt, Hannah, *Responsibility and judgement* (first published in 1971 and reprinted by Shocken Books, New York, 2003).

Aristotle, *Nicomachean ethics* (Revised edition, Penguin Classics edition, London, 2004).

Ashby, Simon, Tommaso Palermo, and Michael Power, 'Risk culture in financial organisation: an interim report' (2012), http://www.lse.ac.uk/accounting/assets/CARR/documents/Risk-Culture-in-Financial-Organisations/Risk-culture-interim-report.pdf (accessed 24 April 2019).

Ashforth, Blake and Yitzhak Fried, 'The mindlessness of organizational behaviors' (1988) *Human Relations*, 41, 305–329.

229

Ashforth, Blake and Raymond Lee, 'Defensive behavior in organizations: a pre-liminary model' (1990) *Human Relations, 43*(7), 642.

Ashforth, Blake, 'The organizationally induced helplessness syndrome: a pre-liminary model' (1990) *Canadian Journal of Administrative Sciences,* 7(3), 30–36.

Aven, Terje, *Risk, surprises and black swans: fundamental ideas and concepts in risk assessment and risk management* (Routledge, Abingdon, England, 2014).

Baldwin, Robert, Martin Cave, and Martin Lodge, *Understanding regulation: theory, strategy, and practice* (Oxford University Press, Oxford, 2012).

Bank of England

Bank of England, 'Future of finance: review on the outlook for the UK financial system – what it means for the Bank of England' (June 2019), https://www.bankofengland.co.uk/-/media/boe/files/report/2019/future-of-finance-report.pdf?la=en&hash=59CEFAEF01C71AA551E7182262E933A699E952FC (accessed 9 March 2020).

Bank of England and FCA, 'Machine learning in UK financial services' (October 2019), https://www.fca.org.uk/publication/research/research-note-on-machine-learning-in-uk-financial-services.pdf (accessed 7 March 2020).

Bank of England/PRA/FCA, 'Discussion paper: building the UK financial sector's opera-tional resilience', Bank of England DP01/18, PRA DP01/18, FCA DP18/04 (July 2018), https://www.bankofengland.co.uk/-/media/boe/files/prudential-regulation/discussion-paper/2018/dp118.pdf?la=en&hash=4238F3B14D839EBE6BEFBD6B5E5634FB95197D8A (accessed 25 May 2002).

Bank of England, 'Fair and effective markets review final report' (June 2015), https://www.bankofengland.co.uk/report/2015/fair-and-effective-markets-review---final-report (accessed 14 June 2020).

Banking Standards Board

Banking Standards Board, 'BSB statement of principles for strengthening pro-fessionalism' (March 2018), https://bankingstandardsboard.org.uk/bsb-statement-of-principles-for-strengthening-professionalism/ (accessed 6 May 2020).

Banking Standards Board, 'Annual review 2018/19', https://www.bankingstandardsboard.org.uk/pdf/banking-standards-annual-review-2018-2019.pdf (accessed 15 April 2019).

Barclays Bank in 2000, Barclays archive, https://www.archive.barclays.com/items/show/5366 (accessed 4 June 2020).

Bar-Yosef, Rivka and E.O. Schild, 'Pressures and defenses in bureaucratic roles' (1966) *American Journal of Sociology, 75*, 665–673.

Basel Committee on Banking Supervision ('Basel Committee'), 'Compliance and the compliance function in banks' (April 2005), https://www.bis.org/publ/bcbs113.pdf (accessed 15 April 2020).

Beaudouin, Valérie and others, 'Identifying the 'right' level of explanation in a given situation' (March 2020), hal-02507316, https://hal.telecom-paristech.fr/hal-02507316/document (accessed 10 April 2020).

Bedan, Matthew, 'Compliance culture, culture eats compliance for lunch:

behavioral science lessons from the Wells Fargo scandal' (28 November 2018), *The Anti-Corruption Report*, 7(24), https://www.forensicrisk.com/wp-content/uploads/The-Anti-Corruption-Report-the-definitive-source-of-actionable-intelligence-covering-anti-corruption-laws-around-the-globe-_-Article_-_p_Culture-Eats-Compliance-fo-002.pdf (accessed 28 March 2020).

Beggs, Jeri and Kathy Dean, 'Legislated ethics or ethics education? Faculty views in the post-Enron era' (2007) *Journal of Business Ethics*, 71, 15–37.

Benhabib, Seyla, 'Judgment and the moral foundations of politics in Arendt's thought' (1988) *Political Theory*, 16(1), 29–51.

Benjamin, Ruha, *Race after technology: abolitionist tools for the new Jim code* (Polity, Cambridge, England, 2019).

Berenbaum, Howard, M. Tyler Boden, and John Baker, 'Emotional salience, emotional awareness, peculiar beliefs, and magical thinking' (2009) *Emotion*, 9(2), 197–205.

Beyer, Janice and others, 'The selective perception of managers revisited' (June 1997) *Academy of Management Journal; Briarcliff Manor*, 40(3), 716–737.

Black, Julia

Black, Julia, 'Forms and paradoxes of principles-based regulation' (2008) *Capital Markets Law Journal*, 3(4), 425–457.

Black, Julia, 'The emergence of risk-based regulation and the new public risk management in the United Kingdom' (Autumn 2005) *Public Law*, 512–548.

Bourdieu, Pierre, *Outline of a theory of practice*, Richard Nice (tr) (Cambridge University Press, Cambridge, 1977).

Brener, Alan

Brener, Alan, 'Developing the senior managers regime' in Costanza Russo, Rosa Lastra, and William Blair (eds.) *Research handbook on law and ethics in banking and finance* (Edward Elgar Publishing, Northampton, 2019).

Brener, Alan, 'Payment service directive II and its implications' in T. Lynn (ed.) *Disrupting finance* (Springer, 2018), 104.

Brener, Alan, 'The golden threads of compliance' (1995) *Journal of Financial Regulation and Compliance*, 3(4), 344–349.

Bunyan, John, *The pilgrim's progress, part 1* (originally published in 1678, Wordsworth Edition, Ware, Hertfordshire, 1996).

Burke, Edmund, *Speeches on America. On conciliation with America*, Arthur Innes (ed.) (first published 1775, Cambridge University Press, Cambridge, 1906).

Burns, Robert, 'A man's a man for a' that' (1795) Scottish Poetry Library, https://www.scottishpoetrylibrary.org.uk/poem/mans-man-0/ (accessed 29 April 2020).

Caldwell, David and Charles O'Reilly, 'Responses to failure: the effects of choice and responsibility on impression management' (1982) *Academy of Management Journal*, 25(1), 121–136.

Capili, April, 'The created ego in Levinas 'totality and infinity'' (2011) *Sophia*, 50(4), 677–692.

Champ, Norm, 'Building effective relationships with regulators', Harvard Law

School forum on Corporate Governance website (22 October 2015), https://corpgov.law.harvard.edu/2015/10/22/building-effective-relationships-with-regulators/ (accessed 19 February 2020).

Chen, Hui and Eugene Soltes, 'Why compliance programs fail—and how to fix them' (March/April 2018), *Harvard Business Review*, https://hbr.org/2018/03/why-compliance-programs-fail (accessed 8 April 2020).

Chiu, Iris H.-Y., *Regulating (from) the inside* (Bloomsbury, London, 2015).

Coffee, John, *Gatekeepers: the professions and corporate governance* (Oxford University Press, Oxford, 2006).

Connelly, Michael and Jean Clandinin, 'Stories of experience and narrative inquiry' (1990) *Educational Researcher*, *19*(5), 2–14.

Conrad, Joseph, *Lord Jim* (first published 1900, Penguin Classics, London, 1957).

Consumer Financial Protection Bureau, 'Fair lending report' (June 2019), Federal Register/Vol 84, No. 130/Monday, July 8, 2019/Notices, 32423, https://www.govinfo.gov/content/pkg/FR-2019-07-08/pdf/2019-14384.pdf (accessed 1 July 2020).

Cuno, James, 'Telling stories: rhetoric and leadership, a case study' (2005) *Leadership*, *1*(2), 205–213.

Curtis, Mary and John Williams, 'The impact of culture and training on code of conduct effectiveness: reporting of observed unethical behavior' in *Research on professional responsibility and ethics in accounting* (Emerald Group Publishing, Bingley, England), 18, 1–31.

Davies, Howard and Maria Zhivitskaya, 'Three lines of defence: a robust organising framework, or just lines in the sand?' (2018) *Global Policy*, *9*(Suppl 1), 40, https://onlinelibrary.wiley.com/doi/pdf/10.1111/1758-5899.12568 (accessed 11 May 2020).

Davis, Michael, 'Avoiding the tragedy of whistleblowing' (Winter 1989) *Business and Professional Ethics Journal*, *8*(4), 3–19.

Deloitte Center for Financial Services, 'Kicking it up a notch. Taking retail bank cross-selling to the next level' (2013), https://www2.deloitte.com/content/dam/Deloitte/us/Documents/financial-services/us-kickingitupanotch-092614.pdf (accessed 28 March 2020).

Deloitte Touche Tohmatsu, 'The changing role of compliance' (2015), https://www2.deloitte.com/content/dam/Deloitte/gr/Documents/financial-services/gr_fs_the_changing_role_of_compliance_en_noexp.pdf (accessed 20 April 2020).

Demott, Deborah, '*The stages of scandal and the roles of the general counsel*' (2012) *Wisconsin Law Review*, 463–493.

Denning, Stephen, 'Using stories to spark organizational change' (2002) *Storytelling Foundation International*, http://providersedge.com/docs/km_articles/Using_Stories_to_Spark_Organizational_Change.pdf (accessed 30 April 2020).

Department of Business, Energy and Industrial Strategy, 'Confidentiality clauses: response to the government consultation on proposals to prevent misuse in situations of workplace harassment or discrimination' (July 2019), https://assets.publishing.service.gov.uk/government/uploads/system/uploads/attachment_data/file/818324/confidentiality-clause-consultation-govt-response.pdf (accessed 28 April 2020).

Department of Business, Innovation and Skills, 'Whistleblowing, guidance for employers and code of practice' (2015), https://assets.publishing.service.gov.uk/government/uploads/system/uploads/attachment_data/file/415175/bis-15-200-whistleblowing-guidance-for-employers-and-code-of-practice.pdf (accessed 1 January 2020).

Schwab, Charles, 'The rise of robo: Americans' perspectives and predictions on the use of digital advice' (November 2018), https://content.schwab.com/web/retail/public/about-schwab/charles_schwab_rise_of_robo_report_findings_2018.pdf (accessed 4 March 2020).

US Department of Justice (DOJ)

Department of Justice (DoJ) and SEC, 'A resource guide to the US Foreign Corrupt Practices Act' (November 2012), 79, https://www.justice.gov/sites/default/files/criminal-fraud/legacy/2015/01/16/guide.pdf (accessed 21 May 2020).

Dobbin, Frank and Alexandra Kalev, 'Why diversity programs fail' (July/August 2016), *Harvard Business Review*, https://hbr.org/2016/07/why-diversity-programs-fail (accessed 15 November 2019).

Doughty, Robert, *The seeds of disaster, the development of French Army doctrine 1919–1939* (Stackpole Books, Mechanicsburg, PA, 1985), 129–140.

EenkHoorn, Piet and Johan Graafland, 'Lying in business: insights from Hannah Arendt's 'Lying in politics'' (2011) *Business Ethics: A European Review*, 20(4), 359–374.

English, Stacey and Susannah Hammond, 'Cost of compliance: global survey' (2018), Thomson Reuters, 28, https://legal.thomsonreuters.com/content/dam/ewp-m/documents/legal/en/pdf/reports/cost-of-compliance-special-report-2018.pdf (accessed 20 April 2020).

Evensky, Jerry, *Adam Smith's moral philosophy, a historical and contemporary perspective on markets, law, ethics and culture* (Cambridge University Press, Cambridge, 2005).

Federal Reserve, Federal Reserve Letter to all Federal Reserve Boards, Staff and Regulated Firms, 'Compliance risk management programs and oversight at large banking organizations with complex compliance profiles' (16 October 2008), SR 08-8/CA 08-11, https://www.federalreserve.gov/boarddocs/srletters/2008/SR0808.htm (accessed 15 April 2020).

Feldman, Yuval and Yotam Kaplan, 'Behavioral ethics as compliance' in Van Rooij and Sokol (eds.) *Cambridge handbook of compliance* (September 2019), Bar Ilan University Faculty of Law Research Paper No. 19-18, Forthcoming, https://ssrn.com/abstract=3458582 or http://dx.doi.org/10.2139/ssrn.3458582 (accessed 16 December 2019).

The Editor's Desk, 'Memorable headlines' (2009), https://editdesk.wordpress.com/2009/08/28/memorable-headlines-gotcha/ (accessed 25 May 2020).

US Department of Justice (DOJ) Criminal Division, 'Evaluation of corporate compliance programs, guidance document updated' (April 2019), https://www.justice.gov/criminal-fraud/page/file/937501/download (accessed 11 February 2020).

Financial Conduct Authority

2020

FCA, *'Proposals to enhance climate-related disclosures by listed issuers and clarification of existing disclosure obligations'*, Consultation Paper, CP20/3

(March 2020), https://www.fca.org.uk/publication/consultation/cp20-3.pdf (accessed 10 March 2020).

FCA, 'Sector views' (February 2020), https://www.fca.org.uk/publication/corporate/sector-views-2020.pdf (accessed 9 March 2020).

FCA Business Plan (2019/20), https://www.fca.org.uk/publication/business-plans/business-plan-2019-20.pdf (accessed 1 July 2020).

FCA Letter to Board Directors, 'Portfolio strategy letter to firms in the Personal & Commercial Lines Insurer (PL&CL) portfolio: identifying and remedying harms' (8 January 2020), https://www.fca.org.uk/publication/correspondence/letter-firms-personal-commercial-lines-insurer-portfolio-identifying-remedying-harms.pdf (accessed 17 January 2020).

FCA Rule book (known as the 'handbook'), SYSC 6.1.1R, 'Senior arrangements, systems and controls, Chapter 6 compliance, internal audit and financial crime', *SYSC 6/12 Release 48* (March 2020), https://www.handbook.fca.org.uk/handbook/SYSC/6.pdf (accessed 15 April 2020).

2019

FCA, 'Fair pricing in financial services: summary of responses and next steps feedback statement' (FS19/04, July 2019), https://www.fca.org.uk/publication/feedback/fs19-04.pdf (accessed 4 May 2020).

FCA, *'Business plan 2019/20'* (April 2019), https://www.fca.org.uk/publication/business-plans/business-plan-2019-20.pdf (accessed 22 April 2019).

FCA 'Dear CEO' Letter, 'Firms' approval of financial promotions: the FCA expectations' (11 April 2019), https://www.fca.org.uk/publication/correspondence/dear-ceo-letter-firms-approvals-financial-promotions-fcas-expectations.pdf (accessed 22 April 2019).

FCA letter of 9 January 2019, clarity in promotions about regulated and unregulated business: the FCA's expectations, https://www.fca.org.uk/publication/correspondence/dear-ceo-letter-promotions-regulated-unregulated-business.pdf (accessed 22 April 2019).

FCA's Mission, 'Approach to supervision' (April 2019), https://www.fca.org.uk/publication/corporate/our-approach-supervision.pdf (accessed 29 April 2019).

2018

FCA, 'Retail and wholesale banking: review of firms' whistleblowing arrangements' (14 November 2018), https://www.fca.org.uk/publications/multi-firm-reviews/retail-and-wholesale-banking-review-firms-whistleblowing-arrangements (accessed 27 November 2019).

FCA, 'Fair pricing in financial services – discussion paper 18/9' (October 2018), https://www.fca.org.uk/publication/discussion/dp18-09.pdf (accessed 22 April 2019).

FCA, 'Price discrimination in the cash savings market discussion paper' (DP18/6 July 2018), https://www.fca.org.uk/publication/discussion/dp18-06.pdf (accessed 21 November 2019).

FCA, 'Approach to supervision' (April 2019), https://www.fca.org.uk/publication/corporate/our-approach-supervision-final-report-feedback-statement.pdf (accessed 25 November 2019).

2017

FCA, 'The compliance function in wholesale banks' (November 2017), https://fca.org.uk/publication/research/the-compliance-function-in-wholesale-banks.pdf (accessed 13 May 2019).

Financial Conduct Authority – Enforcement Notices/Upper Tribunal

2020

FCA Final Notice, Commerzbank (17 June 2020), https://www.fca.org.uk/publication/final-notices/commerzbank-ag-2020.pdf (accessed 2 July 2020).

FCA Final Notice, Lloyds Bank (11 June 2020), https://www.fca.org.uk/publication/final-notices/lloyds-bank-plc-bank-of-scotland-plc-the-mortgage-business-plc-2020.pdf.

2019

FCA Final Notice, Standard Life Assurance (23 July 2019), https://www.fca.org.uk/publication/final-notices/standard-life-assurance-limited-2019.pdf (11 December 2019).

FCA Final Notice, Linear Investments (29 April 2019), https://www.fca.org.uk/publication/final-notices/linear-investments-ltd-final-notice-2019.pdf (accessed 1 May 2019).

FCA Final Notice, Standard Chartered Bank (5 February 2019), https://www.fca.org.uk/publication/decision-notices/standard-chartered-bank-2019.pdf (accessed 21 November 2019).

2018

FCA Final Notice Santander (November 2018), https://www.fca.org.uk/publication/final-notices/santander-uk-plc-2018.pdf (accessed 10 April 2019).

FCA Final Notice, Liberty Mutual Insurance Europe (29 October 2018), https://www.fca.org.uk/publication/final-notices/liberty-mutual-insurance-europe-se-2018.pdf (accessed 21 November 2019).

2017

FCA Final Notice, 'Gregory Nathan re his proposed appointment to be the compliance officer and money laundering reporting officer at Goldenway Global Investments' (21 August 2017), https://www.fca.org.uk/publication/final-notices/goldenway-global-investments-uk-limited.pdf (accessed 14 May 2019).

FCA Final Notice, David Watters (July 2017), https://www.fca.org.uk/publication/final-notices/david-samuel-watters.pdf (accessed 16 May 2019).

2016

FCA Final Notice, Steven Smith (October 2016), https://www.fca.org.uk/publication/final-notices/steven-smith-2016.pdf (accessed 17 May 2019).

FCA Final Notice, Peter Johnson (May 2016), https://www.fca.org.uk/publication/final-notices/peter-francis-johnson.pdf (accessed 15 May 2019).

Revised FCA Final Notice re Carrimjee, https://www.fca.org.uk/publication/final-notices/tariq-carrimjee-2016.pdf (accessed 17 May 2019).

2016 Upper Tribunal Case Tariq Carrimjee v FCA [2016] UKUT 0447 (TCC), http://taxandchancery_ut.decisions.tribunals.gov.uk/Documents/decisions/Carrimjee%20v%20FCA%20for%20website.pdf (accessed 17 May 2019).

2015

FCA, Georgina Philippou, acting director of enforcement, FCA press release re Bank of Beirut (5 March 2015), https://www.fca.org.uk/news/press-releases/financial-conduct-authority-imposes-£21m-fine-and-places-restriction-bank-beirut (accessed 16 May 2020).

FCA, Georgina Philippou, acting director of enforcement, FCA press release re Stephen Bell (13 March 2015), https://www.fca.org.uk/news/press-releases/fca-fines-and-prohibits-mr-stephen-bell-former-director-network-financial-group (accessed 17 May 2020).

FCA Final Notice, Deutsche Bank AG (April 2015), https://www.fca.org.uk/publication/final-notices/deutsche-bank-ag-2015.pdf (accessed 8 May 2019).

FCA Final Notice, Anthony Wills (March 2015), https://www.fca.org.uk/publication/final-notices/anthony-rendell-boyd-wills.pdf (accessed 15 May 2019).

FCA Final Notice, Robert Addison (March 2015), https://www.fca.org.uk/publication/final-notices/robert-addison.pdf (accessed 21 May 2019).

FCA Final Notice, Stephen Bell (March 2015), https://www.fca.org.uk/publication/final-notices/stephen-edward-bell.pdf (accessed 16 March 2019).

FCA press release re Sam Kenny (13 March 2015), https://www.fca.org.uk/news/press-releases/former-chief-executive-stockbroker-firm-fined-£450000-and-banned, https://www.fca.org.uk/news/press-releases/former-chief-executive-stockbroker-firm-fined-£450000-and-banned (accessed 17 May 2020).

Upper Tribunal, Robert Addison v FCA [2015] UKUT 0013 (TCC), http://taxandchancery_ut.decisions.tribunals.gov.uk/Documents/decisions/Arch-v-FCA.pdf (accessed 21 May 2019).

2013

FCA Final Notice, Lloyds TSB (10 December 2013), https://www.fca.org.uk/publication/final-notices/lloyds-tsb-bank-and-bank-of-scotland.pdf (accessed 4 December 2019).

2012

FSA, Coutts & Company Final Notice (23 March 2012), https://www.fca.org.uk/publication/final-notices/coutts-mar12.pdf (accessed 3 December 2019).

FSA Final Notice, Carl Davey (December 2012), https://www.fca.org.uk/publication/final-notices/carl-davey.pdf (accessed 19 May 2019).

FSA Final Notice, UBS AG, 25 November 2012 – re Kweku Adoboli, https://www.fca.org.uk/publication/final-notices/ubs-ag.pdf (accessed 23 April 2019).

FSA Final Notice, Alexander Ten-Holter (January 2012), https://www.fca.org.uk/publication/final-notices/ten-holter-greenlight.pdf (accessed 21 May 2019).

2011

FSA, Coutts & Company, Final Notice (7 November 2011), https://www.fca.org.uk/publication/final-notices/coutts.pdf (accessed 3 December 2019).

FSA, Final Notice Credit Suisse UK (25 October 2011) https://www.fca.org.uk/publication/final-notices/credit-suisse25oct11.pdf (accessed 3 December 2019).

FSA, Final Notice Oluwole Fagbulu (September 2011), https://www.fca.org.uk/publication/final-notices/oluwole_fagbulu.pdf (accessed 22 May 2019).

FSA , Final Notice, Barclays Bank (14 January 2011), https://www.fca.org.uk/publication/final-notices/barclays_jan11.pdf (accessed 14 December 2019).

Oluwole Modupe Fagbulu v FSA [2011] FS/2010/0001 FS/2010/0006, http://taxandchancery_ut.decisions.tribunals.gov.uk/Documents/decisions/VisserandFagbulu_v_FSA.pdf (accessed 22 May 2019).

2010

FSA Final Notice, re Standard Life Assurance (20 January 2010), https://www.fca.org.uk/publication/final-notices/slal.pdf (accessed 11 December 2019).

2008

FSA Final Notice, Alliance & Leicester (October 2008), https://www.fca.org.uk/publication/final-notices/alliance_leicester.pdf (accessed 5 May 2019).

2003

FSA Final Notice, Lloyds TSB, 24 September 2003, https://www.fca.org.uk/publication/final-notices/lloyds-tsb_24sept03.pdf (accessed 29 November 2019).

Financial Reporting Council

Annual Review of the UK Corporate Governance Code (January 2020), https://www.frc.org.uk/getattachment/53799a2d-824e-4e15-9325-33eb6a30f063/Annual-Review-of-the-UK-Corporate-Governance-Code,-Jan-2020_Final.pdf (accessed 10 January 2020).

Financial Reporting Council, 'Corporate culture and the role of boards: report of observations' (July 2016), https://www.frc.org.uk/getattachment/3851b9c5-92d3-4695-aeb2-87c9052dc8c1/Corporate-Culture-and-the-Role-of-Boards-Report-of-Observations.pdf (accessed 27 November 2019).

Financial Stability Board, 'Task force on climate-related financial disclosures: recommendations: Final report' (June 2017), https://www.fsb-tcfd.org/wp-content/uploads/2017/06/FINAL-2017-TCFD-Report-11052018.pdf (accessed 9 March 2020).

Fink, Larry, Chairman and Chief Executive Officer, Letter to the CEOs of companies in which BlackRock is a shareholder, 'A fundamental reshaping of finance', BlackRock website, https://www.blackrock.com/corporate/investor-relations/larry-fink-ceo-letter (accessed 10 March 2020).

Fleming, David, 'Narrative leadership: using the power of stories' (2001) *Strategy and Leadership*, 29(4), 34–36.

Forster Lloyd, William, *Two lectures on the checks to population* (Collingwood, Oxford, 1833).

Fox, Craig and Gülden Ülkümen, 'Distinguishing two dimensions of uncertainty' in Wibecke Brun and others (eds.) *Perspectives on thinking, judging, and decision making* (Universitetsforlaget, Oslo, 2011).

Francesca, Gino and Max Bazerman, 'When misconduct goes unnoticed: the acceptability of gradual erosion in others' unethical behavior' (2009) *Journal of Experimental Social Psychology*, 45, 708–719.

Freedman, David, *Statistical models: theory and practice* (Cambridge University Press, Cambridge, England, 2009).

Freund, Rudolf, William Wilson, and Ping Sa, *Regression analysis: statistical modeling of a response variable* (Elsevier Science and Technology, San Diego, California, 2006).

Galbraith, John S., 'The 'turbulent frontier' as a factor in British expansion' (1960) *Comparative Studies in Society and History*, 2(2), 150.

Ganz, Marshall, 'Public narrative, collective action, and power' in Sina Odugbemi and Taeku Lee (eds.) *Accountability through public opinion: from inertia to public action* (The World Bank, Washington, DC, 2011) 273–289.

Gilad, Sharon, 'Institutionalizing fairness in financial markets: mission impossible?' (2011) *Regulation and Governance*, 5(3), 309–332.

Gillis, Talia, 'False dreams of algorithmic fairness: the case of credit pricing' (November 2019), https://scholar.harvard.edu/files/gillis/files/gillis_jmp_191101.pdf (accessed 1 July 2020).

Goodnight, Thomas and Sandy Green, 'Rhetoric, risk, and markets: the dot-com bubble' (2010) *Quarterly Journal of Speech*, 96(2), 115–140.

Gowler, Dan and Karen Legge, 'The meaning of management and the management of meaning: a view from social anthropology' in *Perspectives on management: a multidisciplinary analysis* (Oxford University Press, Oxford, 1983).

Graham, Jill, 'Principled organizational dissent' (1983), Northwestern University, ProQuest Dissertations Publishing.

Gratton, Peter, 'An Arendtian approach to business ethics' in Mollie Painter-Morland and Patricia Werhane (eds.) *Cutting-edge issues in business ethics* (Springer, New York, 2008), 202–214.

Gray, Edwin, 'Warnings ignored: the politics of the crisis' (1990) *Stanford Law and Policy Review*, 2, 138–146.

Hauser, Christian, 'Fighting against corruption: does anti-corruption training make any difference?' (2019) *Journal of Business Ethics*, 159(1), 281–299.

Herald of Free Enterprise Report of Court No. 8074 Formal Investigation (HMSO,

1987), Mr Justice Sheen, Wreck Commissioner, https://assets.publishing.service. gov.uk/media/54c1704ce5274a15b6000025/FormalInvestigation_HeraldofFree Enterprise-MSA1894.pdf (accessed 1 January 2020).

Howard, Ebenezer, *Tomorrow a peaceful path to real reform* (Swan Sonnenschein, London, 1898).

Huxley, Aldous, *The devils of Loudon* (first published 1952, Harper Colophon, New York, 1965).

Jackman, David, *The compliance revolution: how compliance needs to change to survive* (John Wiley, Singapore, 2015).

Kant, Immanuel, *Critic of practical reason*, Werner Phuhar (tr) (first published 1788, Hackett, Indianapolis, 2002).

Kelly, Christopher, 'Failings in management and governance: report of the independent review into the events leading to the Co-operative Bank's capital shortfall' (30 April 2014), https://assets.ctfassets.net/5ywmq66472jr/ 3LpckmtCnuWiuuuEM2qAsw/9bc99b1cd941261bca5d674724873deb/kelly-review.pdf (accessed 7 July 2020).

Kim, Sung Hui, 'Inside lawyers: friends or gatekeepers?' (2016) *Fordham Law Review*, 84, 1867–1897.

Kleinhesselink, Randall and Richard Edwards, 'Seeking and avoiding belief-discrepant information as a function of its perceived refutability' (1975) *Journal at Personality and Social Psychology*, 31(5), 787–790.

Koriat, Asher, Sarah Lichtenstein, and Baruch Fischhoff, 'Reasons for confidence' (1980) *Journal of Experimental Psychology*, 6, 107–118.

Lambert, Richard, Banking standards review' (May 2014), https:// bankingstandardsboard.org.uk/pdf/banking-standards-review.pdf (accessed 7 May 2020).

Langevoort, Donald, 'Getting (too) comfortable: in-house lawyers, enterprise risk and the financial crisis' (2011), Georgetown University Law Center, Georgetown Public Law and Legal Theory Research Paper No. 11-135, https://pdfs. semanticscholar.org/998e/3dee456132aa2bfd6bd753db30df606aa5c7.pdf?_ga= 2.211922004.1127191784.1589123726-894506139.1589123726 (accessed 10 May 2020).

Larsen, Anelia and others, 'Psychopathology, defence mechanisms, and the psychosocial work environment' (November 2010) *International Journal of Social Psychiatry*, 56(6), 563–577.

Last, Rhian, 'Using patient stories to shape better services' (2012), *Practice Nurse*, 42(13), 33–37.

Leveson, Nancy, 'Applying systems thinking to analyze and learn from events' (2011) *Safety Science*, 49, 55–64.

Llewellyn, David, *The economic rationale for financial regulation* (Financial Services Authority, London, 1999), Occasional Paper No. 1, 1–57.

Locke, John, *An essay concerning human understanding* (first published 1710, Thomas Tegg, London, 1846), Book IV.

Lozano, Josep, 'Ethics and corporate culture: a critical relationship' (1998) *Ethical Perspectives*, 5, 53–70.

Lu, Yi, Karen Marais, and Shu-guang Zhang, 'Conceptual modeling of training and organizational risk dynamics' (2014) *Procedia Engineering*, 80, 313–328.

Mamet, David, *Glengarry Glen Ross* (Methuen, London, 1984).

Mannion, Russell and Huw Davies, 'Cultures of silence and cultures of voice: the role of whistleblowing in healthcare organisations' (June 2015) *International Journal of Health Policy and Management*, 4(8), 503–505 http://www.ijhpm.com/article_3047_e3dccd77b82c18e7e7a717063215ec06.pdf (accessed 8 January 2020).

Manyika, James, Jake Silberg and Brittany Presten, 'What do we do about the biases in AI?' (25 October 2019) *Harvard Business Review*, https://hbr.org/2019/10/what-do-we-do-about-the-biases-in-ai (accessed 12 April 2020).

Martin, Sean, Jennifer Kish-Gephart, and James Detert, 'Blind forces: ethical infrastructures and moral disengagement in organizations' (2014) *Organizational Psychology Review*, 4(4), 295–325.

Massey, Stephen, Kant on self-respect' (January 1983) *Journal of the History of Philosophy*, 21(1), 57–73.

McCollom, Marian, 'Organisational stories in a family-owned business' (Spring 1992) *Family Business Review*, 5(1), 3–24.

Mid Staffordshire Independent inquiry into care provided by Mid Staffordshire NHS Foundation Trust (January 2005–March 2009), HC375-I, Vol 1, https://assets.publishing.service.gov.uk/government/uploads/system/uploads/attachment_data/file/279109/0375_i.pdf (accessed 27 April 2020).

Miller, Arthur, *Death of a salesman: certain private conversations in two Acts and a Requiem* (first published 1949, Penguin Modern Classics, London, 2000).

Moorhead, Richard, 'Mapping the moral compass: the relationships between in-house lawyers' role, professional orientations, team cultures, organisational pressures, ethical infrastructure and ethical inclination' (June 2016), *UCL Centre for Ethics and Law*, https://discovery.ucl.ac.uk/id/eprint/1497048/1/Moorhead%20et%20al%202016%20Mapping%20the%20Moral%20Compass.pdf (accessed 19 April 2020).

Moorhead, Richard, 'Ethics and NDAs' (April 2018) *UCL Centre for Ethics and Law*, https://www.ucl.ac.uk/laws/sites/laws/files/ethics_and_ndas.pdf (accessed 28 April 2020).

Moorhead, Richard and Steven Vaughan, *'Legal risk: definition, management and ethics'* (2015) *UCL Centre for Ethics and Law*, 19, SSRN-id2594228.pdf (accessed 19 April 2020).

Moulton, Carroll, 'Antiphon the Sophist, on truth' (1972) *Transactions and Proceedings of the American Philological Association*, 103, 329–366.

Mowat, Charles (ed.) *The New Cambridge modern history* (Cambridge University Press, Cambridge, 1968), 496–499.

Murphy, Patrick, 'Creating ethical corporate structures' (1989) *Sloan Management Review*, 30(2), 81–87.

National Audit Office Report, 'Financial services mis-selling: regulation and redress' (24 February 2016), HC 851 Session 2015–16, https://www.nao.org.uk/wp-content/uploads/2016/02/Financial-services-mis-selling-regulation-and-redress.a.pdf (accessed 27 November 2019).

National Health Service (NHS) England, 'NHS Staff Survey 2018 National results briefing' (February 2019), 32, https://www.nhsstaffsurveys.com/Caches/Files/ST18_National%20briefing_FINAL_20190225.pdf (accessed 31 December 2019).

Newell, Lauren, 'Happiness at the house of mouse: how Disney negotiates to create the 'happiest place on Earth' (July 2012) *Pepperdine Dispute Resolution Law Journal*, 12, 415–528, https://ssrn.com/abstract=2109491 (accessed 12 January 2020).

Norton, Juliet, 'Interview with Dan Hill, author of emotionomics' (2011) *Strategic Direction*, 27(3), 32–34.

Ofwat, 'Ofwat's final decision to impose a financial penalty on Southern Water Services' (10 October 2019), https://www.ofwat.gov.uk/wp-content/uploads/2019/06/Ofwat's-final-decision-to-impose-a-financial-penalty-on-Southern-Water-Services-Limited.pdf (accessed 25 July 2020).

Paganelli, Maria Pia, 'Recent engagements with Adam Smith and the Scottish Enlightenment' (2015) *History of Political Economy*, 47(3), 363–394.

Paige, Mark, Audrey Amrein-Beardsley, and Kevin Close, 'Tennessee's national impact on teacher evaluation law and policy: an assessment of value-added model litigation' (Winter 2019) *Tennessee Journal of Law and Policy*, 13(2), 564.

Paine, Lynn, 'Managing for organizational integrity' (1994) *Harvard Business Review*, 72(2), 106–117.

Painter-Morland, Mollie, 'Redefining accountability as relational responsiveness' in Mollie Painter-Morland and Patricia Werhane (eds.) *Cutting-edge issues in business ethics* (Springer, New York, 2008), 33–45.

Palermo, Tommaso, Michael Power, and Simon Ashby, 'Navigating institutional complexity: the production of risk culture in the financial sector' (March 2017) *Journal of Management Studies*, 54(2), 154–181, 165.

Panichas, George, 'The moral sense in Joseph Conrad's Lord Jim' (2000) *Humanitas*, 13(1), 10–30.

UK Corporate Governance Code (April 2016), https://www.frc.org.uk/getattachment/ca7e94c4-b9a9-49e2-a824-ad76a322873c/UK-Corporate-Governance-Code-April-2016.pdf (accessed 12 January 2020).

UK Corporate Governance Code (July 2018), https://www.frc.org.uk/getattachment/88bd8c45-50ea-4841-95b0-d2f4f48069a2/2018-UK-Corporate-Governance-Code-FINAL.pdf (accessed 12 January 2020).

Parliament

Parliamentary Commission on Banking Standards

2013 Answers to Qs 511 and 512, Helen Weir, Principal Retail Distribution, 2008–10 and CFO, 2004–08, Lloyds Banking Group (21 January 2013), oral evidence to Sub-Committee on cross-selling and mis-selling of the Parliamentary Commission on Banking Standards, https://publications.parliament.uk/pa/jt201213/jtselect/jtpcbs/uc860-iii/uc86001.htm (accessed 5 May 2019).

Daniels, Eric (former CEO of Lloyds Bank), oral evidence to the PCBS (14 February 2013) answer to question 4247, https://publications.parliament.uk/pa/jt201213/jtselect/jtpcbs/uc606-xxxvi/uc60601.htm (accessed 4 June 2020).

House of Lords and House of Commons, 'Changing banking for good', Report of the Parliamentary Commission on Banking Standards Vol. II: Chapters 1 to 11 and Annexes, together with formal minutes, https://www.parliament.uk/documents/banking-commission/Banking-final-report-vol-ii.pdf (accessed 10 May 2020).

Parliamentary Commission for Banking Standards, Vol 1, 'Changing banking for good report' (June 2013) HL Paper 27-I HC 175-I, https://www.parliament.uk/documents/banking-commission/Banking-final-report-volume-i.pdf (accessed 8 May 2020).

Parliamentary Commission on Banking Standards, 'An accident waiting to happen: the failure of HBOS', Fourth Report of Session 2012–13, Vol I: Report, together with formal minutes, HL Paper 144 HC 705 (Published on 4 April 2013), https://publications.parliament.uk/pa/jt201213/jtselect/jtpcbs/144/144.pdf (accessed 21 November 2019).

Parliamentary Commission on Banking Standards, Paul Moore written evidence (13 May 2013), https://publications.parliament.uk/pa/jt201314/jtselect/jtpcbs/27/27v_we94.htm (accessed 24 February 2020).

2013 Parliamentary Commission on Banking Standards – oral evidence of Martin Woods to the PCBS (14 February 2013), https://publications.parliament.uk/pa/jt201314/jtselect/jtpcbs/27/27v_we107.htm(accessed30 December 2019).

Parliamentary Commission on Banking Standards – Minutes of Evidence HL Paper 27-III/HC 175-III, Q3013, McFadden MP (29 January 2013), https://publications.parliament.uk/pa/jt201314/jtselect/jtpcbs/27/130129.htm (accessed 3 June 2020).

Written Evidence from Public Concern at Work (24 June 2013), https://publications.parliament.uk/pa/jt201314/jtselect/jtpcbs/27/27v_we27.htm (accessed 27 April 2020).

Parliamentary Commission on Banking Standards, Written evidence from Lloyds Banking Group (4 January 2013), https://publications.parliament.uk/pa/jt201314/jtselect/jtpcbs/27/27ix_we_j04.htm (accessed 27 November 2019).

Parliamentary Banking Commission of Banking Standards, Written evidence from the Financial Services Authority (11 December 2012), https://publications.parliament.uk/pa/jt201314/jtselect/jtpcbs/27/27v_we78.htm (accessed 28 April 2020).

Parliamentary Banking Commission of Banking Standards, Written evidence from public concern at work (7 September 2012), https://publications.parliament.uk/pa/jt201314/jtselect/jtpcbs/27/27v_we27.htm (accessed 28 April 2020).

2012 Parliamentary Commission on Banking Standards, Minutes of Evidence Session 2013–14, HL Paper 27-VIII/HC 175-VIII (28 November 2012), https://publications.parliament.uk/pa/jt201314/jtselect/jtpcbs/27/27viii_121128d.htm (accessed 18 February 2020).

Sub-committee D, Panel on corporate governance below board level (1 November 2012), oral evidence of Ali Parsa in answer to Q7 from Baroness Kramer, https://publications.parliament.uk/pa/jt201213/jtselect/jtpcbs/uc706/uc70601.htm (accessed 27 April 2020).

Other parliamentary papers

2019 Hansard, 'Debate on whistleblowing' (3 July 2019), 662, https://hansard.parliament.uk/commons/2019-07-03/debates/AA9B34FC-1CA3-4A24-9EEB-E37F6DE8EBF2/Whistleblowing (accessed 27 April 2020).

1993 Hansard, Written reply by Anthony Nelson MP, Economic Secretary to the Treasury (9 March 1993), 220, col. 503.

House Committee on Financial Services, Subcommittee on Capital Markets, Securities, and Investment, Evidence given by Stephanie Avakian and Steven

Peikin SEC Co-Directors, Division of Enforcement (16 May 2018), https://www. sec.gov/news/testimony/testimony-oversight-secs-division-enforcement (accessed 24 May 2019).

House of Commons, 'Financial advice market review and the Retail Distribution Review', Briefing Paper No. 5528 (14 March 2015), https://researchbriefings. parliament.uk/ResearchBriefing/Summary/SN05528 (accessed 4 March 2020).

Parliament, House of Commons Treasury Committee, 'IT failures in the financial services sector', *Second Report of Session 2019–20* (22 October 2019), 3, https:// publications.parliament.uk/pa/cm201919/cmselect/cmtreasy/224/224.pdf (accessed 1 July 2020).

Patel, Keyur, *Professional bodies and the financial services sector* (The Centre for the Study of Financial Innovation, London, 2014), https://static1.squarespace. com/static/54d620fce4b049bf4cd5be9b/t/55dde01fe4b02fcd4471b848/ 1440604191144/Setting+Standards_by+Keyur+Patel.pdf (accessed 7 May 2020).

Payment Systems Regulator, 'Data in the payments industry: Responses to our Discussion Paper' (DP18/1 September 2019), https://www.psr.org.uk/sites/default/ files/media/PDF/PSR-Responses-to-DP18-1_.pdf (accessed 24 November 2019).

Pinter, Harold, (2005) 'Art, truth and politics', Nobel Prize Lecture, Stockholm, https://www.nobelprize.org/prizes/literature/2005/pinter/25621-harold-pinter-nobel-lecture-2005/.

Porter, Roddy, 'Higher command and staff course staff ride paper: As the experience of the French and German armies in 1940 demonstrates, doctrine not equipment is the key to success in modern warfare. Discuss' (2003) *Defence Studies*, 3(1), 138.

Power, Michael, 'The nature of risk: the risk management of everything' (2004) *Balance Sheet*, 12(5), 19–28.

Prudential Regulatory Authority

Anand, Rohini and Mary-Frances Winters, 'A retrospective view of corporate diversity training from 1964 to the present' (2008) *Academy of Management Learning and Education*, 7(3), 356–372, 356, http://www.wintersgroup.com/ corporate-diversity-training-1964-to-present.pdf (accessed 15 November 2019).

PRA's Written Notice, 'Application for imposition of new requirements pursuant to s55M (5) of FSMA 2000' (23 December 2019), https://www.bankofengland.co.uk/-/media/boe/ files/prudential-regulation/regulatory-action/written-notice-from-the-pra-to-the-society-of-lloyds.pdf?la=en&hash=825F21DB1C8FB24BD5854BB8E374E0DFF63C5E3C (accessed 23 December 2019).

PRA, 'Consultation Paper (CP30/19), Outsourcing and third party risk management' (December 2019), https://www.bankofengland.co.uk/-/media/boe/files/prudential-regulation/consultation-paper/2019/cp3019.pdf?la=en&hash=4766BFA4EA8C278B FBE77CADB37C8F34308C97D5 (accessed 28 May 2020).

PRA, 'Supervisory Statement (SS3/19), Enhancing banks' and insurers' approaches to managing the financial risks from climate change' (April 2019), https://www. bankofengland.co.uk/-/media/boe/files/prudential-regulation/supervisory-statement/ 2019/ss319.pdf?la=en&hash=7BA9824BAC5FB313F42C00889D4E3A6104881C44 (accessed 9 March 2020).

2017 PRA Final Notice re The Bank of Tokyo Mitsubishi UFJ Limited and MUFG

Securities EMEA (9 February 2017), https://www.bankofengland.co.uk/-/media/boe/files/prudential-regulation/enforcement-notice/en090217.pdf?la=en&hash=58442B59B07D7F5FB9A14CCD51224BE338BD0CF5 (accessed 14 January 2020).

2015 PRA and FCA report on the failure of HBOS Plc (November 2015), https://www.bankofengland.co.uk/-/media/boe/files/prudential-regulation/publication/hbos-complete-report (accessed 20 November 2019).

PRA Final Notice, Raphael Bank (November 2015), https://www.bankofengland.co.uk/-/media/boe/files/prudential-regulation/enforcement-notice/en271115 (accessed 7 May 2019).

PRA and FCA, 'Consultation Paper, FCA CP14/13 and PRA CP14/14 Strengthening accountability in banking: a new regulatory framework for individuals' (April 2014), https://www.fca.org.uk/publication/consultation/cp14-13.pdf (accessed 12 May 2020).

Quong, Terry, Allan Walker, and Peter Bodycott, 'Exploring and interpreting leadership stories' (1999) *School Leadership and Management*, 19(4), 441–453.

Racanelli, Vito, 'World's most respected companies' (29 June 2015) *Barron's*, 95(26), 23–24.

Rasmussen, Jens, 'Risk management in a dynamic society: a modelling problem' (1997) *Safety Science*, 27, 183–213.

Reader, Tom and Paul O'Connor, 'The Deepwater Horizon explosion: non-technical skills, safety culture, and system complexity' (2014) *Journal of Risk Research*, 17(3), 405–424.

Rechtbank Den Haag, Nederlands Juristen Comité voor de Mensenrechten/Staat Der Nederlanden, 1878 – Den Haag, 05-02-2020 / C-09-550982-HA ZA 18-388 (5 February 2020) https://uitspraken.rechtspraak.nl/inziendocument?id=ECLI:NL:RBDHA:2020:1878 (English translation).

Registry of Friendly Societies, *Grays Building Society – investigation under section 110 of the Building Society Act 1962'* (May 1979), HMSO Cmnd 7557.

Report of the Mid Staffordshire NHS Foundation Trust Public Inquiry ('Robert Francis's Report') (HMSO, London 2013), HC 898-III, Vol 3, 1381, https://webarchive.nationalarchives.gov.uk/20150407084231/http://www.midstaffspublicinquiry.com/report (accessed 8 January 2020).

Rhodes, Carl, 'Organizational justice' in Mollie Painter-Morland and René Ten Bos (eds.) *Business ethics and continental philosophy* (Cambridge University Press, Cambridge, 2011) 141–161.

Rostain, Tanina, 'General counsel in the age of compliance: preliminary findings and new research Questions' (2008) *Georgetown Journal of Legal Ethics*, 21, 465–490.

2013 Salz Review: An independent review of Barclays' business practices (April 2013), 91, https://online.wsj.com/public/resources/documents/SalzReview04032013.pdf (accessed 15 April 2019).

Sarbin, Theodore, 'The narrative as a root metaphor for psychology' in Theordore Sarbin (ed.) *Narrative psychology: the storied nature of human conduct* (Praeger, New York, 1986).

Sarbin, Theodore, 'The poetics of identity' (1997) *Theory and Psychology*, 7(1), 67–82.

BIBLIOGRAPHY

Securities and Exchange Commission

2020

SEC Report, 'Examination priorities' (2020), https://www.sec.gov/about/offices/ocie/national-examination-program-priorities-2020.pdf (accessed 21 May 2020).

2019

2019 SEC Whistleblower Program, Annual Report to Congress (2019), https://www.sec.gov/files/sec-2019-annual%20report-whistleblower%20program.pdf (accessed 28 April 2020).

2018

SEC, Thaddeus North, Review of disciplinary action taken by FINRA, Release No. 84500 (29 October 2018), https://www.sec.gov/litigation/opinions/2018/34-84500.pdf (accessed 23 May 2019).

2017

2017 SEC File No. 3-18280, Release No. 82070 (14 November 2017), https://www.sec.gov/litigation/admin/2017/34-82070.pdf (accessed 22 May 2019).

2017 SEC Order making findings and imposing remedial sanctions (15 August 2017), https://www.sec.gov/litigation/admin/2017/34-81405.pdf (accessed 22 May 2019).

SEC, Office of Compliance Inspections and Examinations (OCIE), 'The five most frequent compliance topics identified in OCIE examinations of investment advisers', *OCIE National Exam Program Risk Alert*, VI(3) (7 February 2017), https://www.sec.gov/ocie/Article/risk-alert-5-most-frequent-ia-compliance-topics.pdf (accessed 30 May 2020).

2010

SEC, 17 CFR Parts 240 and 249, Release No. 34-63237; File No. S7-33-10] RIN 3235-AK78 Proposed rules for implementing the whistleblower provisions of Sec 21F of the Securities Exchange Act of 1934 (2010), https://www.sec.gov/rules/proposed/2010/34-63237.pdf (accessed 30 May 2020).

2004 and earlier

HM Treasury and FCA, 'Financial advice market review – final report' (March 2016), https://www.fca.org.uk/publication/corporate/famr-final-report.pdf (accessed 4 March 2020).

Markowski, Michael, Release No. 43259 (2000) WL 1264292, IV, https://www.sec.gov/litigation/opinions/34-43259.htm (accessed 23 May 2019).

Rouse, Richard, Release No. 32658 (1993), WL 276149, https://www.sec.gov/news/digest/1993/dig072693.pdf (accessed 23 May 2109).

SEC, Castle Sec Corporation, Corp., Exchange Act Release No. 39523 (1998) WL 3456, https://www.sec.gov/litigation/opinions/34-39523.txt (accessed 23 May 2019).

SEC, 'Compliance programs of investment companies and investment advisers', 17 CFR Parts 270, 275, and 279 [Release Nos. IA–2204; IC–26299; File No. S7–03–03] RIN 3235–AI77, Federal Register/Vol. 68, No. 247 (24 December 2003), https://www.sec.gov/rules/final/ia-2204.pdf (accessed 15 April 2020).

SEC, Final Rule: compliance programs of investment companies and investment advisers, 17 CFR Parts 270 and 275, [Release Nos. IA-2204; IC-26299; File No. S7-03-03], RIN 3235-AI77 (2004), https://www.sec.gov/rules/final/ia-2204.htm (accessed 20 May 2020).

Shah, Atul, *The politics of financial risk, audit and regulation: a case study of HBOS* (Routledge, Abingdon, 2017).

Slaughter and May, 'Independent review of TSB's 2018 migration to a new IT platform' (December 2019), https://www.slaughterandmay.com/news-and-recent-work/news/slaughter-and-may-s-independent-review-of-tsb-s-2018-migration-to-a-new-it-platform/ (accessed 25 February 2020).

Slim, William, 'Leadership in management' (June 2003) *Australian Army Journal*, 1(1), 143–148.

Sole, Deborah and Daniel Wilson, *The power and traps of using stories to share knowledge in organizations* (Learning Innovations Laboratories, Harvard Graduate School of Education, Cambridge, 2002), 1–12, https://www.researchgate.net/publication/242189756_Storytelling_in_Organizations_The_power_and_traps_of_using_stories_to_share_knowledge_in_organizations (accessed 29 April 2020).

Spicer, Andre and others, 'A report on the culture of British retail banking' (2014), *New City Agenda and Cass Business School*, http://newcityagenda.co.uk/wp-content/uploads/2014/11/Online-version.pdf (accessed 31 March 2020).

Staats, Bradley, K.C. Diwas Singh and Francesca Gino, 'Maintaining beliefs in the face of negative news: the moderating role of experience' (February 2018) *Management Science*, 64(2), 804–824.

Stanton, Thomas, Submission to the Federal Reserve Board, 'Enhanced prudential standards and early remediation requirements for covered companies' (13 February 2012), https://www.federalreserve.gov/SECRS/2012/February/20120215/R-1438/R-1438_021312_105398_555068728868_1.pdf (accessed 27 March 2020).

Steele, Logan and others, 'How do we know what works? A review and critique of current practices in ethics training evaluation' (2016) *Accountability in Research*, 23(6), 319–350.

Straumann, Tobias, 'The UBS crisis in historical perspective', in *Expert Opinion for UBS AG* (University of Zurich, Institute for Empirical Research in Economics, 2010), 1–16.

Tayan, Brian, 'The Wells Fargo cross-selling scandal' (8 January 2019) *Stanford Closer Look Series*, 2, https://www.gsb.stanford.edu/sites/gsb/files/publication-pdf/cgri-closer-look-62-wells-fargo-cross-selling-scandal.pdf (accessed 27 March 2020).

Tenbrunsel, Ann and David Messick, 'Ethical fading: the role of self-deception in unethical behavior' (2004) *Social Justice Research*, 17(2), 223–236.

Tett, Gillian, *The silo effect* (Abacus, London, 2016).

Todman, Dan, 'The grand lamasery revisited: general headquarters the Western Front 1914–1918', in Gary Sheffield and Dan Todman (eds.) *Command and control on the Western Front* (Spellmount, Staplehurst, 2004).

Treviño, Linda and others, 'Legitimating the legitimate: a grounded theory study of legitimacy work among Ethics and Compliance Officers' (2014) *Organizational Behavior and Human Decision Processes*, *123*, 186–205.

Tyner, Andrew, 'Action, judgment, and imagination in Hannah Arendt's thought' (September 2017) *Political Research Quarterly*, *70*(3), 523–534, https://www.jstor.org/stable/pdf/26384921.pdf?refreqid=excelsior%3A752f019ddf2b6dca7ad be633807e28d4 (accessed 31 April 2020).

US Senate, An examination of Wells Fargo unauthorized accounts and the regulatory response hearing before the Committee on Banking, Housing and Urban Affairs, United States Senate, 114 Congress, Second Session (20 September 2016) *S. HRG.* 114–510, https://www.govinfo.gov/content/pkg/CHRG-114shrg23001/pdf/CHRG-114shrg23001.pdf (accessed 27 March 2020).

White, Thomas, Release No. 34398 (1994) WL 389903, https://www.sec.gov/news/digest/1994/dig072694.pdf (accessed 23 May 2019).

US Department of Justice

US Department of Justice Criminal Division, 'Evaluation of corporate compliance programs, guidance document updated' (April 2019), JM 9-28.800, https://www.justice.gov/criminal-fraud/page/file/937501/download (accessed 11 February 2020).

US Department of Justice Letter to Nortek Inc. (3 June 2016), https://www.justice.gov/criminal-fraud/file/865406/download (accessed 11 December 2019).

US Federal Trade Commission (FTC), 'Data security improvement orders directed at a number of specific companies' (6 January 2020), https://www.ftc.gov/news-events/blogs/business-blog/2020/01/new-improved-ftc-data-security-orders-better-guidance (accessed 16 January 2020).

Van Creveld, Martin, *Command In war* (Harvard University Press, Cambridge, 1985).

Walker, Sir David, 'A review of corporate governance in UK banks and other financial industry entities: Final recommendations' (November 2009), http://webarchive.nationalarchives.gov.uk/+/http:/www.hm-treasury.gov.uk/d/walker_review_261109.pdf (accessed 5 June 2020).

Wells Fargo

Independent Directors of the Board of Wells Fargo, 'Sales practices investigation report' (April 2017), https://www08.wellsfargomedia.com/assets/pdf/about/investor-relations/presentations/2017/board-report.pdf (accessed 29 October 2018).

Wells Fargo (2016), SEC Proxy Statement, Schedule 14A, https://www.sec.gov/Archives/edgar/data/72971/000119312516506771/d897049ddef14a.htm (accessed 31 March 2020).

Wells Fargo Annual Report (2013) 'The right people. The right markets. The right model', https://qjubs3y9ggo1neukf3sc81r19vv-wpengine.netdna-ssl.com/assets/pdf/annual-reports/2013-annual-report.pdf (accessed 28 March 2020).

Wells Fargo, 'Corporate social responsibility report (2013). The right people. The right passion. The right focus - serving communities in the real economy', https://www08.wellsfargomedia.com/assets/pdf/about/corporate-responsibility/2013-social-responsibility-report.pdf (accessed 27 March 2020).

Wells Fargo, '*Investor conference – final*' (14 May 2010), Fair Disclosure Wire.

Wells Fargo, https://qjubs3y9ggo1neukf3sc81r19vv-wpengine.netdna-ssl.com/assets/pdf/annual-reports/2010-annual-report.pdf (accessed 28 March 2020).

Winnefeld, James, Christopher Kirchhoff and David Upton, 'Cybersecurity's human factor: lessons from the Pentagon' (2015) *Harvard Business Review*, *93*(9), 88–96, https://hbr.org/2015/09/cybersecuritys-human-factor-lessons-from-the-pentagon (accessed 18 May 2020).

Wittmann, Jochen, 'Auftragstaktik for business organizations in volatile and uncertain environments: a competence-based view' (Autumn 2017) *IAFOR Journal of Business and Management*, 2(2), 29–49, https://www.researchgate.net/publication/321756066_Auftragstaktik_for_Business_Organizations_in_Volatile_and_Uncertain_Environments_a_Competence-Based_View (accessed 24 April 2019).

Woike, Jan and Sebastian Hafenbrädl, 'Rivals without a cause? Relative performance feedback creates destructive competition despite aligned incentives' (2020) *Journal of Behavioral Decision Making*, 1–15, https://www.researchgate.net/publication/339233864_Rivals_without_a_cause_Relative_performance_feedback_creates_destructive_competition_despite_aligned_incentives (accessed 2 March 2020).

Zetzsche, Dirk, Douglas Arner, Ross Buckley, and Brian Tang, 'Artificial intelligence in finance: putting the human in the loop' (February 2020), 1, *Centre for Finance, Technology and Entrepreneurship Academic Paper Series*, https://ssrn.com/abstract=3531711 (accessed 7 March 2020).

Speeches

Au, Alan, Executive Director (Banking Conduct), Hong Kong Monetary Authority, quoting Carl Jung, 'Our journey towards sound bank culture – reflections and beyond', *Speech* (14 January 2020), https://www.hkma.gov.hk/eng/news-and-media/speeches/2020/01/20200114-2/ (accessed 22 January 2020).

Bailey, Andrew, 'The supervisory approach of the Prudential Regulation Authority' (19 May 2011), https://www.bankofengland.co.uk/-/media/boe/files/speech/2011/the-supervisory-approach-of-the-pra-speech-by-andrew-bailey.pdf?la=en&hash=722C36565F17942C503A2F355F0B1251CA689575 (accessed 20 April 2020).

Bailey, Andrew, 'The future of financial conduct regulation', *Speech* (23 April 2019), https://www.fca.org.uk/news/speeches/future-financial-conduct-regulation (accessed 24 April 2019).

Brandeis, Louis, Former Associate Justice of the Supreme Court of the United States, Business–a profession, an address delivered at Brown University Commencement Day (1912), https://louisville.edu/law/library/special-collections/the-louis-d.-brandeis-collection/business-a-profession-chapter-1 (accessed 7 May 2020).

Butler, Megan, FCA Executive Director of Supervision – Investment, Wholesale and Specialists, 'Cyber and technology resilience in UK financial services', *Speech* (27 November 2017), https://www.fca.org.uk/news/speeches/cyber-and-technology-resilience-uk-financial-services (accessed 29 April 2019).

Carney, Mark, 'Breaking the tragedy of the horizon – climate change and financial stability', *Speech given at Lloyd's of London* (29 September 2015), https://www.bankofengland.co.uk/-/media/boe/files/speech/2015/breaking-the-tragedy-of-the-horizon-climate-change-and-financial-stability.pdf?la=en&hash=7C67E785651862457D99511147C7424FF5EA0C1A (accessed 9 March 2020).

Ceresney, Andrew, SEC Director of the Division of Enforcement, Keynote Address at Compliance Week 2014, Washington DC (20 May 2014), https://www.sec.gov/news/speech/2014-spch052014ajc (accessed 23 May 2019).

Davidson, Jonathan, FCA's, Director of Supervision, 'Getting culture and conduct right – the role of the regulator', *Speech* (13 July 2016), https://www.fca.org.uk/news/speeches/getting-culture-and-conduct-right-role-regulator (accessed 27 November 2019).

Gracie, Andrew, Executive Director, Resolution, Bank of England, 'Managing cyber risk – the global banking perspective', *Speech at the British Bankers' Association Cyber Conference, London* (10 June 2014), https://www.bankofengland.co.uk/-/media/boe/files/speech/2014/managing-cyber-risk-the-global-banking-perspective.pdf?la=en&hash=E3DB03D027D9443D5D00C80A79BFDA24AB0EE22A (accessed 30 April 2019).

McTeague, Karina, FCA, Director of General Insurance and Conduct Specialists Supervision, 'Leading the way on regulation', *Speech* (16 May 2019), https://www.fca.org.uk/news/speeches/leading-way-regulation (accessed 19 May 2019).

Osofsky, Lisa, Serious Fraud Office, Director, 'Fighting fraud and corruption in a shrinking world', *Speaking at the Royal United Services Institute in London* (3 April 2019), https://www.sfo.gov.uk/2019/04/03/fighting-fraud-and-corruption-in-a-shrinking-world/ (accessed 5 April 2019).

Peirce, Hester, SEC Commissioner Remarks at the National Membership Conference of the National Society of Compliance Professionals (30 October 2018), https://www.sec.gov/news/speech/speech-peirce-103018 (accessed 23 May 2019).

Sants, Hector, 'Delivering intensive supervision and credible deterrence', *at the Reuters Newsmakers event, speech* (12 March 2009), https://webarchive.nationalarchives.gov.uk/20090320233408/http://www.fsa.gov.uk/pages/Library/Communication/Speeches/2009/0312_hs.shtml (accessed 19 December 2019).

Walsh, John, Chief Counsel, Office of Compliance Inspections and Examinations, Securities and Exchange Commission, 'What makes compliance a profession?', *NRS Symposium on the Compliance Profession, Miami Beach* (11 April 2002), https://www.sec.gov/news/speech/spch558.htm (accessed 4 May 2020).

Wheatley, Martin, Speech, 'FSA launches initiative to outlaw flawed sales bonuses that encourage mis-selling' (5 September 2012), https://webarchive.nationalarchives.gov.uk/20121003062553/http://www.fsa.gov.uk/library/communication/pr/2012/084.shtml (accessed 4 December 2019).

Woolard, Christopher, FCA, 'The future of regulation: AI for consumer good', *Speech* (16 July 2019), https://www.fca.org.uk/news/speeches/future-regulation-ai-consumer-good (accessed 24 November 2019).

Websites

Bangor University website, https://www.bangor.ac.uk/courses/postgraduate/banking-and-finance-msc (accessed 4 February 2020).

Banking Standards Board website, 'Statement of principles for strengthening professionalism' (March 2019), https://bankingstandardsboard.org.uk/bsb-statement-of-principles-for-strengthening-professionalism/ (accessed 20 April 2020).

BBC News website

BBC News website, 'TSB customers hit by online banking outage' (1 April 2020), https://www.bbc.co.uk/news/technology-52121990 (accessed 28 May 2020).

BBC News website, 'TSB loses 16,000 customers after IT meltdown' (24 October 2018), https://www.bbc.co.uk/news/business-45952283 (accessed 25 February 2020).

BBC News website, 'Mid Staffs: Helene Donnelly and Julie Bailey honoured' (30 December 2013), https://www.bbc.co.uk/news/health-25549054 (accessed 28 April 2020).

Boston University website, https://www.bu.edu/law/academics/llm-masters-degrees/banking-financial-law/courses-of-study/ (accessed 4 February 2020).

Boston College's website, https://www.bc.edu/content/bc-web/schools/law/academics-faculty/fusion-search.html (accessed 4 February 2020).

Bristol University website, https://www.bris.ac.uk/unit-programme-catalogue/RouteStructure.jsa?byCohort=N&ayrCode=20/21&programmeCode=9EFIM007T (accessed 4 February 2020).

Chartered Banker Institute (CBI) website, 'Speak out', https://www.charteredbanker.com/member-homepage/speak-out.html (accessed 1 January 2020).

Clayton Christensen Institute website, 'Innovation worth watching: Mursion', https://www.christenseninstitute.org/blog/innovators-worth-watching-mursion/ (accessed 15 November 2019).

Disney websites, https://www.thewaltdisneycompany.com/about/ and https://dpep.disney.com/parks-and-experiences/ (accessed 12 January 2020).

Peter Bonisch website, 'Thinking about strategy and uncertainty', 'Excuse me, how many lines of defence? The new financial Maginot Lines' (18 March 2013), https://paradigmrisk.wordpress.com/2013/03/18/excuse-me-how-many-lines-of-defence-the-new-financial-maginot-lines/ (accessed 10 May 2020).

Financial Conduct Authority website

FCA website, Magnus Falk, 'Artificial intelligence in the boardroom', https://www.fca.org.uk/insight/author/magnus-falk (accessed 24 November 2019).

FCA website, 'Automated investment services - our expectations' (May 2018), https://www.fca.org.uk/publications/multi-firm-reviews/automated-investment-services-our-expectations (accessed 28 February 2020).

FCA website, 'FCA encourages firms to develop purposeful cultures' (5 March 2020), https://www.fca.org.uk/news/news-stories/fca-encourages-firms-develop-purposeful-cultures (accessed 10 March 2020).

FCA website, 'The retail intermediary market 2018' (June 2019), https://www.fca.org.uk/data/retail-intermediary-market-2018 (accessed 4 March 2020).

FCA website, 'Use of attestation letters', Exchange of letters between Clive Adamson, FCA director of supervision and Graham Beale, Chairman of the FCA Practitioner

Panel clarifying the FCA's use of Attestations (28 August 2014), https://www.fca. org.uk/news/news-stories/fca-use-attestations (accessed 18 May 2020).

2019 'Psychological safety' (18 February 2019), https://www.fca.org.uk/culture- and-governance/psychological-safety (accessed 23 January 2020).

2018 'Retail and wholesale banking: review of firms' whistleblowing arrangements' (14 November 2018), https://www.fca.org.uk/publications/multi-firm- reviews/retail-and-wholesale-banking-review-firms-whistleblowing- arrangements (accessed 27 April 2020).

'Whistleblowing', https://www.fca.org.uk/firms/whistleblowing (accessed 1 January 2020).

Financial Crimes Enforcement Network (FinCEN) website

FinCEN press release, 'Haider Settlement' (4 May 2020), https://www.fincen.gov/ sites/default/files/2017-05/HaiderSettlement_050417.pdf (accessed 21 July 2020).

FinCEN website, 'FinCEN Penalizes US Bank Official for Corporate Anti-Money Laundering Failures' (4 March 2020), https://www.fincen.gov/news/news- releases/fincen-penalizes-us-bank-official-corporate-anti-money-laundering- failures (accessed 19 March 2020).

FinCEN assessment of a civil money penalty against Michael LaFontaine (4 March 2020), https://www.fincen.gov/sites/default/files/enforcement_action/2020-03-04/ Michael%20LaFontaine-Assessment-02.26.20_508.pdf (accessed 24 March 2020).

FinCEN's assessment of a civil money penalty against Wachovia Bank (4 March 2010), https://www.fincen.gov/sites/default/files/enforcement_action/100316095447.pdf (accessed 24 March 2020).

Financial Planning website, Todd Cipperman, 'Voices: my predictions for 2019's reg- ulatory agenda' (7 January 2019), https://www.financial-planning.com/opinion/sec- intensifies-scrutiny-on-doubled-up-compliance-officers (accessed 21 May 2020).

Financial Reporting Council (FRC) website, Improved governance and reporting required to promote sustainability and trust in business' (9 January 2020), https:// www.frc.org.uk/news/january-2020/improved-governance-and-reporting- required-to-prom (accessed 9 January 2020).

Forbes website, Erika Kelton, 'Seven ingredients for a successful whistleblower program' (21 March 2012), https://www.forbes.com/sites/erikakelton/2012/03/ 21/seven-ingredients-for-a-successful-whistleblower-program/#4cd7ad9b390c (accessed 28 April 2020).

Gallup Great Workplace Awards website, https://www.gallup.com/events/178865/gallup- great-workplace-award-current-previous-win-ners.aspx (accessed 28 March 2020).

International Association of Risk and Compliance Professionals (IARCP), website, The Chief Compliance Officer, https://www.chief-compliance-officer.org (ac- cessed 24 May 2019).

Irish Institute of Banking, website, Certified Bank Director course, https://iob.ie/ programme/certified-bank-director (accessed 26 June 2020).

Marketplace website, Interview transcript: Kai Ryssdal interviewing John Stumpf (10 June 2008), https://www.marketplace.org/2008/06/10/interview-transcript- john-stumpf/ (accessed 26 March 2020).

Medical Practitioners Society website, 'An inconvenient truth' (29 August 2017), https://www.medicalprotection.org/uk/articles/an-inconvenient-truth (accessed 31 December 2019).

Occupational Safety and Health Administration (OSHA) website, 'OSHA orders Wells Fargo to reinstate whistleblower, fully restore lost earnings banking industry' (3 April 2017), https://www.dol.gov/newsroom/releases/osha/osha20170403 (accessed 29 March 2020).

PACE University website, https://www.pace.edu/lubin/departments-and-research-centers/center-for-global-governance-reporting-and-regulation/ccrp (accessed 4 February 2020).

Reading University website, https://www.icmacentre.ac.uk/study/masters/masters-in-capital-markets-regulation-and-compliance#%20entry-requirements (accessed 4 February 2020).

Reuters website, 'Former MoneyGram executive settles closely watched U.S. money laundering case' (4 May 2017), https://www.reuters.com/article/us-moneygram-intl-moneylaundering-idUSKBN1802P3 (accessed 21 July 2020).

Royal College of Nursing (RCN) website, 'Raising concerns: guidance for RCN members', https://www.rcn.org.uk/employment-and-pay/raising-concerns/guidance-for-rcn-members (accessed 1 January 2020).

SEC website

Aguilar, Luis, SEC website, Public Statement, 'The role of chief compliance officers must be supported' (29 June 2015), https://www.sec.gov/news/statement/supporting-role-of-chief-compliance-officers.html (accessed 21 May 2020).

Queen Mary University London website, https://www.qmul.ac.uk/law/postgraduate/courses/llm/modules/ (accessed 4 February 2020).

SEC, 'SFX Financial Advisory Management Enterprises, Inc. and Eugene S. Mason' (15 June 2015), Administrative proceedings, File No. 3-16591, https://www.sec.gov/litigation/admin/2015/ia-4116.pdf (accessed 21 July 2020).

SEC Officer of the Whistleblower website, https://www.sec.gov/whistleblower (accessed 28 April 2020).

SEC website, 'Compliance Programs of Investment Companies and Investment Advisers', Rule 206(4)-7 for investment advisers and Rule 38a-1 for investment companies, SEC Final Rule:17 CFR Parts 270 and 275, [Release Nos. IA-2204; IC-26299; File No. S7-03-03], RIN 3235-AI77, https://www.sec.gov/rules/final/ia-2204.htm (accessed 24 May 2019).

SEC website, 'Enforcement actions: FCPA cases', https://www.sec.gov/spotlight/fcpa/fcpa-cases.shtml (accessed 21 May 2020).

Statistical Analysis System website, DataFlux Quality Knowledge Base (QKB), https://support.sas.com/software/products/qkb/index.html (accessed 13 May 2019).

UCL website, https://www.ucl.ac.uk/laws/study/llm-master-laws/llm-modules-2020-21 (accessed 4 February 2020).

Online media

'Auditor in court' video, available on YouTube, https://www.youtube.com/watch?v=oEgCMZRgJLs (accessed 13 November 2019).

Newspapers

American Banker magazine website (13 November 2013), https://www.americanbanker.com/news/wells-fargos-john-stumpf-the-2013-banker-of-the-year (accessed 28 March 2020).

Compliance Week, 'In focus: 2016 compliance trends survey' (2016), https://www2.deloitte.com/content/dam/Deloitte/us/Documents/governance-risk-compliance/us-advisory-compliance-week-survey.pdf (accessed 8 April 2020).

The Charlotte Observer, 'Some at Wells Fargo say they fear using 'ethics line,' even as bank vows to fix it' (11 November 2016), https://www.charlotteobserver.com/news/business/banking/bank-watch-blog/article114171173.html (accessed 29 March 2020).

Financial Times

'Lloyd's lapse draws tighter BoE scrutiny of whistleblower systems' (23 December 2019), https://www.ft.com/content/8eabd3fe-2578-11ea-9305-4234e74b0ef3 (accessed 23 December 2019).

2019 'PPI scandal hits £50bn after claims rise at Lloyds and Barclays' (9 September 2019).

2019 'Trading floor culture remains a barrier for senior female staff' (9 August 2019), https://www.ft.com/content/16cbf8da-b9d7-11e9-96bd-8e884d3ea203 (accessed 23December2019).

2019 'Southern Water hit by £126m penalty for 'serious failures' (25 June 2019), https://www.ft.com/content/518b21fa-9711-11e9-9573-ee5cbb98ed36 (accessed 25 July 2020).

2019 'Investec shuts robo-advice service due to 'low appetite' (16 May 2019).

2017 'Wells Fargo's independent directors hire lobbying firm' (22 February 2017), https://www.ft.com/content/e27d7446-f921-11e6-bd4e-68d53499ed71 (accessed 6 April 2020).

2015 'Pension firms report increased demand for DB transfer quotes: Members of 'gold plated' final salary schemes are increasingly tempted to cash them in' (1 May 2015), https://www.ft.com/content/eb9b0de2-f011-11e4-ab73-00144feab7de (accessed 16 May 2020).

1992 'Royal Life agent on £69,000 charge' (6/7 October 1992).

Dill, Alexander, 'Banks have learnt their lesson on risk management' (16 December 2019).

The Guardian, 'Mid Staffs whistleblower Julie Bailey: 'I don't go out here on my own any more' (27 October 2013), https://www.theguardian.com/society/2013/oct/27/julie-bailey-mid-staffordshire-nhs-whistleblower (accessed 28 April 2020).

The Herald, Scotland, 'Royal Bank subsidiary fined record amount for mis-selling endowments' (1 December 2000), https://www.heraldscotland.com/news/12165500.royal-bank-subsidiary-fined-record-amount-for-mis-selling-endowments/ (accessed 14 April 2020).

Los Angeles Times, 'Wells Fargo's pressure-cooker sales culture comes at a cost' (21 December 2013), https://www.latimes.com/business/la-fi-wells-fargo-sale-pressure-20131222-story.html (accessed 29 March 2020).

New Statesman, 'We should look at the Quakers who founded Barclays for an example of banking with values' (20 December 2013), https://www.

newstatesman.com/business/2013/12/we-should-look-quakers-who-founded-barclays-example-banking-values (accessed 29 April 2020).

New York Times, 'Charles Keating, 90, key figure in '80s savings and loan crisis, dies' (2 April 2014), https://www.nytimes.com/2014/04/02/business/charles-keating-key-figure-in-the-1980s-savings-and-loan-crisis-dies-at-90.html (accessed 3 June 2020).

Nursing Times, 'Whistleblowing Mid Staffs nurse too scared to walk to car after shift' (17 October 2011), https://www.nursingtimes.net/clinical-archive/accident-and-emergency/whistleblowing-mid-staffs-nurse-too-scared-to-walk-to-car-after-shift-17-10-2011/ (accessed 18 April 2020).

People Management, 'NHS to be banned from using NDAs to gag whistleblowers' (23 April 2019), https://www.peoplemanagement.co.uk/news/articles/nhs-to-be-banned-using-ndas-gag-whistleblowers (accessed 28 April 2020).

The Telegraph, 'Another fine insurance mess' (3 December 2000), https://www.telegraph.co.uk/finance/personalfinance/comment/4474186/Another-fine-insurance-mess.html (accessed 3 May 2019).

Legislation – EU

Payment Services Directive (PSD) II (EU) 2015/2366.

Legislation – US

2010 Dodd–Frank Wall Street Reform and Consumer Protection Act, Public law No. 111-203, § 922(a) amended Securities Exchange Act of 1934, 124 Stat. 1841 (2010).

15 U.S.C. § 78dd-1 and 9-47.000 – Policy Concerning Criminal Investigations and Prosecutions of the Foreign Corrupt Practices Act, https://www.justice.gov/jm/jm-9-47000-foreign-corrupt-practices-act-1977 (accessed 10 December 2019).

Legislation – UK

The Money Laundering, *Terrorist Financing and Transfer of Funds (Information on the Payer) Regulations* 2017.

Money Laundering Regulations 2007.

s60A, Vetting of candidates by relevant authorised persons, Financial Services and Markets Act (2000).

Regulation – UK

FCA, Handbook, 'TC App 1.1 Activities and Products/Sectors to which TC applies subject', https://www.handbook.fca.org.uk/handbook/TC/App/1/1.html (accessed 16 June 2020).

TC TP 3 Regulated Mortgage Contracts: assessments of competence under the Mortgage Code Compliance Board Rules, https://www.handbook.fca.org.uk/handbook/TC/TP/3/3.html (accessed 12 May 2020).

BIBLIOGRAPHY

Cases

English and Scottish

R (British Bankers Association) v FSA and others [2011] EWHC 999 (Admin), 20 April 2011, https://www.bailii.org/ew/cases/EWHC/Admin/2011/999.html (accessed 27 April 2020).

Scottish Courts and Tribunals, Royal Scottish Assurance PLC v Scottish Equitable Life PLC [2006] CSIH 47, https://www.scotcourts.gov.uk/search-judgments/judgment?id=ef4886a6-8980-69d2-b500-ff0000d74aa7 (accessed 14 April 2020).

US

Houston Federation of Teachers, *Local 2415v. Houston School District* (2017) 251F. Supp. 3d 1168.

INDEX